Noble Warrior

Noble Warrior

The Story of Maj. Gen. James E. Livingston, USMC
(Ret.), Medal of Honor

James E. Livingston with
Colin D. Heaton and Anne-Marie Lewis

ZENITH PRESS

First published in 2010 by Zenith Press, an imprint of MBI Publishing Company, 400 First Avenue North, Suite 300, Minneapolis, MN 55401 USA

Zenith Press titles are also available at discounts in bulk quantity for industrial or sales-promotional use. For details write to Special Sales Manager at MBI Publishing Company, 400 First Avenue North, Suite 300, Minneapolis, MN 55401 USA.

To find out more about our books, join us online at www.zenithpress.com.

Library of Congress Cataloging-in-Publication Data
Livingston, James E., 1940–
   Noble warrior : the life and times of Maj. Gen. James E. Livingston, USMC (Ret.), Medal of Honor / James E. Livingston, Colin D. Heaton, and Anne-Marie Lewis.
      p. cm.
   Includes bibliographical references.
   ISBN 978-0-7603-3807-0 (hbk. w/jkt)
   1. Livingston, James E., 1940- 2. Generals--United States--Biography. 3. United States. Marine Corps--Officers--Biography. 4. Medal of Honor--Biography. 5. Vietnam War, 1961-1975--Personal narratives, American. 6. Quang Tri (Vietnam : Province)--History, Military--20th century. 7. United States. Marine Corps. Regiment, 4th. Battalion, 2nd. Echo Company. 8. Vietnam War, 1961-1975--Regimental histories--United States. I. Heaton, Colin D. II. Lewis, Anne-Marie. III. Title.
   E840.5.L58A3 2010
   355.0092--dc22
   [B]   2010005413

On the cover: Marine squad in the assault. *U.S. National Archives* **Inset:** Capt. James E. Livingston with Medal of Honor, circa 1970. *James E. Livingston*
On the back cover: Marines moving from landing zone into ambush positions. *U.S. National Archives*

Design Manager: Brenda C. Canales
Layout by: Helena Shimizu
Maps by: Trevor Burks, based on official USMC maps provided by William Weise.

Printed in the United States of America

Courage is doing what you are afraid of.
There is no courage without fear.
—Captain Eddie Rickenbacker,
U.S. Army Air Service

The enemy will not perish himself.
—Mao Tse Tung

Only the dead have seen the end of war.
—Plato

For the Marines who never returned from the world's battlefields,
and those Marines who are fighting against terrorism today.

Certain proceeds from this book will support the 2nd Battalion, 4th Marine
Regiment War Memorial Fund and 2/4 Marine Association, as well as the
Wounded Warrior Project.

This book is especially dedicated to my mother, Ruth.
God never made a better mom.

—*James E. Livingston*

Contents

Foreword

GENERAL AL GRAY, USMC (RET.),
29TH COMMANDANT

IT IS A SPECIAL honor for me to write a foreword to this rich memoir of a truly noble warrior who has distinguished himself in both war and peace. General Jim Livingston's inspirational leadership and dauntless courage during a critical battle in the Vietnam War is well known to all who serve our nation's Marine Corps.

Serving under another great warrior, Bill Weise, whose bravery and indomitable leadership under fire earned him the Navy Cross (our nation's second-highest award), Jim's valor at the Battle of Dai Do in northern Quang Tri Province enriched the legacy of the Marine Corp and surely places him in the first rank of the pantheon of Marine heroes. Readers will be riveted as Jim leads his beloved Echo Company, 2nd Battalion, 4th Marines, across the rice fields of the Cua Viet River complex to meet an entrenched, resourceful, and determined North Vietnamese force in the spring of 1968.

During those days in 1968 when Jim, Bill, Jay Vargas (another noble warrior who earned the Medal of Honor), and many other brave men of our armed forces distinguished themselves, our nation was in upheaval. The echo had hardly faded from the Tet Offensive with its resultant turmoil, and Americans were becoming divided on the war. American and Allied forces were scattered from the Demilitarized Zone (which separated South and North Vietnam) to the Mekong Delta. They were fighting a ruthless enemy whose guerilla warfare included terrorism, skillful propaganda, and relentless persecution of innocent civilians. However, the North Vietnamese and Viet Cong underestimated the resilience, courage, and dedication to duty of our forces.

It has been my pleasure to know and admire Jim, both professionally and personally, for over thirty-five years. While I was the commanding officer of the 4th Marines, he joined the regiment after serving as an instructor at the Army's Advanced Infantry Course at Fort Benning, Georgia, in late summer 1974. Due to his background and knowledge, I assigned then-Captain Livingston to be the Regimental Operations Officer even though this is normally a senior major's billet. He became an outstanding staff officer who quickly fit into the team. In addition to upgrading the training and operations procedures, he served with great professionalism in a complex, brigade-sized amphibious exercise in the Southern Philippines later that fall.

In the spring of 1975, while afloat with me in the South China Sea as part of our Regimental Landing Team (RLT) assigned to the 9th Marine Amphibious Brigade preparing for the evacuation of South Vietnam, higher command opted to place a small group from Okinawa in Saigon as an advanced party for coordination. As they were not familiar with the ongoing planning, I provided Jim Livingston to the group for continuity. As expected, his performance was superb, attending to myriad details in and around the principal evacuation site of Tan Son Nhut Air Base. During my daily reconnaissance throughout the Saigon area, I frequently observed Jim in action. His contributions—along with another courageous and superb effort by the 2nd Battalion, 4th Marines, under the brilliant leadership of George Slade—were most commendable.

Our paths crossed again in the early 1980s when I was privileged to command the 2nd Marine Division at Camp Lejeune, North Carolina. Jim commanded our 6th Marine Regiment with his customary outstanding leadership, and it was a pleasure to see him grow with increased responsibilities. Always a hard charger, he pushed himself to his limits and beyond. He pushed his Marines just as hard, leading by example, and never allowed anyone to take the easy way out. Later in my career, Jim was a general officer who continued to make vital contributions to our Corps. For example, he served with distinction as the first commanding general of our 4th Marine Forces Reserve (our Reserve Air/Ground/Logistics Team) and upgraded to total readiness our Reserve Forces.

Jim Livingston's commitment to his country, his Corps, and to the people around him "who make it happen" remains steadfast today. His success as a businessman and as a civilian leader has won him additional acclaim. Through it all, he has remained humble and true to himself. Many years ago a colleague of ours in the 4th Marines was asked about Jim's character and his Medal of Honor. A man of few words, our colleague said, "He wears the medal well." That says it all, for he meant that Jim, like other Medal of Honor recipients, does not wear the title "hero" comfortably. There are too many names on the wall of the Vietnam Veterans Memorial representing the real heroes, as our Medal of Honor holders (and all true leaders in the profession of arms) would agree. This book includes these men and highlights their actions. They represent all branches of our armed forces who gallantly served their nation.

Readers of military history will find this book hard to put down. Marines will find it an indispensable addition to their professional development. Americans in general, even if they have not served in uniform, will find within it a piece of history that is little known but important, since it tells us once again why we are a great nation.

For our warriors around the globe in these difficult times, I salute you. Take care of yourselves, take care of each other, may God bless, and Semper Fidelis.

BRIGADIER GENERAL WILLIAM WEISE, USMC (RET.)

The Jim Livingston I knew during the Vietnam War was a true warrior, a Marine's Marine. He was a tiger in combat, but he was much more than that. He knew how to train and whip a disorganized unit into shape. He knew how to motivate his Marines and sailors using both the stick and the carrot. He was tough but fair. He was a superb combat leader. He loved his Marines and sailors, although many of them didn't realize it at first. He loved them enough to make them do the right things even when they were exhausted. Jim developed "battle smarts"—that rare gift few leaders have. In the chaos of close combat, when things were going to hell in a hurry, he would sense and immediately apply a workable solution. He proved his battle smarts in heavy fighting at Lam Xuan (East), Vinh Quan Thuong, Dai Do, and numerous smaller actions.

I first met Jim in Vietnam when he reported in to the 2nd Battalion, 4th Marines (2/4), at the end of October, 1967, at Dong Ha Combat Base, close to the demilitarized zone (DMZ). He was a tall, muscular, serious officer who was eager to command a rifle company. At that time I had been commander of the "Magnificent Bastards" of 2/4 only a few days.

During the preceding two months, 2/4 had suffered heavy losses against North Vietnamese Army units along the demilitarized zone. My predecessor had been wounded and evacuated. The battalion executive officer had been killed, along with a number of other key leaders. All five company commanders, including Livingston, were newly assigned. The battalion commander, executive officer, operations officer, and logistics officer, plus about half of the other officers and senior noncommissioned officers, had also recently joined.

Our job was to reorganize, train, and get 2/4 ready for battle quickly. There was little time to do this. In less than seven days, we were assigned to the First Marine Regiment to eliminate a serious guerrilla threat to the Quang Tri Airfield, then under construction by U.S. Navy Sea Bees. This was the hectic environment in which Livingston had to whip his Echo Company into shape, and he had to train his company while performing combat missions in a hostile enemy environment. Talk about a leadership challenge!

Throughout 2/4 there were bad habits to overcome as a result of what I call "combat lethargy" among the Old Salts (Marines who had been in 2/4 more than two months). Combat lethargy is a dullness or apathy that overcomes many soldiers and Marines who have faced the horrors of close combat with little rest, constant fear, inadequate nourishment, and loss of both close friends and trusted leaders over an extensive period. Combat lethargy is often accompanied by a sense of hopelessness, a feeling of "What's the use? I'll never survive thirteen months of this hell."

A Marine in this condition forgets or ignores the basics he needs for survival—keeping his weapon clean, staying alert, maintaining personal hygiene, maintaining camouflage, and the like. Other bad habits resulted from poor training or just plain laziness: machine gun teams that did not carry the tripod on combat operations, poor or nonexistent camouflage, inadequate patrol orders and patrol debriefings, and so on.

Overcoming bad habits requires very strong leadership. Jim Livingston supplied that leadership and more. Some of his methods, which proved very effective at that time, may seem draconian by today's standards. To impress the importance of clean weapons, for example, when he discovered a Marine with a dirty weapon, Livingston made the Marine's platoon commander clean every weapon in his platoon. This happened rarely because the word got out quickly. Soon every small-unit leader in Echo Company made cleaning weapons a high priority. Similar methods overcame other bad habits. Strong leadership developed down to the small-unit level and led to repeated success in battle. Livingston's high standards and tough love kept his Marines and sailors on their toes and kept battle casualties to a minimum.

Livingston always led by personal example. His Marines knew that he would not ask them to do anything that he would not do himself. He was brave but not foolish. In battle he placed himself where he could best influence the action of his company, regardless of the danger. If necessary, he would lead the final assault himself, just as he did at Dai Do. To him, it was mission first, his Marines and sailors next, and himself last.

I have followed Jim Livingston's distinguished military and civilian careers for more than four decades. He remains humble despite many successes in different areas. He has not changed. He continues to inspire those who know him, and I am fortunate and proud to call him my friend.

Semper Fidelis

GENERAL PAUL X. KELLEY, USMC (RET.), 28TH COMMANDANT

We must remember that one man is much the same as another, and that he is best who is trained in the severest school.
— Thucydides, *History of the Peloponnesian War*

From its creation in 1775, the United States Marine Corps has been an integral part of our great nation's history. If I were to capture it in one word, that word would be *pride*. The pride of young recruits as they stand tall at their graduation from boot camp and are called *Marine* for the first time. The pride of a young second lieutenant as he or she first pins on the brown bar. The pride of five Marines and one U.S. Navy corpsman as they raised a flag atop Mount Surabachi during World War II, giving the world a powerful message of victory. There are two more words, Latin words, which have always given Marines hope and inspiration: *Semper Fidelis*—always faithful—to their country, to their Corps, to each other.

Major General Jim Livingston, truly a Marine's Marine in every sense, has given us a memorable autobiography, one which will adorn bookshelves in "every clime and place." This is a story about combat as seen through the eyes of the grunts, a nickname for our Marine infantrymen. The story is tough, deadly, and often sad—a saga of raw emotions and self-sacrifice. Jim commanded a Marine rifle company with 2nd Battalion, 4th Marines during the 1968 battle of Dai Do, in the vicinity of Dong Ha, Quang Tri Province. By coincidence, I commanded the same battalion in Vietnam during early 1966. An earlier commanding officer had given us the nickname "Magnificent Bastards"—and that we were and still are.

I truly believe that Vietnam was a military victory and a political defeat. And let me shout from the highest hilltop, let me say it for all to read: despite meddling by the White House, despite indecision by the Congress, despite inaccurate sensationalism by the liberal press— despite all of them—the U.S. Soldiers, Sailors, Airmen, Coastguardsmen, and Marines who fought under the Stars and Stripes in Vietnam have every right to be proud of their accomplishments. They stopped the growth of communism in southeast Asia, and that was their mission. They showed the world an awesome display of firepower and the ability to employ it. But most of all, they proved what courage, determination, and patriotism can accomplish on the battlefield. To each I say, "Stand tall and be proud. You are patriotic Americans, and I salute you!"

Preface

COLIN D. HEATON

AS BOTH AN ENLISTED U.S. Army soldier and a U.S. Marine (serving in both branches), I had the experience of serving under and becoming acquainted with several different types of officers, from platoon leaders to commanding generals. Often this experience included foreign military officers from around the world. In addition, during many years of interviewing veterans from many nations and conflicts and publishing their life stories, I often had the privilege of getting to know the veterans very well. Many of these meetings established long-standing friendships.

Serving as a Marine scout-sniper in Surveillance, Target, and Acquisition (STA) Platoon in 1st Battalion, 6th Marines, at Camp Lejeune, I never had the privilege of meeting our regimental commander, then Col. James E. Livingston, on a one-to-one basis personally. However, his legend within the Marine Corps matched his professional bearing. He was judged (as are all officers) by his men to be a hard and unyielding leader, yet a man who led by example. The concepts of compromise and mediocrity were not part of his character. This was evidenced by his leading the units on six-mile runs at a pace that was the standard for his men, who, for the most part, were more than half his age.

Within the 6th Marine Regiment, Livingston had many nicknames, which I will not state here. Suffice it to say, they were all spoken warmly and with the utmost respect. I once even spoke with a Marine who had been given the colonel's office hours, which was very unusual. These were normally handled at the company level or, on rare occasions, at the battalion level. Regimental office hours were unheard of. I cannot remember the Marine's offense, but if memory serves, it was a failure to salute superior officers and a disrespect charge. Although he was reduced by at least one pay grade and given restriction to quarters, he flatly stated, "Hell, at least the colonel was polite about it all. It could have been much worse for me." I saw this Marine picking up trash around the base on the weekends for as long as I can remember.

The most important things that Marines look for in their leaders are consistency, willingness to provide advancement opportunities based on personal merit, and unilateral fairness. Livingston always extolled those ideals. He may have been hard, but no one could say that he was unfair in his application of discipline. I cannot say that about all the other officers I ever served under.

Livingston hated being behind a desk. It was clear that he much preferred being in the field with his men; his hands-on training programs would pay the same dividends for the U.S. Marines of the 1980s through today as they did during his days in Vietnam. His methods saved lives, helped liberate nations, freed those living under tyranny, and built upon the existing *esprit de corps* that sets the Marine Corps apart from the other forces.

In 2005 I first sat down to speak with General Livingston at length about doing an interview for *Vietnam* magazine, and I learned some new things about him. First, his modesty about his career and actions made it hard to get detailed combat information from him. I actually learned more regarding his actions at Dai Do by reading his Medal of Honor citation than from the information he initially gave me over a period of several months. Statements from those around him, such as Wally Nunn, who had seen General Livingston in action, were also illuminating:

Forty-one years ago, as a young army door gunner on a Huey, I had the privilege of witnessing an awesome site: a U.S. Marine company fixing bayonets and, along with three other companies, defeating a North

Vietnamese Army (NVA) division. Years later I read the novel *Gates of Fire* about the battle of Thermopylae (the same historical battle behind the movie *300*). It came to me that what I had witnessed was nothing less than the spirit of Leonidas and his Spartan warriors standing against the Persian horde—only it was Capt. Jim Livingston, Lt. Col. William Weise, Capt. Jay Vargas, and a group of Marines, every one of whom would have made any Spartan mother proud. Very few of those Marines walked away from the battlefield, and had it taken every one of them to defeat the enemy. I have no doubt that, like the three hundred Spartans, they would have fought to the last man.

Just as the three hundred saved Greece, the sacrifices made by the 2nd Battalion, 4th Marines, saved Dong Ha, which, in fact, saved this nation from a great defeat. Can you imagine what the reaction would have been if the NVA flag flew above the largest Marine combat base in Vietnam for even a brief moment? Not only would the left, which was running amuck in our streets, have used it as a rallying cry, but also every newspaper in the world would have had a front page story: "Marine Base Falls to the Communists." Our nation's morale, which was already very low, would have collapsed, and Congress would have folded. I believe there was a real possibility that we would have lost the war had that happened. Yes, 2/4's sacrifice was for a reason.

Even Spartans need leaders, and very few leaders would compare to Gen. James Livingston. His story is not just one of heroism, for one can be heroic and not be a leader. As you read this book, you find yourself in awe that this man who was capable of such heroics was also a man who cared so deeply for his men. But most importantly, he cared for his nation and his faith.

I know that as long as there is a Marine Corps and men like General Livingston to lead it, I and those who come after me will live as free people.[1]

Finally, after almost a year of regular contact and meetings, General Livingston finally relaxed and allowed me to explore the more complex aspects of his personality and details of his career.

However, once the interviews were underway, I think he realized that his story was not just a personal narrative, but also a very important piece of military, political, and especially Marine Corps history. He knew before I did that we had a book in the making. Once he agreed to the project, I felt as if I had won the lottery, whereas he probably felt that he had, for the first time in his life, been beaten into submission.

Regardless, I secured the opportunity to chronicle and document the life of this man I had grown to respect, which is an honor that comes to a historian once in a lifetime. Upon securing the agreement, I immediately brought Anne-Marie Lewis and her special talents on board. I have written books and interviewed some very famous (most not so famous) and amazing people within the worldwide military community. James Livingston is, and perhaps will always be, the pinnacle of this success.

General Livingston, to his great credit, wished to ensure that all the persons involved in his life and career were mentioned. This desire will explain why many persons and their individual actions, as well as their personal comments and narratives, are included in specific chapters. Men who fight do not function in a vacuum; they are all integral parts of an organic machine, each man depending upon others for their mutual survival. This book will illustrate just how critical teamwork is.

What this book will not tell the readers is exactly how many thousands of American lives (and others) Livingston may have actually saved during his almost thirty-four-year career as a U.S. Marine officer. This number is impossible to determine and is subject to speculation. Whether due to his never-ending and sometimes ruthless training programs and methodology, or the self-confidence and knowledge he imparted to the Marines under his command spanning two generations, the ripple effect of his command is still being felt throughout the Corps. I can assure the readers that the insurgents in Iraq and Afghanistan are today feeling the end result of that particular brand of "Livingstonism."

Our military men and women today are engaged in the life-and-death struggle against global terrorism around the world, particularly in Iraq and Afghanistan, and previously in Somalia, Sierra Leone, Liberia, Grenada, Lebanon, and other flash points. Tradition goes a long way, but the discipline, consistency, repetition of training, and *esprit de corps* Livingston extolled will outlive all of us. Thanks to my coauthor, Anne-Marie, and the many men mentioned in this book, we hope we have done his life story justice.

In assisting General Livingston in writing this book, we have paid particular attention to citing the relevant secondary and primary historical sources, as well as direct quotations from the distinguished participants.

Acknowledgments

WE WISH TO THANK American Military University with assisting in financing the research expenses, as well as the following persons for both their direct or indirect support of this project. Many people came together to assist us, and their efforts must not go unnoticed.

The following persons, in their own ways, have smoothed the path, making this work possible: Wilma Bonvillian; Gregory M. Kopatch; Col. Jay Vargas, USMC (Ret., Medal of Honor recipient); Brig. Gen. Bill Weise, USMC (Ret., Navy Cross recipient); Lt. Col. Vic Taylor, USMC (Ret.); Joey Reynolds; Scott Laidig; Steve Wilson; Albert Wunsch III; James "Doc" Swann; Lt. Col. George "Fritz" Warren, USMC (Ret.); Dave Jones; Rod Forman; Jack E. Wilmot; Jesse Brooks; and all the members of 2nd Battalion 4th Marines Association and the 196th Infantry Brigade.

Special thanks to John Valdez for his reading list, recommendations, photographs, and emails, and to Ken Crouse, secretary of the Fall of Saigon Marines Association, for his recollections on Saigon and for other information. Also we wish to thank the United States Marine Corps Historical Division for chronicling this and other areas of Marine Corps history for future generations.

We also need to thank Wally Nunn, Ken Johnson, and Sam Davis of the 174th Assault Helicopter Company, who participated in the Battle of Dong Ha. These kind and brave gentlemen assisted with the army air operations, after-action report details, comments, and some of the photos included within this book. Thanks also to Jim Winsness for proofreading and assisting with editing. His keen eye really helped us throughout the process.

Prologue

Freedom is measured by those willing to preserve it.
—Gen. Dwight D. Eisenhower

My MOTHER, RUTH LEONA BROWNING, married my father, Myret Barrett Livingston, and they had two sons; I was born on January 12, 1940, and my brother, Donald Barrett Livingston (who is now deceased) was born on August 23, 1943. We grew up in Telfair County, in Towns, Georgia. My father was a farmer and construction worker, and according to Mother, "There had never been two boys more loved by their father than these boys . . . He was very proud of James."[1] She only wished Dad could have lived to see me become a general-grade officer. Dad never spanked us boys as a form of punishment. My mother always considered me a smart boy, a quiet boy, businesslike and serious all my life.[2]

During my early years, the Great Depression that had gripped the country since 1929 was slowly fading, although the effects were still felt throughout most of the United States. Most of the damage control was due to the massive government building projects inaugurated by the Franklin D. Roosevelt administration. Projects such as the prewar Banking Act federalizing all banking institutions and the Tennessee Valley Authority Project, along with other civil-service programs, assisted the country in slowly climbing out of the economic quagmire. However, like many regions in the American South, Georgia was not a direct recipient of massive government aid.

Our family was fortunate enough to own and operate a three-thousand-acre farm, a self-sustaining environment that produced hard-working, honest, and ethical people. Despite the strict segregation and Jim Crow laws of the day, we never subscribed to this socially induced form of discrimination against African Americans. The years of hard work, our religious faith, and the benefits of a rural upbringing helped shape us boys into the men we became. I always believed in what Dr. Martin Luther King Jr. said during those tumultuous years of the Civil Rights Movement: that a man "should be judged by the content of his character and not by the color of his skin."

This was never truer than on the field of battle, and it is one of the great hallmarks of our beloved Marine Corps. We were all green; it was just that some were a lighter shade of green than others. I have always tried to judge men by their actions, and any man who served with me, such as the men mentioned in this book, know this. (And my coauthor, Colin Heaton, will attest to that fact.)

I attended grammar school in Towns, Georgia, and junior high and high school in Lumber City, Georgia. When I graduated in 1957, my father decided that I needed more structure, so he sent young me to attend North Georgia College. One year later I transferred to Auburn University. While there, I joined the Sigma Pi fraternity. I tended to party more than study, and my grades reflected this. When I returned home, my father led me to a tractor, telling me, "Son, you need to go back to school and do better, or ride this tractor for the rest of your life." I took those words to heart and returned to Auburn, applied myself, and earned a bachelor's degree in civil engineering.

During the tumultuous years of the 1960s, conscription was still part of the American social and political fabric. One day I visited the Auburn University student union and spoke with several of my classmates about military service and the draft. I admittedly knew nothing about the Marine Corps, as I did not come from a military family. My father and relatives had been exempted from World War II and the Korean War because they were farmers.

I knew that I would be called upon to serve my country, so I decided to do it on my own terms. Upon receiving my draft notice in 1961, I decided to join the United States Marine Corps in Birmingham, Alabama, in 1962. My decision was simple. I wanted to be with a very

aggressive outfit. Therefore, instead of attending the initial officers'
training course over two summers, at six weeks respectively, I went
through the entire course in one session.

Upon completing Junior Platoon Leaders Class in 1961 we walked
the twenty-five miles to mainside to attend Senior Platoon Leaders
Class, where we learned we would start our basic training all over again.
The following morning, 65 percent of the men I had arrived with had
withdrawn, not wanting to relive the experience. I remained to attend
the platoon leaders course. Due to my size, I was weighed down by
carrying the water-cooled Browning .30 caliber machine gun, which
was not a prime weapon in high demand for grunts "on the hump," in
addition to the full rucksack and additional items we all carried.

Upon completion of the platoon leaders classes at Quantico,
Virginia, and graduation from Auburn University, I received my
commission as a second lieutenant in the United States Marine Corps
Reserve in June 1962, and attended the Basic School, Class 1-62. I did
not want a regular commission, since I did not intend on staying in the
Corps beyond my three-year term. In fact, the other incentive for my
joining the reserve was that reserve officers received a three-hundred-
dollar stipend towards uniform purchases, which the regular officers
did not enjoy. I remained at Quantico for two months, operating as a
platoon leader and working as an aggressor-unit commander against
the new officer trainees.

Shortly thereafter, I soon received orders to report to Camp
Pendleton, California, where I joined the 2nd Battalion, 5th Marines.
Living in San Clemente was a new experience for me, a young man
coming from a farm in Georgia. Soon the unit boarded ships out of
San Diego for a Far East unit deployment on what would be a fifteen-
month cruise. When asked what she thought about my decision to join
the Corps, my mom said, "You know good and well I was worried." She
was worried even when my parents came with me and I brought my
Corvette to California.

Spending a month on board ship and enduring sea sickness, the
unit managed to spend five days in Hawaii, enjoying the local flavor and
drinking mai tais. The battalion had been designated 3rd Battalion, 3rd

Marines, from 2/5, and I was a Lima Company platoon commander. We all ventured forward to see exotic places, such as Hong Kong and the Philippine Islands, with an interesting stint in Olongopo, a Philippine city most Marines and sailors know of all too well.

We remained off the coast of Vietnam as a combat-support group and as security and observers for the airfield at Da Nang. However, this trip to Vietnam would not prove to be very adventurous. After completing this tour, I was reassigned to Cherry Point, North Carolina, as an air intelligence officer, which was an assignment I loathed. I did finally secure a position as a series training officer at Marine Recruit Depot on Parris Island, South Carolina, in 1965, and that assignment was more suited to my talents and ambitions. After that stint, I was reassigned to Weapons Training Battalion for the next seven months, where I also functioned as a company commander.

South Carolina was where I met and fell in love with a local Beaufort school teacher and University of South Carolina graduate, the former Sara Craft from Swansea, South Carolina. Teachers often worked in military locations due to the higher wages offered, and Sara was one of those who chose this option. She was from the area and wanted to remain close to home. Within nine months of meeting, we were married on June 10, 1966—sort of a whirlwind romance, I guess. And within a month of the wedding, I was deployed again for the next two and half years.

In late June 1966 I reported to the aircraft carrier USS *Wasp* (CV-17) berthed in Boston, Massachusetts, where I remained for nine months. Twice the ship ran aground in its role of chasing Soviet submarines. I then found myself in charge of the ship's nuclear weapons and its security detachment of fifty Marines. Being me, I always wanted to gather as much intelligence as possible, so I placed a few of my best Marines as aides to the ship's commander, Captain Etheridge, and the fleet admiral. I also knew that their daughters liked dating Marines, so I soon had my own internal intelligence pipeline, as my Marines collected data on future operations while on their respective dates.

I finally tired of being at sea and offered my resignation unless I was given another command. I was planning on a return to civilian life as an engineer, putting my degree to good use unless I could have a transfer. I volunteered for duty in Vietnam, and this wish was soon granted in September 1967. In October I arrived at the 3rd Marine Division headquarters in Da Nang, Quang Tri Province, in the Republic of Vietnam, and was assigned to 2nd Battalion, 4th Marines. Following my in-processing and assignment posting, I took command of Echo Company 2/4 (E 2/4) on October 31, 1967. Just twenty days earlier, the unit had suffered 60 percent casualties. During this time, 2/4 was redesignated Battalion Landing Team 2/4 (BLT 2/4) as the ground element of Special Landing Force Alpha, embarked on the navy ships of the Amphibious Ready Group.

My battalion was under the command of the Lt. Col. William Weise, perhaps the most outstanding combat officer I ever served under in the field. We have been the best of friends for four decades, and I know of no one who does not admire and respect him. Soon afterward we moved to Phu Bai in order to be a reaction force in case Hue City was threatened, and we were designated as a Special Landing Force. Fate would dictate that we would miss the Battle of Hue City by only two days, but I was not going to miss any action following the launching of the Tet Offensive. We were soon to make history.

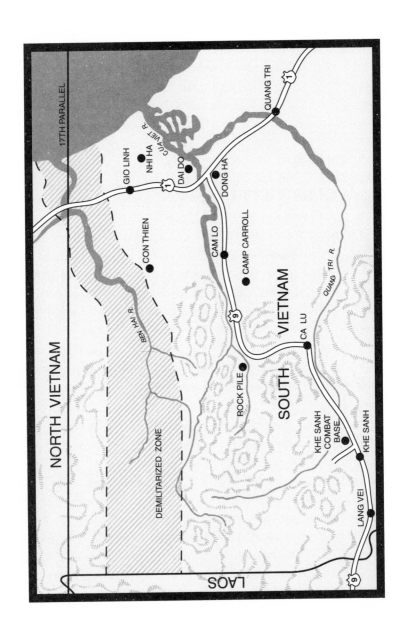

Area of 2/4 operations in Northern I Corps, Quang Tri Province.

CHAPTER 1

Quang Tri Province, 1967–68

Once the bullets fly by and men start dying, what you do next is the most important decision of your life and theirs. It had better be the right one. You may not get a second chance to make a bad mistake.
— Col. James Nicholas Rowe, U.S. Army Special Forces

OUR ENTRY INTO THE northern province of Quang Tri saw us participate in several operations after I assumed command of Echo 2/4 on October 31, 1967. The combat experience we gained during this period steeled us for what would later occur. Initially, I know that I earned the enmity of the many long-serving veterans. I enforced close haircuts, clean gear, and no mustaches. Daily shaving and rigid discipline were my unyielding methods. I never believed in idle down time.

In my mind, if a Marine was not fighting, he should be cleaning weapons or training. If not training, he should be doing physical fitness, or be getting the necessary rest for the next day's events after he cleaned weapons again. One of my first decisions was to have a heart-to-heart with my platoon leaders. I told them that if they did not perform, they would be relieved, and to enforce this ethos, I had them clean all the company's weapons. I also told my lieutenants to inspect their men and ensure they had clean gear, socks, and all the items necessary to keep them in fighting shape. And I meant business. I was and always have been uncompromising. A lot of leaders were beginning to lower

Thoughts on the New Skipper
—1st Lt. Dave R. Jones

I met Jim in October 1967, when he and I and all the other lieutenants in the company were brand new. He was all business. He interviewed all four lieutenants for the executive officer position (number two in the company), and I got the job. I was pretty proud of myself and asked him how I got it. He said it really didn't have anything to do with my performance during the interview; it was the fact that I had been in the USMC a couple of months longer than the other lieutenants. That pretty much popped my bubble!

[Livingston] was big on discipline from the very beginning of our relationship. Shaves (even though I had very little to shave), haircuts, clean weapons, and the wearing of flack jackets in the rear were the norm for our company. We also did all kinds of tactical training and physical training. I have secretly, and jokingly, told his wife that I am the one who really kept Jim alive during those months because of how much the troops hated physical training (PT) and training in a combat zone.

We were getting up at 0530, before the other companies, and running around the area doing our morning exercises. That was kind of a local joke within the battalion. We hated it, but we always felt we were the most ready.[1]

their expectations for their Marines. I kept my Marines looking like Marines. I was death on keeping weapons cleaned, and we were famous for conducting office hours in foxholes.

I lived up to my threats, but not just to be a hard ass. I knew what all good leaders knew: men need not fear authority, but they must respect it. And when Marines look and feel like Marines, they perform like Marines. I also knew the unit had suffered terrible casualties before my arrival, and raising the morale and confidence of the men was my primary ambition. I led by example and was always shaved, kept my gear in order, and was always in the front of a fight or PT run. You have to lead from the front, which is what the word *lead* means. Anyone can shout orders from the rear, but I would not want to follow such "leaders" into harm's way either. I had to be a leader. I even had the men dig fighting positions large enough so that they could do push-ups and sit-ups without being wounded by enemy fire.

To most of the Marines in E 2/4, I must have been a shock wave reminiscent of boot camp. The older veterans knew they had a real leader. The 2nd Battalion, 4th Marines, known as "the Magnificent Bastards," had earned a tough reputation. During Operation Choctaw in June 1967 to October 1967, the North Vietnamese Army (NVA) had reduced the unit to one-third of its normal operational strength, down to about three hundred Marines after their battle on September 11, 1967, at the bridge site near Cam Lo.[3] Most of those wounded in these engagements were flown to the USS *Repose*, USS *Tripoli*, and other ships waiting out in the Gulf of Tonkin or positioned off the coast of Da Nang. Lieutenant Colonel William Weise had taken over 2/4 at the end of Operation Kingfisher.

"We blamed the skipper for our woes because it seemed he was always volunteering us. A lot of us figured he would win the Medal of Honor, or die trying. We used to gripe and bitch among ourselves that he would probably kill us all getting it, but he definitely had our respect and, secretly, our admiration. I can think of no other officer I would rather have around when the shit hit the fan." [2]
— Pfc. Michael Helms

Bill Weise was, and is, an exceptional man, a quality commander, a true leader, and a Marine who inspired confidence. With him at the helm, you knew the job would get done and the Marines would prevail. He is just a great Marine and a great man.

Weise was a graduate of the U.S. Army's Command and General Staff College, Special Warfare Officer's School, Ranger School, Airborne School, and the U.S. Navy Scuba School. In Korea he commanded a rifle platoon and a mortar section and served as a rifle-company executive officer. In peacetime he commanded a rifle company, served as a battalion operations officer, and spent five years in two different force reconnaissance companies.

BLT 2/4 presented Weise and his company commanders with many problems. In addition to having new personnel in all key billets, as well as many new replacements, he perceived a lack of professionalism. There was laxity in applying noise and light discipline, improper use of listening and observation posts, poor patrolling and security procedures, poor weapons maintenance, and sloppiness in other basics.

Weise incorporated his ranger training as soon as he took command, and he initiated an in-the-field training program. He explained, "When I first took over the battalion, these guys [M-60 gunners] weren't carrying their tripods. They were shooting John Wayne style with a bipod or from the hip. We had to kick ass on that one. I threatened to relieve one company commander if he didn't get the tripods back on his machine guns. It was a matter of . . . requiring them to do what most of them already knew how to do."[4] In an article for *Marine Corps Gazette*, Weise also said, "In addition, we trained continuously in military basics appropriate to our area: assaults on fortified positions, small arms marksmanship, patrolling, crew served weapons, ambushes, calls for supporting arms, camouflage, etc. Emphasis was placed on complete paragraph orders at every level. Special emphasis was placed on patrol preparation, patrol orders, and thorough patrol briefings. When not in actual combat, the reserve company followed a formal training schedule."[5]

Prior to my joining the unit, BLT 2/4 had joined Operation Kingfisher on September 11, 1967, from its base at Camp Evans. Severe firefights and ambushes had wreaked havoc on the unit, and Golf Company endured heavy assaults. Sixteen Marines were killed in action (KIA) and 118 more wounded in action (WIA) as a result of the September 11 engagement. On October 14, 1967, BLT 2/4, while defending Bastard's Bridge on Route 61, made contact with the NVA as the latter first probed Hotel Company and then struck Golf Company with heavy rocket propelled grenades (RPG) and tear-gas attacks.[6]

Commanding in Quang Tri
—1st Lt. Dave R. Jones

While I was XO (executive officer), I was also the platoon commander of any of the platoons that may have been without an officer, and that was frequently. I got to know more of the men in the company as a result and had a pretty good feel for morale and the strengths that each platoon and platoon member possessed. Our first sergeant, Charles (Charlie) Otto was the man who really ran the company office (my primary assignment) and he had great respect for Jim Livingston. "Top" was in the field with his company more often than he was in the rear with records and other paperwork. Charlie also 'trained' me on how not to make too many dumb lieutenant-type mistakes.[7]

The fighting became close quarters up to the battalion command post.[8] The Marines suffered twenty-one KIA and twenty-three WIA, and twenty-four NVA dead were left behind.[9] The next mission on October 25 was uneventful until later that evening, when 2/4 and 3/3 engaged each other by accident. The word was passed that all units were to remain in place. Anything that moved from that point on was "unfriendly."

My fights were usually with the Viet Cong (VC) guerrillas. Around the Ai Tu Airfield near Quang Tri in November through December 1967 it was a cat-and-mouse game. The thing you had to watch carefully in Quang Tri was the VC would take pot shots at you—quick engagements at a distance—and run. We figured out that they would try and channel you into areas where they had booby traps, where they could hit you or get you tied down.

In this crash course in combat, I figured out how to fight them. The way to beat them was to use more ambushes along the trails, figure out the trail system and what area they were moving through. Put out just one small ambush with a fire team of four or five Marines, in multiple trail locations, and you would hit them. They would run, try to break contact by using another trail, and I would hit them again. We were hitting them with multiple ambushes, and they did not know how to get out of them. Then they would fragment into smaller teams, which would make our smaller ambushes more effective. I learned how to get into their mind, their tactics. We kicked their ass pretty well at Quang Tri. It took a month to figure it out, but I finally did. I was very successful down there.

> "During April 1968, our night patrols and ambushes were particularly productive. Most of our kills were at night with very few friendly casualties. We even conducted a successful battalion night attack. We literally took the night away from the enemy. I firmly believe the enemy began to avoid our area because he was consistently getting his ass kicked." [10]
> —Brig. Gen. William Weise

It is always good for any commander to obtain the perspectives and evaluations of his subordinates. The men under you will always see most of what you see, but in many cases, given the amount of responsibility a commander is burdened with, these observations by subordinate Marines often become invaluable. The commander cannot be everywhere all the time.

Our success was manifested by the decrease in casualties, both from enemy fire and booby traps. My men knew the terrain, and they came to know the people. Establishing trust among the indigenous personnel was the root of any "hearts and minds" campaign. Such campaigns were mostly touted by the famed Green Berets, great soldiers specially trained, designated, and deployed to cultivate relationships with the locals.

I think we Marines also knew how to work the hearts-and-minds battle, because we understood the Kit Carson Scouts, men who had been NVA and VC and who had decided that fighting for freedom and being truly free meant joining the American cause. We also understood the integration in the Combined Action Platoon Program, which was a real success in the areas of operation where we would do MEDCAPS

(Medical Civil Action Programs) and those kinds of things. So there was a good template on how to fight the hearts-and-minds war, but it was never really exploited properly, in my mind.

The secret to success on the battlefield was to have local support at all levels; hence, once the military application was applied, the political application fell into place. Our Marines would have made any A-Team detachment proud. You'd spend more time out there and get dirty with the locals, and you stayed there until you got shot or you got rotated. That's how our Marines earned the trust of the locals, which is the most critical component in reducing any insurgency operation.

The Kit Carson Scouts were OK, and the last one I had was a pretty good guy. He sent us gifts and cried like a baby when we left. He really wanted to be a Marine. He had been a VC chief. I could not tell you what happened to the guy after we left. I suspect the VC were aware of him and killed him when we pulled out. But he was very helpful—not as great as I thought he would be, but pretty damned good. The mistake the military would make was they would not put you where a Kit Carson Scout was from, where he really knew the people and the area. The dialects changed, and if he wasn't from the area of operations, his knowledge of the terrain was no better than ours; he was just as lost as anyone else.

Bill Weise used the slow down in operations to train the unit, while still assisting with Operation Osceola near the Ai Tu Airfield in Quang Tri. All the standard high-speed infantry training methods were used: crossing danger areas, fording streams, entering villages, patrolling, locating booby traps, employing camouflage, firing and maneuvering, etc. This gave me a chance to have a great training ground for my company before we got involved with the big stuff up north. We had about two months at the area, and I emphasized training, training, training the whole time we were there, doing all the fundamentals— patrolling, learning tactics, making sure my platoons and platoon leaders were all up to speed. It was constant. We used missions against the guerrilla threat we had around Quang Tri as a method of keeping us honest. So when we got into the fight up around Cua Viet, we were ready to fight.

Captain James Laney (Jim) Williams had his own perspective on the PT sessions:

> We company commanders thought the idea of doing PT in a battle zone and running in cadence in company formations was a little much. Admittedly, we were in a kind of rear area, but we were certainly within range of artillery and rockets. We thought it was hokey and not very tactical, not very safe, but we came around. We never did take any incoming, and it did get us back to thinking like Marines again. Gradually, Weise got our confidence and we found out he was a little flamboyant and hot doggy, but he had the substance to go with it.[11]

BLT 2/4 earned a legendary reputation across Vietnam with our willingness to look for the enemy, not just respond to threats, as Captain Williams describes: "We were just a really aggressive outfit, and the initiative was ours. Other units were always waiting for the enemy to do something. With us it was exactly the opposite. We were doing it to them. You have to put the credit right at the top. I witnessed this extraordinary evolution of a battalion that was on its ass in proficiency, morale, esprit, and discipline—the four indicators of leadership—as Weise turned it into probably the finest fighting outfit in Vietnam."[12]

During this time, I kept my men in the field, learning the terrain, working on tactics (especially the aforementioned ambushes), tracking, patrolling, and using noise and light discipline. I believed in Field Marshal Erwin Rommel's credo that "sweat saves blood," and believe me, I made them sweat. I hammered into them that you didn't stop your attack when a man went down, but I assured them that once the attack was launched and the mission completed, the wounded and the dead would be retrieved.

For all the discomfort, pain, hunger, and exhaustion incurred by 2/4 and by Echo Company in particular, what we achieved was competence, confidence, and *esprit de corps*. And the men had faith in their skipper. Men grumble and complain about their leaders. That is as true today as it was in the time of Alexander the Great. However, men under fire or the threat of fire will endure anything for a commander who shares their pain, discomfort, and danger, and who they know will be there for them. This is important, and I think the sharing of hardship

Nothing Stops a Marine
—Capt. James Laney Willams

Our Marines, trained from the first day of boot camp to look out for one another, were allowing their attachment to their buddies to jeopardize all of us. When one youngster would get hit, three more would stop their assault fire and forward movement and run over to assist their fallen buddy.

This phenomenon was particularly troublesome in the attacks on Vinh Quan Thuong and Lam Xuan East and Jim Livingston and I, along with some encouragement from Weise, resolved to do something about it. During the lull in the action in April, we cordoned off an area in front of our perimeter at Mai Xa Chanh [West] and drilled our squads and platoons in live fire assaults. We stressed the fact that in the attack, continued momentum is essential and once committed to the assault, nothing must stop them . . . I don't care if it is your mother going down, you leave her lying there and you keep going.[13]

does more than just bond a unit together; it also instills a sense of integrity and discipline that cannot be achieved otherwise.

I also knew that if men fear a leader, they will fight for him; but if they love and respect him, they will die for him and the cause for which they are fighting. That was the way I felt about Bill Weise. This concept goes up the rank structure as well as down. Loyalty goes a long way, but it is a two-way street. That concept was also reflected by the men under Captain Williams and Capt. Jay Vargas, as well as under our battalion commanding officer (CO). Vargas said, "The three of us knew that if anything went wrong, the other guy was going to come hell for broke."[16] All of us company skippers had complete faith in our fellow company commanders and the battalion CO, and vice versa. That was our strength, and that fact alone would prove to be our greatest weapon. It was a comfortable feeling to know that if one company was in trouble, the others would move heaven and earth to assist the unit under threat, even at the risk of their own lives. The men knew this, and they could count on that fact.

Williams, Vargas, and Weise were cut of the same cloth. Leading men into danger was preferable to following those men into comfort or issuing orders from the rear, which is not the Marine way of doing business. My Quang Tri operations against the Viet Cong had brought me invaluable experience, which I later utilized at places such as Vinh Quan Thuong. I also learned a lot about my men; I was able to see their strengths and weaknesses, and compensate accordingly, by placing the right man in the right place at the right time.

The two months spent at Ai Tu, from November to December, had cost 2/4 six KIA and seventy-eight WIA versus seventeen enemy KIA and two enemy prisoners of war (POWs). By January 6, 1968, the battalion (newly redesignated BLT 2/4) was deployed to Subic Bay, Philippines, for rest, refit, and further training. Weise said that "the training and rehabilitation, scheduled for a month, lasted only seven days. Although many personnel were joined, the BLT was not brought up to full table-of-organization (T/O) strength. The increase in enemy activity in Vietnam was the reason 2/4's stay in the Philippines was cut short." [15] The immediate future would prove that we would need every minute of rest, every weapon ready, and every fresh Marine we could get.

The 3rd Marine Division began a program of civic action as part of the ongoing hearts-and-minds campaign in the province. Creating a user-friendly environment among the civilian population was deemed critical. They had been badly abused, and getting to know the people and obtaining their trust was important. We did that, and that was a good thing. At the end of the day, having a population that was friendly and reliable took a lot of pressure off of us. We did a good job, and it paid off.

So there I was, the new skipper of a combat-tested rifle company. I took them to the next level, reinforced their training, built their confidence, and made them tough. I knew that they would need it. I just had no idea just how soon that preparation would pay off.

CHAPTER 2

Enemy Push to Dong Ha

Often when you feel your weakest, events unfold that force you to do your very best.

—Lt. Gen. Marion Carl, USMC

THE YEAR 1968 WAS a watershed for the United States in Vietnam. In true Damoclesian fashion, the American military defeated the NVA and Viet Cong in the field on many fronts during and after the Tet Offensive. However, the year proved to be a double-edged sword. The perceived success by the Communists as portrayed in the American media was erroneous, yet forever damaging to our cause. The media failed to inform the American people of the success we had at killing the enemy, often at a ten-to-one ratio, if not more.

U.S. forces were stretched thin, especially within I Corps. Operation Scotland II involving Khe Sanh and Operation Delaware in the A Shau Valley kept a large percentage of American forces and the Army of the Republic of Vietnam (ARVN) busy.[1] This fact was the catalyst for the various attacks the NVA launched throughout South Vietnam. Due to the scattered nature of our collective forces, the enemy felt emboldened to launch the Tet Offensive. The enemy hoped that our attention would be diverted, and thus our assets focused to the south and west. So they decided to launch an incursion that April. (This chain of events is clearly stated in the book *U.S. Marines in Vietnam: The Defining Year, 1968*.[2])

At this point it is important to distinguish between the small town of Dong Ha and the Dong Ha Combat Base (DHCB). The DHCB was the largest and most important combat and combat-support base in the DMZ. The headquarters of the 3rd Marine Division, it was occupied and defended by Marine support troops and was located immediately south of Dong Ha town. Dong Ha town occupied the junction of two very important highways: Highway 1, running north and south, and Highway 9, running east and west. The town also lay on both sides of the Bo Dieu/Cua Viet River and the important bridge crossing that river. Dong Ha town was the command post of the 2nd ARVN Regiment and was defended by Vietnamese Army troops. The Bo Dieu/Cua Viet River flowed west to east from Dong Ha town into the South China Sea. More than 90 percent of the supplies for all allied forces in the northern part of South Vietnam were off-loaded from ships in the South China Sea onto lighter navy craft, ferried up the Bo Dieu/Cua Viet River, off-loaded at a ramp at Dong Ha town, and transported by truck to DHCB.

The NVA 320th Division was tasked with taking the area from Dong Ha and Quang Tri province down to Da Nang, thereby severing the river routes necessary for American supplies. These supplies were substantial; according to U.S. Marines in Vietnam: The Defining Year, 1968, "nearly 63,000 tons of supplies came in by sea at the Cua Viet port facility for the 3rd Marine Division and then were shipped up the Cua Viet to Dong Ha."[3] If the NVA could cut this area off from the rest of I Corps, it would be a strategic defeat, and our ability to fight the war would have been compromised.

The NVA had learned their tactics from fighting the French a decade earlier until their final victory in May 1954. They also learned from us, and the Communists were determined to control the region, including Routes 1 and 9 to Highway 1, in total.

One of the main problems with the field tactics employed was that the overall commander of U.S. forces, U.S. Army Gen. William C. Westmoreland, wanted to operate on the "search and destroy" method, where he hoped to weaken the North's resolve through combat and materiel attrition. In a 1994 interview, Westmoreland stated: "I felt that being mobile, and highly efficient, we would be able to wear the enemy down. With the Air Force, Navy and Marine air assets hitting the Ho Chi Minh Trail, and all other resupply routes, the NVA and VC would wither on the vine. What we could not interdict with any proficiency were the sanctuaries they enjoyed in Laos and Cambodia. Being denied these areas, they were able to regroup, refit and reengage at will."[4]

This fact mentioned by Westmoreland must be addressed. He was very correct in his assertion that our inability to openly attack across the Laotian and Cambodian borders was at the very least a great hindrance. In my humble opinion, handcuffing us and not allowing us to pursue the enemy, no matter where they went, made about as much sense as backseat driving at the Indianapolis 500.

Lieutenant General Victor H. Krulak, the commanding general of the Fleet Marine Force Pacific (FMFPAC) knew the method employed by Westmoreland was flawed, as did I, Weise, and any other Marine officer, and he could look to the last several years of operations to prove it. Krulak, NVA general Vo Nguyen Giap, as well as Ho Chi Minh, all knew that large battles were not the only key to success. Controlling the waterways and villages, interdicting and controlling the flow of men and materiel, as well as gathering local support through hearts and minds (or through terror, in the case of the Communists), was the way to win this type of war. Unlike the U.S military, the Communists did not answer to an elected civilian government, and public opinion back home in Hanoi was irrelevant. To us, the dead dictated policy. To them, the dead were martyrs for a greater revolutionary cause. Unfortunately for the Marines, Krulak was not calling the shots.

The NVA and VC used the borders with Laos, Cambodia, and North Vietnam as sanctuaries from which to launch attacks and then to withdraw to, knowing that large-scale conventional forces were prevented from pursuing in force. We did deploy small special-operations units, which had their value, but these groups were very limited in their capabilities, and therefore not able to provide as much of an impact on the larger picture as we needed.

Hanoi knew what Washington mandated, and the NVA used it to their advantage. The enemy also knew that they could not survive and emerge victorious in the field, either in a conventional or unconventional war, if engaging U.S. forces *en masse* on a regular basis. This was especially true of engaging our Marines. What had really disturbed me was the fact that politicians in Washington, being more concerned with foreign and domestic opinion, tried to piecemeal our way through the war, sending in units in varying stages and incrementally. We should have gone in right away in 1965 with everything we had, reserves included, and finished the job in about four to five years. Instead we struggled through that war for a decade.

It was at this point that the war became more of a struggle politically than militarily, and propaganda became the most effective weapon. The NVA did not win a significant battle in the whole Tet Offensive. They won a strategic battle in the political arena, but not a significant tactical battle. Where they won was when Walter Cronkite came out and said there were all these problems; the rest of the press picked up on that message, then Congress started to echo the polemic. We started having riots here in the States, so everything turned against the war and in favor of this sort of strategic environment that the press had painted—the image that we were losing (just like the press did in Iraq before the surge in 2007).

Once BLT 2/4 returned to Vietnam in January 1968, Lieutenant Colonel Weise had his Marines and sailors moving in the direction he desired. Nonetheless, training continued even during combat operations. Training from this point forward focused on differences in the enemy and tactical situations, which varied from operation to operation. The unit participated in both Operation Ballistic Armor and Operation Fortress Attack from January 22 to 31, 1968.[5] The Tet Offensive had placed 2/4 north of Camp Carrol in February 1968 during Operation Lancaster II, where it suffered ten KIA and ninety-eight WIA, while inflicting thirty-five confirmed enemy kills.[6]

One of Weise's crown jewels was Maj. George F. "Fritz" Warren, his new S-3 (operations officer), who joined the unit on February 19, 1968.[7] Warren was a former enlisted man who attended the U.S. Naval Academy at Annapolis, and he was highly regarded by his battalion C.O. and the company commanders. On March 5, 1968, BLT 2/4 relived the 3rd Battalion, 1st Marines, commanded by Lt. Col. Max McGowan, at Mai Xa Chanh, on the north bank of the Bo Dieu/Cua Viet River. The BLT 2/4 tactical area of responsibility (TAOR) encompassed major North Vietnamese Army infiltration routes. The area had been the scene of many violent clashes over the years.

The Battle for Dai Do was to unfold as part of a larger and more complex battle for the region of Dong Ha in Quang Tri Province. Understanding the events that led up to our actions is critical to understanding the nature of the buildup. A series of calculated and often unplanned actions came together to create a confusing scenario. However, although the fog of war was present, the presence of mind, training, and experience of the men and the officers prevailed.

The 3rd Marine Division, commanded by Maj. Gen. Rathvon McC. Tompkins (succeeding the deceased Maj. Gen. Bruno Hochmuth) had its headquarters at Dong Ha Combat Base. On its right flank, the unit was reinforced from the U.S. Army's 3rd Battalion, 21st Infantry Regiment, 196th Infantry Brigade of the "Americal" Division.[8] The NVA had pushed thousands of troops into the area. Part of this combined force was 2/4 under the command of Weise. BLT 2/4, stationed on the USS *Iwo Jima*, had been placed under operational control of 3rd Marine Regiment, commanded by Col. Milton A. Hull of the 3rd Marine Division, based in Okinawa, Japan.[9]

The NVA had been hurting from our forces' surprise offensive all over the country. The major objectives had not been secured long term: Hue City was retaken by the Marines; Saigon, including the attack against the U.S. embassy, was unsuccessful from the start; and Khe Sanh, even though the Americans were overwhelmed by superior numbers and under constant artillery barrages, would hold out successfully for over two months. The Central Highlands and the Special Forces fire bases were still intact overall, and the general military picture was quite positive all the way to Washington, D.C.

Operating near the DMZ, a farcical, imaginary line of demarcation supposedly separating the violent south from the unapproachable north, Marine, army, and ARVN units had been hit hard, but not hard enough. Placing U.S. forces in this static position only assisted the enemy, who were under no movement and targeting restrictions, unlike American forces commanded by Westmoreland. He was attempting to manage a controlled war according to the mandates of Washington and President Lyndon Baines Johnson, which I thought was a ludicrous way to wage a war.

The NVA and their VC allies knew that direct confrontation against us was not feasible unless they had overwhelming numerical superiority, which on occasion they achieved, although it really never mattered. What they did not factor in was the professionalism and tenacity of the Marines and soldiers in front of them. Many of our men may have been conscripts, but unlike our enemy, they were not illiterate peasants, led from the rear with a rifle in their backs. Our men were better trained, although not always as experienced. The NVA decided to target the softer and less motivated ARVN troops whenever possible, forcing many an American commander to lose sleep over the "allies" supporting his flank. I can tell the world that Weise was no exception. It was not just the questionable loyalty of these troops, which tended to shift with the wind. It was also oftentimes their lack of training and discipline that caused us concern.

BLT 2/4 command post had been located at Mai Xa Chanh since March 5, and BLT 2/4 had been operating along the Cua Viet for only seven days when Foxtrot Company was ambushed at Lam Xuan West late in the afternoon on March 12. Foxtrot Company had been lured into a kill zone. Under cover of darkness, with the assistance of Echo Company and the recon platoon, Foxtrot Company reportedly pulled all its wounded to safety. The eighteen Marines reported killed in action were left for evacuation the following day. The number eighteen did not include a photographer from the public affairs office, 3rd Marine Division, who joined Foxtrot the night before the ambush.

At daylight on March 13, the recovery operation for the reported KIAs began. The plan was a simple one. Two companies (Hotel and Golf) were to advance from the south to within 500 meters of Lam Xuan East. Hotel Company, in the lead, was to open fire on the heavily fortified village to make the enemy think the main attack was from the south. Once the enemy was under fire, Echo Company, mounted on amtracs, was to cross Jones Creek and assault the enemy from the west, hopefully achieving surprise. (Prior to the Echo assault, a Foxtrot Marine ran out of Lam Xuan East into Hotel Company positions. He had survived the ambush, but had been knocked unconscious. The Marine had survived the night by pretending to be dead.[10]

I was on the first amtrac that reached the bank of the river, and I thought the amtracs would take us all the way up and drop us on top of the NVA. But instead they became mired, stuck in the mud, and we could not go above the bank because we were taking as much incoming fire from our own forces as we were from the enemy. We were trapped in the middle of an impact area, and artillery from both sides was landing around us. The only way Weise could assist Echo was to have either Golf or Hotel Company (or both) charge across five hundred meters of open terrain, exposing them to the deadly fire from dug in enemy positions. Weise thought that this would be foolhardy and result in too many friendly casualties.

Echo Company and I launched our attack after jumping off the amtracs, and I would imagine the enemy was no more than ten to fifteen feet from us, slightly above and over the embankment from where we were on the edge of the streambed. I have no idea how many were there, but later we found all kinds of foxholes. We also found a mass grave where the enemy had buried our dead, throwing them all in together.

I made the decision not to attack at that time, since rising above the riverbank would have left us highly exposed and vulnerable. As a result of rising this way, five Marines had been shot, and I had to find a way to get them out without risking the rest of the men. I decided to place the wounded Marines on air mattresses inside the amphibious tractors (amtracs), and we floated them out on those air mattresses. We spun the dials on the amtracs, took off all the weapons, and began to pull back from that phase of the operation.

Weise did not wish to sacrifice more of his Marines to recover bodies, and therefore, he decided that he would first order the withdrawal of all three of his companies. He believed he could sufficiently soften the enemy position with supporting arms to enable the recovery of the bodies without heavy friendly losses. For the remainder of the day and through March 14, Lam Xuan East was pounded with air strikes, artillery, and naval gunfire.[11]

These maneuvers were executed so that Hotel and Golf companies would not be exposed on their advance and suffer the same fate as Foxtrot had.[12] The area was tentatively secured on March 15, 1968, and we recovered all eighteen bodies. These KIA were identified, wrapped in ponchos, and laid neatly in one row in a clear area to await evacuation by helicopter. As the first helicopter approached, enemy artillery fire hit the area close to the helicopter landing zone (HLZ) and continued throughout the twenty-minute evacuation. To avoid enemy fire, the H-34 helicopters zigzagged back and forth, approaching and leaving the HLZ, touching down very briefly to allow the bodies to be loaded quickly into their side doors.

The bodies were then delivered to the Dong Ha Combat Base medical company before being transferred to the morgue at Da Nang. The medical company claimed that only seventeen bodies were delivered when they were checked some time later. The unaccounted for Marine body may have fallen out of the open side door of one of the helicopters en route to Dong Ha. Sadly, despite active searches, the body was never located.[13]

In a twist of irony, higher command believed that Weise had not been aggressive enough and that he should have recovered the bodies on March 13. This belief was not shared by me or any of the other company commanders. Weise sensed that the enemy was building up to something much larger. This assessment was to be proven true on March 18 at Vinh Quan Thuong, when a recon platoon under 1st Lt. William C. Muter managed to identify the enemy before a similar ambush could be launched against the Marines.[14] Echo and Hotel laid down a base of fire from the east for Golf Company to assault the fortified ville from the north, as Golf attacked the exposed enemy flank. The actual assault was to begin immediately following a scheduled air strike at 7 a.m. For unknown reasons, the air strike was not delivered on time.

Then, without orders, Jim Williams and I both jumped up, each emboldening the other; he was armed with an e-tool [entrenching tool], while I was armed with a burp gun. Given the tactical advantage as I saw it, the enemy would not expect an outright attack from so small a group of Marines. So we led the final assault for both companies into the village of Vinh Quan Thuong under an intense artillery and rocket barrage. We attacked from across the open ground. At this time, Weise ordered Golf Company to support this attack from the north.

We were coming around to the right, and when we started, we were still down in the sand dunes. We were taking extensive incoming enemy fire from small arms and rockets—the whole works, including offensive artillery. Captain Williams was inside the hedgerow at the wood line, and he and I were both moving forward. At that point, Weise pulled me around, and we began to consolidate with Hotel.

What is very interesting and should be mentioned was that just prior to our assault, this mission witnessed the battalion's last active use of flamethrowers. We pulled flamethrowers over to the left of Vinh Quan Thuong. This really panicked the North Vietnamese, who were entrenched in typical A-frame bunkers and spider holes. They were all dug in, so you really had to get right up on top of them to find them. They had obviously been there for quite a while, and when they were exposed to those flamethrowers, they began pouring on the fire and pouring on the artillery. I guess that was the first time they had been exposed to flamethrowers, which are excellent psychological weapons and force multipliers. The flamethrowers really frightened the devil out of those guys. During this time, Jay Vargas came in on the flank aboard amtracs, and all three companies moved in. It was a slugfest. However, we had sixteen to eighteen Marines killed very quickly on that mission.

One strange and funny thing was this: before the operation, Sgt. Charlie Otto and I were coming from Mao Tse Tung and Mai Tse Tai across the rice paddies and were receiving four deuce [U.S. 4.2-inch] mortars. We took some short rounds, which almost landed right on top of Otto and me, and the only thing that saved us was that they landed and buried themselves in the rice paddy. Consequently, the mortar rounds did not explode, but instead produced just a "whump-thuck" sucking sound that we were glad to hear.

I must say that we had some idea of the enemy's dedication and intent, especially when we were on the mission to recover the bodies of our dead Marines from the earlier actions in March at Nhi Ha, Lam Xuan East, and Lam Xuan West. Several of us were in the field collecting the dead and loading them onto helicopters when we started taking serious incoming. Weise and I took a dive into the same foxhole when the rounds came in. To this day, we still joke about how we both somehow made ourselves fit into it. However, the humor of that situation was seriously offset by the gravity of recovering the fourteen or fifteen bodies that were left behind at Lam Xuan by Foxtrot Company. It was a sad time, but we were not going to leave our Marines behind.

That recovery happened the evening after the operation was over and we had overrun the enemy position. The NVA were trying to escape. I was tired, and the Marines were tired. We had been slugging it out since three that morning. At 9 p.m., after we had secured the terrain and consolidated our position, I sort of just passed out. Well, the company gunny, Wayne Thomas, shot one of the enemy in the perimeter as he was trying to escape, and the guy fell dead across my legs. It was not until a couple of hours later that I woke up to find this corpse lying across me. I had never heard the shot or even felt the guy land on me. The gunny, an original Irish character, smiled at me as I woke up and saw this NVA on top of me. He must have seen the surprise and confusion on my face. He said, "I didn't want to wake you up, sir." (Thomas was a guy who would make runs to get the cigars and the Tabasco sauce, and could always come up with onions—everything.)

The Marines finally secured Vinh Quan Thuong after heavy fighting. Williams and I would both receive Silver Stars for our actions.[15] General Westmoreland even sent a congratulatory message to BLT 2/4 for its success.[16]

The following mission, Operation Kilo, which ran from March 31 to April 2, 1968, was a combined USMC-ARVN operation to clear the enemy from the area between Highway 1 on the west, the South China Sea on the east, the Bo Dieu/Cua Viet River on the south, and the DMZ on the north. The 2nd ARVN Regiment was responsible for the area between Highway 1 on the west and Jones Creek on the east. BLT 2/4 tied in with the 2nd ARVN Regiment and the 1st Amtrac Battalion. BLT 2/4 was in the center, with the ARVN unit on its left along Jones

Creek and 1st Amtrac on its right. The operation began at the Bo Dieu/ Cua Viet River and continued north to the DMZ. All units jumped off at the same time. Weise used three companies for the sweep, with one in reserve. Golf Company, under Capt. Robert Mastrion, was on the left; Hotel Company, under Capt. Jim Williams, was on the right; and Echo Company, under me, followed in trace. Foxtrot Company, under 1st Lt. Michael Gavlick, remained at Mai Xa Chanh.[17]

As Golf Company moved into the open area north of Lam Xuan East, it received heavy artillery fire from the north and heavy machine-gun fire from its west. The heavy machine-gun fire came from the "friendly" ARVN unit to its left. Fortunately, the machine-gun fire was high, and the artillery rounds landed in soft ground, which absorbed much of the shrapnel and explosive force. It took a long time to get the friendly ARVN to stop firing at Golf. There was nothing Golf could do except lay prone all day and pray.[18]

Mastrion, who was recently assigned as the commanding officer of Golf Company (relieving the twice-wounded Capt. Jay R. Vargas), kept his cool, and his company suffered no serious casualties. Mastrion's former enlisted infantry experience served him well, despite his previous assignment as a supply officer before reporting to 2/4. Bill Weise said Mastrion "was a tough, competent, no-nonsense leader who had a wonderful sense of humor. During the enemy artillery barrage, he was injured but refused evacuation in order to remain with his company. Despite his injuries, he remained calm, and his coolness permeated Golf Company, whose Marines and sailors lay hugging the ground for many hours. Mastrion showed his sense of humor, despite the pain from his wounds."

During one of the many radio contacts Mastrion had with Weise, he was asked how he was doing. He replied, "I'm OK, Dixie Diner Six [Weise's call sign], but this is one hell of a situation for a supply officer."

Finally the ARVN machine-gun fire ceased. For his leadership under continuous enemy fire, despite painful wounds, Mastrion was awarded the Silver Star.[19]

The only significant contact with enemy troops occurred late on the second day of Operation Kilo, when Hotel Company encountered an enemy strongpoint north of Nhi Ha. After a bitter defense by the enemy, Hotel Company, led by Williams, seized the position in a violent, close combat, killing approximately twenty enemy soldiers and suffering ten casualties. One of Hotel's casualties was 1st Lt. Tim Shorten, who was killed during the assault. Surprisingly, the enemy strongpoint turned out to be a cleverly concealed aid station or field hospital with many medical supplies. There was also evidence that casualties had recently been treated there. It appeared that the enemy defenders had delayed Hotel Company long enough for medical personnel and their patients to be evacuated.[20]

The remainder of the sweep all the way to the DMZ was relatively uneventful, except for sporadic enemy artillery and sniper fire. A number of recently vacated positions were discovered. In several of them, Marines discovered personal gear and pots filled with warm, recently cooked rice. Evidently, the positions were vacated in great haste.

As March closed, 2/4 incurred 59 KIA and 360 WIA during the month, and the combined force bagged an estimated 474 NVA. I know that at least a couple of hundred enemy troops were removed by 2/4 during that time.

Padding a body count was not only considered acceptable, but it was also encouraged by Washington, via Westmoreland, to justify the war effort politically.[21] Using the law of probability was also a political way for senior U.S. Army commanders to not have to get into the bush to justify their actions. While it may be true that many commanders, especially in the army, at some point used the estimate, few at the company level in the Marines had that much latitude. I was not a man to guess at anything and neither was Bill Weise. In my opinion, army units tended to use the body-count estimate more liberally than Marines, and in fact, we never used anything resembling an estimate. If it was not tagged, bagged, dragged, and identified, it was not a kill. I believe that this policy in the army was due more to their higher command authority; men who hardly, if ever, went into the bush personally wrote the after-action reports that secured their promotions and enhanced their careers. I call that leadership by proxy.

CHAPTER 3

Entering Dong Ha and Dai Do

I thought commanders who flew in helicopters while their troops were on the ground were assholes. You have to go where the action is to find out what's going on.[1]

— Brig. Gen. Bill Weise, USMC (ret.)

THE FIRST HALF OF April was fairly quiet for 2/4 and the 3rd Marine Division in general. Upon completion of Operation Kilo on April 3, 1968, the rifle companies of BLT 2/4 were relocated as follows: Echo Company moved to Nhi Ha. Golf Company moved to Lam Xuan East. Hotel Company moved to the southwest sector of the BLT's TAOR. Two platoons of Foxtrot Company were located in the eastern sector of Mai Xa Chanh, and its third platoon was stationed at My Loc on the banks of the Cua Viet River. Each of these companies established bases from which to patrol and cover their assigned sectors of responsibility. The BLT 2/4 command post and remaining units— such as the BLT aid station and the engineer, amtrac, communications, and 81mm-mortar platoons (minus one section located at Nhi Ha)—continued at Mai Xa Chanh.[2]

With exception to sporadic nocturnal engagements and the occasional patrol contact, all was fairly quiet on the Dong Ha front, although we had extensive ongoing patrolling operations. Weise liked to know what was out there, where the enemy was and, just as important, where the enemy was not. All four rifle companies patrolled extensively at

Training Never Stopped
—Brig. Gen. William Weise

Despite all [our] preparation and security, training continued unabated. Full five-paragraph patrol orders were mandatory, and thorough patrol briefings were emphasized. All units in the BLT were required to conduct daily physical conditioning except when engaged in combat. The requirement for physical conditioning was grudgingly implemented by most of the unit leaders, but was carried out with enthusiasm by Captain Livingston. The purpose of the seemingly unnecessary requirement for physical conditioning was simple: to keep the Marines from becoming lethargic and careless.[3]

night and set up ambushes and listening posts in areas of likely enemy activity.[4]

Weise, Warren, and others understood this necessity, and eventually all company commanders realized the purpose of what some had originally believed to be bordering on unnecessary harassment. The other company commanders and I practiced the British system of being 100 percent alert from thirty minutes before daybreak until thirty minutes after daybreak. Emphasis was placed on weapons cleaning and the practice of various combat techniques, especially assaults against fortified positions and immediate reaction to ambushes.

During this time, replacements came in, reinvigorating the battalion, and training continued at Ai Tu. Once again we focused on the basics and enhanced the lethality of the battalion in general and my company in particular.

On April 26, 1968, intelligence reports revealed the presence of a large North Vietnamese Army unit in a fortified hamlet at An My, just below the DMZ, north of Nhi Ha and the ARVN position at Alpha 1 (a fortified "dye-marker" position). In less than forty-eight hours, BLT 2/4 planned and executed a night attack against the enemy at An My. The attack plan was simple, but daring. Under cover of darkness, Echo Company was to move from Nhi Ha to an attack position north of An My for a predawn assault. Weise hoped that an attack from the north would be a complete surprise and catch the enemy off guard.[5] Foxtrot Company was to move into a position in the sand dunes east of An My and from there provide a base of fire for the Echo Company attack. Golf Company was to move into a blocking position south of An My, to kill or capture any enemy retreating from the Echo Company assault. Hotel Company, designated BLT Reserve, prepared to move and support the attack if required. All units would move during darkness from their assigned locations.[6]

This mission was to support the overall 3rd Marine Regiment's Operation Napoleon/Saline, scheduled to launch on the night of April 28, 1968.[7] The mission was augmented by the 2nd ARVN Regiment troops located in a fixed strong point seven kilometers northwest of Mai Xa Chanh West, about three miles south of the DMZ. Most Marines had little confidence in the ARVN unit, and I was no exception.[8] (During my final battles in Vietnam, a unit of South Vietnamese Marines would earn my respect, as they fought to the death while other units quit.) We were stationed at the bridge at Dong Ha, but I went up to observe the action along Route 1.

A fly in the ointment resulted because this attack plan needed to be coordinated with the ARVN company located on Alpha 1. Apparently, a mole in the ARVN unit had notified the enemy of the 2/4 attack. Just after darkness, as the BLT 2/4 companies were moving into their assigned positions, the NVA vacated the village and moved south. The NVA bumped into Golf Company, resulting in a night engagement between the enemy battalion and a Marine rifle company.[9]

By 10 p.m., Mastrion had placed Golf Company where the S-2 (intelligence) officer claimed that two thousand NVA would be arriving. Soon one Marine heard voices and called out, initiating the firefight. Mastrion called in the action to the S-2 as the NVA opened up on his men. Green enemy and red Marine tracers intersected as rounds were exchanged.

Weise knew what was happening, and he decided not to send either Foxtrot or Echo company deeper, as the possibility of accidental friendly fire was too high. With that knowledge, Mastrion ordered Lieutenant

Acly to call in artillery, which he did. The fire mission fell to Alpha Battery, 1st Battalion, 12th Marines, and their 105mm guns, based at Dong Ha.[10] Supporting the heavy artillery, 2/4's 81mm mortars were also in the loop. Mastrion assessed the result, relocated his men fifty meters from the contact point, and ordered a medical evacuation as the wounded were collected and placed in litter teams.[11]

A night firefight ensued—violent, unplanned, every man for himself, and close range. Mastrion called Weise for help, but Weise knew that sending reinforcements to Golf Company at night during a firefight would end in disaster, with Marines fighting Marines. So Weise told Mastrion that he was on his own and to do the very best he could. Mastrion and Golf did just that. Golf Company more than held its own, forcing the enemy back. Unfortunately, Mastrion was wounded,

---

The NVA After Tet
—Brig. Gen. William Weise

From a strictly military point of view, the 1968 Tet Offensive was a major failure, and the North Vietnamese knew it, even if our own press did not realize that fact. In a futile attempt to emulate their previous success against the French at Dien Bien Phu in May 1954, the NVA lost thousands of soldiers and inflicted relatively minor damage on the Marine defenders. At Hue City (the ancient capital of Vietnam) the NVA forces were defeated and driven out, despite their initial success at occupying the city. Most important of all, the expected popular uprising throughout South Vietnam did not occur. Instead of welcoming the NVA/VC invaders with open arms, the South Vietnamese Popular Forces (PF) fought for their villages and, in most cases, soundly defeated the many VC units. In fact, as a result of the village PF, the VC military organization was virtually eliminated as a major force throughout South Vietnam.

for the second time in three weeks, by an explosion that blew him into the air, badly bruising his back. Unable to walk, he maintained control of his company despite great pain.[12]

When the fighting subsided, Mastrion reorganized his company and established what he believed to be a secure night HLZ from which to evacuate his most seriously wounded Marines. What Mastrion did not know was that a number of enemy soldiers lay close by, hidden in the darkness.[13] Mastrion retreated Golf Company to Pho Con, a village along Route 1, under Weise's orders—a decision apparently not welcomed by his platoon leaders. They arrived at 3 a.m., and the most severe casualty was a young Marine with a head wound. He had been carried throughout the movement and later died. These events were the precursor to what was about to happen in the larger battle.

Faced with these failures, the North Vietnamese needed a dramatic victory that would convince the American public that it would be futile to continue the war. The defeat of the U.S. Marines and the destruction of DHCB by the North Vietnamese Army would not only prove disastrous to the U.S. military effort, but it would also give a tremendous boost to NVA morale and great encouragement to the American antiwar effort. It was equally an important propaganda requirement and a strategic military necessity.

Penetration of the thinly defended perimeter around the sprawling base would be easy for a well-planned infantry or sapper (an NVA commando-type unit) attack; especially if surprise was achieved. Even if the entire base was not destroyed, the ammunition dump and POL farm, which lay close to Highway 1, could be set ablaze in a massive conflagration that would last for days. Such a spectacle playing nightly on the six o'clock news would have been a major propaganda victory.[14]

When the fight between the ARVN and NVA was over, I took some men forward to look over the battlefield along Route 1 between Dong Ha and Gio Linh, and we had a talk with the ARVN. I saw that the forces they'd been fighting were not the typical VC, but top soldiers. To risk expending these assets meant this terrain meant something to the NVA. I must also say that we were chomping at the bit to get into the fight. That would change soon enough.

I saw one small group from the 2nd ARVN Regiment had tangled with the NVA just about a half mile north of us, at Gio Linh, where there was a small stream with a bridge. (Gio Linh is both the name of a town just south of the DMZ on Highway 1 and the name of the northern district of Quang Tri Province.) The NVA were walking boldly up Highway 1, which meant they were taking our presence in the area seriously. This type of bold exposure was extremely uncommon and daring, and I knew they were playing for real. The ARVN this time had killed many of the NVA, who were really trying to take Dong Ha, because it was such a strategic target. Had they been successful, it would have been a totally catastrophic failure for American forces. The NVA even reaching the bridge where Echo Company was would have been a grave circumstance.

Dong Ha Combat Base—which was located on the west side of Highway 1, approximately fifteen kilometers south of the DMZ—was slightly south of the city of Dong Ha and extended west. It was a sprawling base containing an air strip, the command post of the 3rd Marine Division, an artillery regiment, a huge ammunition dump, a large POL (petroleum, oils, and lubricants) farm, and various combat and combat-support units. It was the major combat/combat-support base in the northern part of South Vietnam, which meant that it was only logical that the NVA would have a real good reason to overrun it.

My company headquarters was located in a run-down building in Nhi Ha on the east bank of Jones Creek. My unit was three kilometers north of Weise's battalion headquarters on the west bank of the river, which was a tributary of the larger Cua Viet River.[15] My adjacent unit was Foxtrot Company, commanded by Capt. James H. Butler, at Mai Xa Chanh East. Weise was under the impression that

"Nhi Ha had always been a staging area for NVA infiltrating south along Jones Creek."[16]

I decided the time had come to attack, and Dave Jones and I planned the mission. Abandoning cumbersome gear and moving light, we would use stealth, speed, and deception to engage the enemy. Abandoning the normal preparatory fires used to mask movement or demoralize and reduce enemy assets, our attack was to be a complete surprise. Hotel Company was to maintain the base of fire, and Mastrion's Golf Company would set up as a blocking force to trap any NVA able to evade the attack. (Echo participated in the attack, and two platoons of Foxtrot were in battalion reserve in Mai Xa Chang.) Williams's Hotel Company was not included in the mission. From their base 2,500 meters southwest of Mai Xa Chanh West, they manned a platoon patrol base.[17] This would be 2/4's first battalion night mission, and Weise led.[18]

At 9:30 p.m., Foxtrot engaged the NVA after detecting movement.[19] At 9:45, Hotel located enemy movement and called in seventy-five rounds, but observed no positive results.[20]

Meanwhile, thinking the enemy had moved to a small hamlet for cover, Mastrion sent a detail to check it out. Soon the H-34 helicopters from the USS *Iwo Jima*, assigned to Heavy Marine Helicopter (HMH) Squadron 362 and known as the "Ugly Angels," called in for a situation report. They were informed that the landing zone (LZ) was four hundred yards from the enemy. A hot LZ at night was not what most pilots hoped for, but Marines will do anything to save fellow Marines. Once the first helicopter turned on its landing lights for a brief visual check, Mastrion realized that he was in the wrong position; his men were in the very spot the NVA had retreated to.[21]

As the H-34 medevac, piloted by Capt. Ben R. Cascio, arrived at the LZ in the darkness, he was not aware of just how close the enemy was. So he set down full on the LZ to load wounded, instead of maintaining a low hover for a rapid under-fire extraction. All hell broke loose as the enemy targeted Cascio's helicopter, and it took heavy fire. Enemy soldiers, hiding in the darkness opened fire with small arms, grenades, and rockets.

Despite numerous rounds shredding the fuselage, Cascio coolly kept his aircraft on the ground until all casualties were loaded. As he was ready to lift off, an enemy grenade or rocket hit the nose of the chopper, blowing off the engine cowling and Plexiglas canopy, severely injuring Cascio and his copilot. The crew chief was also wounded, but managed to crawl forward to check on his pilots as enemy fire continued to hit the aircraft. The copilot was unconscious and Cascio had grenade and Plexiglas fragments all over his body, including his face and head. Cascio was in extreme pain, and the blood from his head and face wounds blinded him.[22] Although unable to see, Cascio managed to regain the controls and pilot his badly damaged helicopter, under the direction of his wounded crew chief. Loaded with eight wounded Golf Company Marines, just feet above the ground, Cascio flew his crippled H-34, dripping fuel and hydraulic fluid, toward the 3rd Marine command post at the mouth of the Ba Dieu/Cua Viet River, ten kilometers away. Just as he reached the south bank of the river mouth, the engine froze, and Cascio crash-landed the helicopter on the navy boat ramp. The chopper was far too damaged to continue on to the *Iwo Jima*.[23] The wounded Marines, including the helicopter crew all survived; however, the copilot later died of his wounds. Cascio would be permanently blinded in one eye as a result of his wounds, but he recovered. Today he is a successful lawyer and very active in community and veterans affairs. He was unanimously inducted into the 2/4 Association, and he adopted the call sign of the "One-eyed, Ugly Magnificent Bastard," which he shortened to "1UB" when signing his emails.

At daylight, Mastrion himself had to be medically evacuated due to excruciating pain. Captain Jay R. Vargas, who was the battalion assistant operations officer and had been relieved by Mastrion in March, resumed command of Golf Company.[24]

Those who were seriously wounded were out of the upcoming fight. They would be the lucky ones.

CHAPTER 4

Into the Hornet's Nest

How many of the enemy you kill means far less than how many of your men you bring home.

—Maj. Gen. Walter Krupinski

O N SUNDAY, APRIL 28, at 4 a.m., my Echo Company and Williams's Hotel Company launched off and entered the empty hamlet. The enemy had hastily left Nhi Ha not long before. Later that day, my Vietnamese guide lured a lone wounded NVA soldier out of a bunker. The man may have been wounded by friendly fire, and he later succumbed to his wounds.

Then, as we crossed a rice paddy, Echo Company came under intense artillery fire from across the DMZ. The exposed Marines hustled out of the impact area, where the soft ground absorbed the impact of the incoming rounds as the men dived into the muddy water, shrapnel flying over their heads and all around us.[1]

At that time, I had only one man slightly wounded. I had managed to save my men and return to Nhi Ha at about the same time Mastrion was being medevaced after losing the feeling in his legs.[2] All units returned to our respective patrol bases. (Ironically, later, during the battle, Nhi Ha would be the designated blocking point for the army's 2/31st "Gimlets," who entered the area on May 1, 1968.[3])

The NVA 320th Division crossed the DMZ on Monday, April 28, 1968, launching the Battle of Dong Ha. There they met two battalions of the 2nd Regiment, 1st ARVN Division, near Gio Linh, a district headquarters about twelve kilometers north of DHCB. The other two 2nd ARVN battalions occupied dye-marker positions. Thus, the town of Dong Ha and the area on both sides of Highway 1, which lay in the 2nd ARVN Regiment TAOR, were evacuated.

The ARVN unit's reliability was somewhat questionable, and Weise believed they were "asleep at the switch."[4] Fritz Warren says it was possible "that the ARVN totally vacated their command-post (CP) area and moved north on Highway 1. They claimed to have met stiff resistance and called for the division reserve, a small motorized/mechanized force, which was ambushed, leaving Dong Ha totally unprotected."[5]

The NVA were trying to take the strategic Cua Viet River "horseshoe" south of the DMZ (I Corps ARVN) and the surrounding area, thus forcing a logistics nightmare as well as a tactical withdrawal of American units in the area, which would have been a strategic loss of the entire province.[6] The best result for the enemy would have been a large contingent of U.S. forces being trapped and having to be supplied by air—not a very attractive proposition for U.S. forces.

The next day, April 29, a small group from Task Force Robbie, the reserve component commanded by and named after Col. Clifford J. Robichard—consisting of Delta Company, 1st Battalion, 9th Marines; an armor company from 3rd Tank Battalion; an amtrac platoon; a platoon of Ontos anti-tank vehicles; four army vehicles including two 40mm "dusters;" and a platoon of engineers—was ambushed en route to assist the 2nd ARVN Regiment. The ARVN was responsible for the defense of Highway 1.[7] The mission of both the ARVN unit and Task Force Robbie was to protect and defend two important bridges on Highway 1 north of DHCB, where Echo 2/4 was under the operational command and control of 3rd Marine Division. Our purpose in Echo was to support the 3rd Marine Division assets and the Dong Ha bridge, among others, along Highway 1.

NVA sappers had blown explosives at a culvert four miles north of us at Dong Ha. Task Force Robbie had eleven dead and twenty wounded, while killing twenty-six of the enemy, and incurred damage to four tanks.[8] Because Echo Company was unavailable, Weise had to order Golf Company to occupy Nhi Ha in addition to Lam Xuan West. With the division reserve and the 2nd ARVN Regiment committed, the entire area between Highway 1 and the left flank of BLT 2/4 was undefended from the Bo Dieu/Cua Viet River north.[9]

However, the enemy had gone nowhere. I knew instinctively that not only were they still around, but they were going also to come at us hard at their first opportunity. They had the entrenched defensive positions, superior numbers, and terrain appreciation. On April 29, at 1:45 a.m., Echo fired at three enemy troops advancing on our position. This occurred again at 5:20 a.m. Both events would yield negative results, although two antitank mines were located and disabled by Foxtrot.[10]

At 5:10 p.m. on April 29, Hotel Company "received nine rounds of enemy artillery, which resulted in two medevacs."[11] This was the catalyst for our next action. The 2/4 after-action report (AAR) says that "[a]t 1715 Echo was helo-lifted to our position north of Dong Ha Bridge. Golf moved east to take responsibility for the two base camps at Nhi Ha and Lam Xuan West. At 2045 one of Golf's LPs called in 81mm mortars, but with exception to a blood trail, no bodies were found at first light."[12]

The Battle of Dai Do was simmering into existence. Dai Do was on a small peninsula defined by the Bo Dieu and Cua Viet rivers and two streams, one flowing into each of the rivers. The peninsula was actually populated by five hamlets: Thuong Do and Dinh To in the northwest, Dai Do and Dong Huan in the middle, and An Lac on the north bank of the Bo Dieu.[13] Nearby hamlets included Bac Vong, just across the stream that flowed into the Cua Viet near Dong Huan, and Dong Lai, west of Dai Do across the stream that flowed into the Bo Dieu.

At 3:30 a.m. on April 30, 1968, the NVA, from its positions at An Lac, started the first of several attacks by rocket and small arms against the navy river boats. Hotel Company, under Jim Williams, saw the fire, and one of his patrols out near Bac Vong witnessed the attack.[14]

At 4 a.m., rocket-propelled grenades (RPGs) and small-arms fire struck a navy landing craft utility (LCU) boat, killing one sailor and six Marines, and wounding others, forcing the LCU to return to Dong Ha. Weise radioed Col. Milton A. Hull, regimental commander of the 3rd Division, informing him of the event, and Hull wanted good intel on the situation regarding Task Force Clearwater, which was in charge of securing the Cua Viet to keep the supplies flowing up the river. Weise had requested a shift of boundaries from Hull, but this shift was the responsibility of the division commander, General Tompkins, who had to give authorization.[15]

The 9th Marine Regiment, along with tank support and augmented by the 1st Amphibious Tractor Battalion, had been brought in for the pending operation. There was limited information coming down the pipeline to us company commanders, and the bulk of the intel was coming from recon patrols and observations. For example, when I inspected a group of NVA dead, I noticed their close haircuts and their new gear, uniforms, and weapons. It was clear to me we had some fresh troops moving down against us (as mentioned by Nolan in his book), and I knew it was for real.[16]

At 7 a.m., Weise received approval for the boundary shift. Weise's command post was located at Mai Xa Chanh, at the south terminus of Jones Creek. He radioed Williams to send a Hotel Company platoon across the stream near Bac Vong to "reconnoiter area from which attack occurred" and "assemble remainder of Hotel, which was widely dispersed."[17] Weise's position at that time was about five thousand meters just northeast of Bac Vong, where Foxtrot assets also were, and one platoon was at My Loc on the Cua Viet River, three thousand meters away to the east. Jay Vargas and Golf Company were three thousand meters to the north, near Lam Xuan and Nhi Ha, straddling Jones Creek on both sides.[18] Weise still had the problem of not being able to move Golf and Foxtrot from the My Loc area without permission from 3rd Division, leaving him with only Hotel and two platoons from Foxtrot. Given this limitation, Weise ordered Captain Butler to take his Foxtrot platoons by amtracs from Mai Xa Chanh to Bac Vong.

At 8:10 a.m., Hotel Company, on the march toward Bac Vong under Jim Williams, saw more NVA fire in the area of Dong Huan north of Bo Dieu.[19] Upon getting a visual contact, scout-sniper Lance Cpl. James L.

O'Neill killed an enemy soldier.[20] Soon a quick maneuver by Cpl. James A. Summey and his squad found five NVA. The 1st Platoon leader, 2nd Lieutenant Boyle, pulled them back from Bac Vong and called for fire across the Cua Viet.[21]

At 8:30 a.m., Hotel entered Bac Vong from Jones Creek, which had been the initial boundary with the 2nd ARVN. Williams and Hotel began taking murderous fire from everything in the NVA inventory, as the NVA were entrenched south across the stream at Dong Huan. Williams radioed his condition, and Weise knew that Williams's small force would not be enough to penetrate the enemy's lines. Assessing the situation, Weise ordered Williams to pull back and await reinforcements from Foxtrot and the remainder of Hotel.[22] Having a better understanding of the situation, Weise then requested permission to send Golf from Nhi Ha and Foxtrot from My Loc to support Hotel at Bac Vong.

The navy patrol boats, called "skimmers," and two LCUs were still running up and down the river, firing upon Dong Huan as 105mm artillery bracketed the target area.[23] Weise decided that he; Sgt. Maj. "Big John" Malnar, the air liaison officer; and three RTOs (radio telephone operators) needed to board a navy LCM-6. He wanted to be up close and see the events. Weise was a commander who knew you had to be where the action was in order to control the action. Weise stated: "The monitor proved to be an ideal command post with good communications and significant firepower . . . a breech loaded 81mm mortar, two 20mm cannons, plus .50 and .30 caliber machine guns."[24]

Weise planned on having the artillery and air assets soften up the target area prior to the ground-force insertion, supporting Williams and Hotel Company as they crossed the stream into Bac Vong. The two tanks, recoilless rifles, and supportive direct fire would then cover Hotel's advance. Once Hotel secured their objective and consolidated, the remaining Foxtrot assets were to join them. Upon completing this maneuver, Foxtrot would create a diversion, drawing fire from Hotel. Then Weise received control of Golf, and he planned a heliborn insertion by Vargas to Mai Xa Chanh.[25] That plan would soon change.

The first wave of helos brought in the mortar section, along with the necessary supplies, but the enemy was watching. Soon afterward the NVA bracketed and then, supported by a ground assault, targeted the LZ with precision and overran it. Vargas was forced to cancel the rest of his company's airborne insertion. Earlier, Colonel Hull had boarded a skimmer, stopping at Dong Huan. He spoke with 1st Lt. Alexander F. "Scotty" Prescott regarding his casualties and condition, then joined Weise on his boat. After conferring with Weise and seeing the battle, Hull told Weise to keep the pressure on, and he promised to release Bravo Company, under 1st Lt. George C. Norris, for the effort. Norris radioed Weise that he was ready and waiting, and Weise briefed him with the situation report.

I was listening on the radio during all of this, and there was a lot going on all around us. The enemy positions, while fixed, were not completely known to us, and the enemy troops on maneuver did so in a very fluid way, supported by their protective fires in hit-and-run operations.

"The initial event at Dai Do was an enemy rocket launched (probably prematurely) at a navy supply vessel on the Cua Viet River," says Fritz Warren.[26] The Marines also received small-arms and recoilless-rifle fire from five hundred meters away, hitting an LCU loaded with casualties, which turned out to be Butler on his way into Dai Do.[27]

Bravo landed north of the Bo Dieu at 4:25 p.m., and Norris positioned his men just south of An Lac. Task Force Clearwater maintained covering fire supporting the Marines, and the second group from Bravo established a rather tenuous beachhead. This beachhead group was in danger of being pushed back into the river by the high volume of fire and the large numbers of NVA to its front and on its flanks. NVA soldiers were actually positioned in and firing from Dai Do, but also launching rockets and indirect fire from Dong Lai, one thousand meters away.[28]

One of the hidden enemy snipers killed Norris, a fine Marine. His loss was truly felt. Bravo Company 1/3 became a shell of its former self. Norris was dead, and the Marines were taking heavy casualties. They could not advance, there were no immediate reinforcements, and the wounded could not be extracted at that time. So Weise ordered them "to halt, reorganize, [and] form a defensive perimeter in the western half of the hamlet." Bravo was alone, almost surrounded, and waiting for help.

Still listening to the action, I was livid—and I mean I was ready to cut and thrust. My men felt the urge, feeling like junkyard dogs tied to a leash. Men were dying—our friends and brothers. I was not a man to ever disobey an order, and I would never leave my security position at the bridge, but I was feeling that the bridge itself had enough Marines and support weapons to allow some of us to move into the battle. Besides, I felt that if we hit the bastards head on and put up a serious blocking force, there would be no attack on Dong Ha. The dead do not advance.

As far as I know, no enemy had actually been spotted in Dai Do as of yet, because they were dug in so well, and Foxtrot had been sent there as an insurance policy to secure the area and divert attention from Hotel. Bac Vong was also to be secured by Hotel to prevent an enemy base of fire on Dong Huan. Upon entry, Hotel found the village vacant

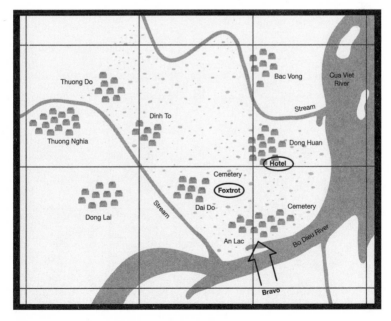

Assault by Bravo Company on An Lac, April 30, 1968. *William Weise*

and therefore secured it with two M-48 tanks and a Marine recon team in support. Crossing the swampy terrain was also slow going, the marsh mud and water proving unstable and deep in points, further complicating movement of the troops.

Air support was on call, and Marine F-4 Phantoms dropped their ordinance (using new experimental, two-thousand-pound bombs) on Dong Huan to prevent the enemy from establishing a firm hold, although there were some NVA firing from the hamlet.[29] Foxtrot was on the move toward Dai Do with the amtracs, but was under heavy fire, as Williams placed 81mm and M-60 fire into Dong Huan in response. Butler and Foxtrot were seven hundred meters away from Williams. Additionally, 2nd Lt. Carl R. Gibson called 105mm and 150mm artillery to hit the target with high explosive (HE) and white phosphorous (WP) rounds, creating smoke to screen the movement.[30] Weise stated, "Foxtrot was hanging on by the skin of its teeth in the

Remembering Dai Do
—Capt. James Laney Willams

Hanoi Hannah was on the radio, they spoke about us when we arrived, knew Weise by name, and we thought it was comical. She would say "All you Marines will die," which we thought was pretty damned funny. That propaganda was right on the open regular radio channels.

When waiting to jump off in the attack, we were having trouble getting Mastrion to jump off, problems with communication, but I took off without him. We called in smoke to cross the five hundred meters to reach the entrenched NVA. What gave us the advantage was that we jumped up and continued the online assault, straight from the book, never stopping, keeping the momentum, and we . . . overran the NVA positions. They had pulled back and left their guys to die, and we caught these guys, eastern edge of Dai Do, and we were pounding enemy positions with artillery, naval gunfire, and organic weapons."[31]

Williams led Hotel Company into the assault and had the suppressive fire lifted as they neared the hamlet; there was no enemy response. The enemy was seen hiding in holes, and Hotel swept through rapidly and cleared them out. At this point, Williams had two problems: the fire mission ordered by Gibson was bringing friendly rounds into Hotel's area, and Williams himself had been wounded by a grenade hurled by a NVA soldier in a hole.[32] The soldier threw another grenade; luckily it was a dud.[33] Williams finally killed the man.[34]

As his executive officer (XO), 1st Lt. Prescott, took command, Williams saw another NVA soldier emerge from a hole near him; the man climbed out, looked at Williams, wounded Staff Sgt. Ronald W. Taylor, and then ran away. Williams would receive his second Silver Star and the Purple Heart for this action (and later a Bronze Star with

those who stayed, anyway. We found the enemy radio operator who was dying, and my Vietnamese interpreter took the radio. He said that the NVA on the other end wanted to know what was happening. My guy told the other operator, "They have been overrun, courtesy of the 2nd Battalion, 4th Marines, the Magnificent Bastards."

I was ironically the first casualty at Dai Do, hit . . . as I was telling everyone to slow down. I was hit by a grenade, but I got that guy. That was when Prescott took charge, and I was sent back with the casualties. They were getting ready to medevac me, and the NVA were still running around. The corpsman . . . wrote down "fragmentation wound left hip." If you were misdiagnosed, you could get bounced around from station to station. He said to me, "Remember, sir, enlisted men get hit in the ass, officers get hit in the hip." After I was medevaced, it was about a year before I learned what happened at Dai Do. [35]

Combat V). Hotel had moved so fast they had bypassed isolated NVA in holes, but the following sweep operation rooted them out. Thirty enemy dead and weapons showed the company's effectiveness.

As Prescott consolidated Hotel Company, gathered the wounded, counted the dead, and called in medevacs, Foxtrot was hit hard near Dai Do. Gibson, married a month before arriving in country, had been there only ten days when he was killed by a sniper. Meanwhile, Williams and six other wounded were loaded onto a boat for the trip to Mai Xa Chanh West.[36] That was where the beachhead was turned into a triage center, and helos were coming in to extract the wounded and fly them to the USS *Iwo Jima*. As the day slowly succumbed to the envelope of night, Hotel Company had performed remarkably.

In Foxtrot Company, an RPG had hit the amtrac carrying Capt. James Butler, wounding the naval gunfire team radioman and several Marines.[37] Looking like a porcupine bristling with radio antennae, the amtrac was a logical target. A second amtrac also had hits and gunfire from Dai Do. Butler had responded by sending 106mm recoilless-rifle fire into the village as his men moved forward. Foxtrot had stalled in the attack on the left due to the volume of enemy fire, while elements on the right managed to get to the edge of Dai Do.[38]

One platoon was trying to save another, and Butler was on the hook for air support. He was, however, lucky enough to get both Marine and air force "fast movers." Each aviation branch had its own method of operations regarding ground support, and the Marines were usually far more effective. The U.S. Air Force F-4 Phantoms, simply by their doctrine, would hit a ground target perpendicular to their flight path, thus minimizing their exposure to ground fire, while Marine aviators would fly down the enemy's throat, getting more punch out of their ordinance, but also running the risk of taking deadly ground fire. There is a great difference between a three- to five-second exposure and a ten- to twenty-second exposure to enemy ground fire. There is also a lot more damage inflicted upon the enemy when more time is spent carefully placing ordinance where it matters most.

This is not an indictment of the air force, whose pilots are as brave as those in any branch, in my opinion. Each branch of service applied close-air-support doctrine differently. The same may be said of navy pilots. Marine pilots are a different breed for a very simple reason: "Every Marine is a rifleman" is more than a motto in the Corps; it is our way of life. Unlike other branches of service, Marine aviators spend time on the ground with the grunts, and a bond is formed. Therefore, a Marine pilot is not simply helping another American in trouble; he is helping another Marine who would run the same risks for him if he were in trouble on the ground or downed following an ejection.

The Marines took close air support from a philosophy and tactics used in the 1920s, during the Nicaragua Campaign and other actions, the so-called "Banana Wars." The Marines turned it into an art form during World War II. Weise's comments here are noteworthy: "Our fixed-wing support had not been responsive during the early months of 1968. Even preplanned strikes were usually late and sometimes cancelled without notice. During March and April, including the first day and a half of the Dai Do battle, close air support was not adequate. We learned to operate without relying on close air support, the king of Marine Corps supporting arms.[39]

The BLT 2/4 operations officer, Major Warren, was working on the regimental command post because his platoon had been returned to division. A heated radio exchange ensued between Warren and the regimental operations officer, Maj. Dennis Murphy. Murphy relayed that Colonel Hull ordered Weise to "belly up" to the NVA. Warren replied that Weise was so close already that the NVA "could slit Weise's belly with a knife."[40] I could not have agreed more.

Murphy cautioned Warren to be careful with his words, as Colonel Hull was listening on his tactical net. Warren replied "that he could care less who was listening" as long as "Weise received the priority of fires and additional assets he requested."[41] Warren later noted, "Additional tanks were never received, but priority of close air support was supplied on the third day of the battle."[42] Friendly forces on the ground really appreciated the air support, and the Marines in this battle needed all the help they could get. Warren was a hell of an officer, and sometimes tact is not the best way to maneuver through a problem. He got his point across.

Despite these positive, albeit slow, developments, Weise had other problems. His fire support and control went through an ARVN command center, and he was reluctant to move his men unless he had operational control. Such was the lack of faith in our ARVN comrades. Listening to the battle events on his radio, Weise knew he would have to commit his reserves, and he ordered Golf Company into the attack. NVA artillery began landing, and Weise suspected two sampans, which had been observed in the river, were spotters. He ordered them destroyed. Meanwhile, Weise and Hull discussed throwing my Echo Company, positioned north of Dong Ha, into the fight. But we were still assigned to 3rd Marine Division.

Weise decided to launch his own surprise attack, and he detailed Echo Company to lead the battalion on a strike: "I (had previously) requested the return of Echo Company [under his command by this time] and permission to move Foxtrot and Golf companies. Permission was granted to move two Foxtrot Company platoons and all of Golf Company. The Foxtrot platoons and company headquarters moved out immediately from Mai Xa Chanh toward Bac Vong aboard amtracs. Golf Company would be moved by helicopter later that afternoon. Echo Company would not return for 36 hours."[43]

Weise was perhaps trying to hold too much ground with too few Marines, and he knew it.[44] At least he had naval gunfire and 4.2-inch mortars if needed. According to Weise:

> Destroyers equipped with five-inch guns were usually on station and within range of the Cua Viet area. Sometimes, powerful eight-inch gun cruisers provided support. Whenever a new navy gunship came on line our naval gunfire officer, Lt. (Jg.) Joe Carrol, U.S. Naval Reserve, was aware of it. He and his naval gunfire support team spent many hours registering the guns of each "new" ship and establishing an operating camaraderie with the shipboard gunners and operating personnel . . . We were happy to get the support, especially when we reported the destruction of targets (which was often). We found naval gunfire support to be accurate, reliable, and, best of all, available when needed.[45]

But air assets were very limited due to the simultaneous operation by the Marines of BLT 3/9 six kilometers away at Thon Cam Vu. In addition, Bravo Company, in its new defensive posture, was still having its own troubles at An Lac, with casualties mounting.[46] There were just not enough assets to go around. What Weise did not know at the time was that the NVA 48th and 52nd Regiments had passed right through the 2nd ARVN Regiment, supposedly undetected, to stage the assault on Dai Do proper. Weise said, "Undetected my ass. Those NVA bastards and their brothers in the ARVN must have had an agreement. We never heard a single shot come from our 'allies,' but we sure heard from our enemy."[47]

Weise then ordered Butler and his Foxtrot Company (actually two full platoons when it started, with only twenty-six men able to fight) to retreat, under the cover of darkness, from the southeastern edge of Dai Do to Dong Huan and join Hotel in securing a stronger perimeter until they could regroup.[48] Weise "did not want to have three separate perimeters that night. Foxtrot Company had difficulty in withdrawing from

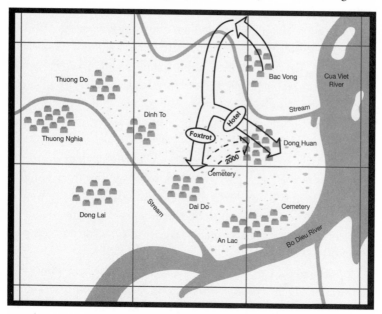

Attacks by Hotel and Foxtrot companies on April 30, 1968. *William Weise*

Dai Do and reorganizing... I was concerned about Foxtrot Company, but there were more pressing problems to deal with that night."[49]

The withdrawal was ad hoc and scattered; Marines were separated, and many ending up walking all night. Weise was less than pleased with Butler's performance as CO, but then, Butler had been in command for only two months and had not seen much action. The daylight began to wane as our Marines were consolidating, and the remaining support groups were still maneuvering.

Not to be forgotten was Capt. Jay Vargas's Golf Company at the patrol base at Lam Xuan West, who had been standing by for a helo lift by CH-46s to Mai Xa Chanh West. Weise had the complete confidence of this CO and his men, as did I. With the LZ untenable, Vargas and his company would walk into hell instead of ride, and do so under continuous indirect fire. Vargas was a seasoned warrior, a skilled leader who never exhibited fear in front of his men. The fates of Vargas and I were to be inextricably intertwined for all time.

As Vargas moved his men, the incoming rounds slammed into the muddy river banks, which cushioned the lethality of the rounds or even prevented them from exploding. The irony was that the friendly artillery, in its role of counter battery fire, lit the night sky, silhouetting the Marines and making them visible to any enemy. The men moved throughout the falling shells, and one shell landed ten feet from Vargas. The wet mud absorbed the impact and cushioned the blast, but the concussion still knocked him off his feet and sent shrapnel into his right leg—his third wound in three months.[50]

In all, over twenty Marines were walking with various degrees of wounds from their rain-of-steel ordeal, suffering over three hundred incoming rounds by the time they reached Mai Xa Chanh West at 11:30 p.m. The entire hump took three hours.[51] To understand the problem, you have to have some background on what was going on with the enemy.

Up around the Cua Viet River, the enemy used artillery, which they had positioned across the Ben Hai River. They could reach us with it, but they would have the artillery reverted into caves in locations where we could not knock it out with air. Then they would pull it out and shoot.

They had little trigger points, and they had forward observers. When you walked through one of those trigger points, then boom, boom, boom! Then you walked out of the point, and the artillery stopped. They had to have it all preregistered, complete with pace counts, as it was just too damned accurate. They were good with mortars of the 62mm and 82mm Soviet variety; they also could fire any rounds they captured from us, and those rounds were good in their mortars as well.

Vargas had the steel splinters removed from his leg, and his Marines were also treated, one suffering a traumatic amputation of the right arm. Vargas was informed by Major Warren that Golf Company would take navy boats the rest of the way to An Lac to assist in the final assault on Dai Do by 4 a.m. on May 1. Hotel Company reported that the enemy may have moved from Dai Do to attack An Lac, probably because of the heavy naval gunfire that pounded the Dai Do area for several hours.[52] Simultaneously, Bravo Company 1/3 caught a platoon-sized element of forty NVA in open field, actually headed for Dai Do, and they opened up on the enemy troops, cutting them down.

Weise stated: "Assessing the situation at the end of the first day, 30 April, I felt we had done well with what we had. But I was frustrated because we did not have enough power to continue the attack on Dai Do. After Hotel Company successfully assaulted Dong Huan, and had the other two companies (Echo and Golf) been available, I was certain we could have seized and held Dai Do. We seemed to have caught a large enemy force off balance, but the two Foxtrot company platoons were not nearly strong enough to take Dai Do."[53]

As the evening of April 30, 1968, wore on, the NVA made several probes into Dong Huan, but Hotel and Foxtrot repelled each attempt. Hotel was in Dong Huan, and Golf and Bravo 1/3 were still viable and in defensive postures, despite Weise's request for A-6 Intruder and eight-inch artillery fire missions receiving no response. The A-6 mission, with a two-thousand-pound delayed-fuse ordinance, followed by napalm and additional ordinance, would have reduced the enemy fortifications, killed many enemy troops, and confused and demoralized the survivors. We could have pushed into the area during that confusion and killed the remaining exposed enemy fleeing the area.

There are many "what ifs" in war, but in my opinion, that potential force multiplier would have paid dividends.

One of the issues with air support came from the method by which it was dispensed, since fixed-wing air support required a thirty-six-hour notice for planning purposes. If we were lucky, and if you had fast movers in the area with ordinance, it was possible to divert them as part of a secondary mission plan. However, relying on this support in this manner would have been foolish, so we had a lot of hope, but not a lot of faith. In addition, the rapid development of the battle, and the very fluid nature of the enemy attacks and our actions, made a thirty-six-hour time line for planning purposes almost impossible. We never knew where we or the enemy would be in that amount of time.

The situation was that General Tompkins did not know for certain exactly where the main enemy assault would come from. For all he knew, Dai Do could have been a diversion, meant to lure our troops away from another critical pressure point the NVA was waiting to exploit. He also had to monitor the situation with 3rd Battalion, 9th Marines, three miles away to the west; they were also fighting in Cam Phu, battling the NVA 320th Division. This was where Task Force Robbie had been engaged the previous day, and Tompkins believed that 3/9 had contained the enemy to his west.[54]

My Echo Company was still chained to the damned bridge at the intersection with Highway 1. I knew we had taken casualties, but it was much later that I would learn that we had lost only sixteen dead and 107 wounded, while killing ninety of the enemy. The only way this operation could have been successful—and it was indeed successful—was for Weise to have properly assessed the threat, secured the men and supportive arms, and tactically outmaneuvered and blocked the attacking enemy with a defensive counterattack. This was not an easy operation to conduct in the best of conditions, and it was even more difficult when a unit is seriously scattered, under strength, and exhausted. I admired Weise for his ability to control what could have been a panic-stricken disaster and to convert it into a masterpiece of parry and thrust.

Weise felt that if Golf and Echo had been available from the start, the situation would be far different. He knew he needed additional support and more Marines on the ground, but the additional Marines, mainly my Echo, had been delayed being chained to the Dong Ha bridge under 3rd Division's command. On the morning of May 1, 1968, Weise, understandably frustrated over his inability to effectively utilize all of his assets as he saw fit, briefed Vargas on the situation as they moved onto the boats loading Golf Company. Weise felt that if Golf and Echo had been available from the start, the situation would be far different. Vargas was told that his men were going straight into the attack upon reaching the muddy river beachhead. The other companies had been shredded by enemy fire and were in no shape to launch an assault. Vargas *was* the main attack force, and he had two M-48 tanks as his support.

The village and surrounding hamlets had been strafed and napalmed by two navy A-4 Skyhawks. The Skyhawks had finished their last run as Golf Company, transported by LCM-8 landing craft, set boots on the beach, moving toward An Lac.[55] Weise explained: "My orders were simple: land south of An Lac, pass around the right flank of Bravo Company, attack northwest, seize and hold the village of Dai Do."[56] The 60mm mortars splashed the ground ahead of Golf with preparatory fire to soften up any lingering resistance. Vargas had wanted heavy artillery, white phosphorous (known as "willy pete") and smoke, laid down heavily to mask his movement, but it was not available because of the battery "checking fire" for the aircraft in the area. The check-fire order should have been engaged only when the aircraft were on the bomb runs, which they would call in, hence lifting the barrage briefly; then fire could be resumed once the fast movers had departed. Golf Company would be entering the area without fire support, and they had seven hundred meters of open terrain to cover between An Lac and Dai Do.[57] Vargas said, "I started out with 123 men, and by the time I got through the village I was down to 41."[58]

The NVA had been routed by the air strike, from what the Marines could observe. And then all hell broke loose. Heavy-weapons fire, including fire from 12.7mm, Soviet-made machine guns and supplemented by artillery and mortars, swept the terrain, wounding and killing Marines in the first few minutes. A report stated that over one hundred NVA were on Vargas's left flank. Elements from Golf were diverted to attack the entrenched enemy with one tank in support, the 90mm cannon offering comfort, if nothing else. RPG and B-40 rocket fire was directed at the Marine advance, so the tank started to retreat in the face of the heavy fire.

Vargas was going to have none of it, and he grabbed the phone at the rear of the tank and told the commander he was going nowhere. The commander explained he was out of ammo, but Vargas explained the psychological assistance armor brought to the fight. The tanker was not interested, but after Vargas threatened to fire up the tank himself, the tanker began to think otherwise. Unknown to Vargas, Weise had been monitoring the scenario by radio, and the battalion commander issued his own order to the tanker in support of Vargas. Weise also threatened to shoot the tank if it returned and to court martial the commander.[59] The next day, May 1, 1968, would be just as bad.

On April 30, despite the high volume of fire, our Marines had managed to kill many NVA as they were static or on the run. Golf Company had tossed smoke grenades along their advance to alert Foxtrot Company of their positions. Likewise, the Foxtrot Marines had shifted fire to the right in order to not incur friendly casualties. The enemy also shifted the artillery fire onto Foxtrot, which explained Foxtrot's situation.[60]

That morning, at 6 a.m., Bravo Company, 1st Battalion, 3rd Marine Regiment, was assigned, and they assaulted their objective, which was the village just southeast of Dai Do. At 10:40 a.m., Golf Company, with two tanks, along with Weise, landed by Mike-8 boats and linked up with Foxtrot, which had been located at My Loc. Weise issued his frag order to attack and seize Dai Do.[61]

On May 1, Lt. Col. William P. Snyder, commanding the 3rd Battalion, 21st Infantry Regiment, of the U.S. Army's 196th Infantry Brigade (commanded by U.S. Army Brig. Gen. William B. Rosson and assigned to 3rd Marine Division as of 7 p.m. on April 30) received an execute order to head towards the DMZ. The first wave was to land at Dong Ha at 9 a.m., and the balance would arrive by 4:13 p.m. from field locations and Fire Support Base Belcher via Marine CH-46 and

CH-53 helicopters, which would land at the 3/21 observation post (OP) at Mai Xa Chanh. The final lift was at 6:41 p.m. and landed at 7 p.m. At 9:30 p.m., Snyder's party departed Cua Viet by squad assault boats and returned to the battalion command post. The army was about to get seriously involved as Tompkins "turned over operational control of the Army battalion to the 3rd Marines to insert into the Nhi Ha and Lam Xuan area."[62]

Foxtrot would approach from the north, and Hotel would approach from the east within four hundred meters of the village, supplying a base of fire and providing a screening force for Golf. Bravo Company, after securing their objective by 7 a.m., were still receiving recoilless-rifle and indirect fire and were located southeast as the BLT reserve. Weise ordered a call for fire that lasted from 11 a.m. to 12:40 p.m. and included air and artillery strikes.[63]

Bravo 1/3 received a report from a recon patrol saying that they had observed the enemy leaving An Lac. The company then secured the village. Likewise, Hotel Company, using small arms and calling in mortars, started a killing spree against sixty NVA in the open as the enemy crossed a rice paddy. Weise believed that these NVA may have been "a reinforcing unit looking for the village of Dai Do . . . or stragglers from An Lac."[64] Following these actions, a short respite ensued, and both sides caught their second wind. We were reconsolidating and resupplying, and I am certain that the NVA were doing the same.

At 12:53 p.m., Golf launched their attack on Dai Do proper. Golf, under Captain Vargas, received an incredible amount of effective enemy fire from the west. Weise then requested that my Echo Company be sent back to the BLT so that we would be in a position to sweep through from the west. This action occurred at 1:30 p.m. Meanwhile, a smoke screen was laid to the west of Golf to hide the Marines' movement; the screen proved effective, and enemy fire ceased.[65]

During all of these actions, all night and day, I had been monitoring the battle by radio from my company command post. Although I was only two kilometers away and could hear the battle, I chafed at being tied to my position, knowing my friends and fellow Marines were fighting and dying within mortar range of my bridge position. I knew that we were in a tactical blocking position to protect the bridge from attack if the NVA broke through. However, as I said before, I was listening to the radio, and we were chomping at the bit to get into this battle. BLT 2/4 was deeply involved in this fight, and they were in a world of hurt. They were not making that much progress, being bogged down and suffering casualties.

I will not say there was anything resembling panic; there was none of that. But those talking over the radio seemed greatly concerned. We had been studying the terrain as best we could, and I spent my time refreshing the lieutenants and squad leaders on what was probably about to transpire. Colonel Hull, Weise, and General Tompkins (who was coming in) were having their dialogues; it was the classic piecemeal undertaking after which some valuable lessons were learned.

The reality was that Weise had few options; he had been forced to spread the battalion out all over the area of operation, including covering all of those areas where he could anticipate enemy aggression. Men were placed into listening and observation posts (LP/OP) and established blocking positions, and they also secured the primary avenues of approach. The units that had been sent in were very small, in contrast to the area they had to operate in.

The preparations I made with my officers and men were the normal troop-leading steps that you would go through preparing the men for a fight. I went through all the various courses of action for whatever we might have had to deal with—contingency planning, plotting the various avenues of approach for us, as well as where the enemy may come from, and ensuring we had primary and supplemental avenues of withdrawal, should that be necessary. This preparation was especially important when getting the wounded out became a factor.

I had little doubt we would be called into the fight. I especially followed the radio traffic from Golf Company, who were supporting BLT 1/3, and they were doing their very best, I had no doubt. It became very apparent to me that this was tough effort, tough going, and they were giving it their best shot. However, it was also very apparent that they were not making the progress that was anticipated, and it was soon very obvious to all of us that the enemy threat was much larger—and perhaps much greater in materiel, for lack of a better word, for the area involved—than we had anticipated.

The one thing that was very apparent in my mind was that BLT 1/3 had attempted to go across the rice paddy and had just gotten hammered. They could not make any forward progress, let alone get inside the village. They were experiencing a combination of both enemy direct and indirect fire. They never penetrated the line, and as a consequence, when they became bogged down in front, the North Vietnamese just knocked the hell out of them.

Given the size of the operational area, the scope of the mission we had, and the collective numbers of both friendly and enemy numbers in such a small area, the enemy defenses, how they were dug in, and their capability to respond to any movement and counterattack framed a battle that was about like a knife fight in a phone booth. This battle was a classic study of a developing situation where both sides, ours and theirs, were not supported by good intelligence.

CHAPTER 5

Echo Company into the Breach

*You will kill ten of our men, and we will kill one of yours. And in the
end it will be you who tire of it.*

—Ho Chi Minh

W EISE FINALLY SECURED ECHO'S release from 3rd
Division, and our orders were to hump as rapidly as possible
toward An Lac. My men had been surprised when, earlier, the trucks
arrived loaded with food, including steaks, soft drinks, and other deli-
cacies. That kind of delivery was rare in the field and a real treat. No
sooner had the items been unloaded than I gave the order to mount up.
The chow would have to wait.

I told my men that we were fixing to go, that the battalion was in
difficulty, and that Echo was ready to get going. There was no hesi-
tation at all. I was very proud of my Echo Marines. Upon receiving
my orders and without even flinching, the Marines of Echo had
secured their gear and moved out on foot. They were ready to get
into the fight. We knew from monitoring the radio that Bravo 1/3
had been pinned down and chewed up, and also that Vargas and
Golf had been effectively torn apart and were basically surrounded.
It was quite obvious that a relief force would have to go in, and
that force was us. We were the only uninvited guests to the party.
The Marines were pretty wound up by the details and specifics, and

Heading for Dai Do
—1st Lt. Dave R. Jones

Echo Company was guarding a bridge on Route 1 north of Dong Ha when we got the word to rejoin the battalion. We were just getting ready to sit down for a steak dinner that Jim and the first sergeant had arranged. That would have been our first hot meal in a long, long time. We immediately saddled up and headed for Dai Do. The Keith Nolan book details that move pretty well. My platoon was leading the company and got shot at several times during the move. We wanted to stop and fight, but Jim told us to get on with the mission.[1]

following the briefings given by their platoon and squad leaders, they were ready.

My XO, 1st Lt. David R. Jones, and I had the typical CO and XO chat regarding the order of movement to the area where we would link up with the battalion headquarters and the residual elements of Bravo 1/3. We planned to have the lead platoon sent out with the screening forces, getting the company out to a particular assembly area from which we would launch the attack, as well as placing the snipers out where they could observe enemy movement and do their work. I placed Jones's 3rd Platoon in the lead, with Sgt. James W. Rogers's squad as point. We were on our way.

Rogers was a very interesting guy, who came in from Marine Barracks Hawaii. He did not know very much about combat operations, but just a very good guy—a typical barracks Marine—who first joined us up around Nhi Ha. I really had great fun with him while on our first patrol and ambush together. I went out with his squad, and we laid out an L-shaped ambush just to the east of Jones Creek, where there was a little village. I was able to watch as he matured. By the time we hit Dai Do, he had become a very steady hand—very stable, helpful, and reliable.

At 2:55 p.m., Foxtrot had recovered a Marine KIA during their earlier, April 30 engagement and were headed to support Hotel when they were hit with enemy artillery, resulting in three more KIAs. This was just the opening bell. At 4:25 p.m., all of the 2/4 assets were under fire, including Echo, which was headed to join Golf. Bravo 1/3 was then ordered to also link up with Golf, which was fighting for its life as the enemy counterattacked. What was evident was that the NVA had decided to launch a massive coordinated assault, believing the Marines to have been rendered ineffective from the concentrated fire.

Bravo 1/3 was just approaching the southeast corner towards Golf's position when they were greeted by intense enemy small-arms and automatic-weapons fire. Bravo had run head on into the NVA force that was trying to outflank Golf. At 5:45 p.m., Bravo 1/3 and Golf 2/4 were ordered into tight defensive perimeters, where they prevented the enemy counterattack from overrunning their positions.[2]

Foxtrot and Hotel 2/4 also received the order to form tight perimeters in the positions held the previous night. At 6:45 p.m., the recon platoon was given the responsibility for medevacing the casualties from Bravo 1/3 and Echo 2/4 at Echo's perimeter. I knew that as we moved in, we had 60mm mortars on call, although we did not really have any mortar support going in, because battalion had the priority of fire. They were using all the 81mm and 105mm and anything they could in support, given the situation and difficulties associated with Golf, Foxtrot, and Hotel companies, as well as the reconnaissance Marines.

It was around mid-afternoon by the time we got in there, and the Marines from our battalion, especially Golf Company, were hanging on by their fingernails. Alpha Company was moving back into the area of An Lac, where they had launched the attack and where Weise and the battalion headquarters were located.

I did not request any specific supportive fire going in, with exception of the 60mm mortars on the left flank. We took advantage of the supportive elements organic to the battalion, using the 60s extensively, and we also took advantage of the snipers. We had two great snipers, and they were able to give us great and very effective suppressive fires against

Waiting for Echo Company
—Brig. Gen. William Weise

My morale went up several notches when I heard that Echo Company had been released by 3rd Marine Division and was en route to my position, now located ashore in An Lac. But Echo Company would not arrive in time to help Golf that second night. I would have to use one of the companies already nearby. I had tried using Foxtrot Company, but it failed. Hotel Company was too weak for a major effort. I decided to use Bravo Company, which had received a new CO, XO, and several experienced staff— noncommissioned officers—from its parent battalion.[3]

the North Vietnamese machine-gun positions, which were north on the little ridge line on the west side of the creek below Dai Do.

I had to rapidly assess the battalion situation on the ground as I saw it, from the viewpoint of eyeball to eyeball with the threat, as opposed to simply collecting traffic over the radio. I collected my men, rallied them, and then organized a proper defense to protect the wounded that were to be later relocated to Mai Xa Chanh West by skimmer boat and otter, and then evacuated by helicopter. We worked with getting Bravo back in to the lines after I deployed my company. They were pretty emotional. They had a lot of dead Marines, and even more were wounded. I had to help get their mind back into the proper framework and help them get reorganized and repositioned.

Golf, Hotel, Foxtrot 2/4, and Bravo 1/3 continued to receive intense artillery, mortar, and rocket fire throughout the late afternoon and early evening.[4] During this time, Vargas (following his early morning meeting with Weise) and his Golf Company were stagnant and choked with wounded. Vargas himself had been hit for the fourth time in the right arm as his men closed on a bunker that had been missed in the initial sweep. Throwing the trap door open, Vargas shot the three NVA hiding inside and followed through with a grenade.[5]

Shortly thereafter, another mortar barrage came down on Golf; then Vargas was informed by radio that the enemy was counterattacking, and there were enemy troops in the open between An Lac and Dai Do.[6] In record time, he managed to call in his needs and pop green smoke to mark his positions. Within a few minutes, naval gunfire, fast movers, indirect fire, and helicopter gun ships arrived on the scene. Cannon, rockets, artillery shells, and napalm shook the ground and darkened the landscape. There were so many enemy troops in the open that the various pilots had trouble deciding who would be the first to go in for the kill.

Vargas ordered his men to pull back. There were too many dead and wounded, and they needed to reorganize rapidly, as the air strikes gave them a brief respite. Vargas placed his men in a large ditch for cover and as a rallying point from which to establish a good defensive position. He knew they would be overrun otherwise, and he wanted a proper count of his men.

As the last Marines fell back onto the new position, they were followed by a large number of enemy soldiers. The Marines immediately opened fire and dropped most of them. Unfortunately, from 7 to 8 p.m., the artillery communication nets were jammed, making any counter-battery fire impossible. By 7:45 p.m., Bravo 1/3 had medevaced its remaining casualties and dropped back five hundred meters south to Echo's location.[7] By 9 p.m., the enemy attack had been stopped, but at high cost to both sides. Thankfully, for the Marines, the night remained rather uneventful.[8]

The platoon of Marines on Vargas's left flank retreating to their new position had previously crashed head on into a like number of NVA, immediately engaging in hand-to-hand combat. Rifles and helmets were used as clubs, and entrenching tools became weapons of convenience. Vargas's men were partially blinded by the saw grass, and they used their rifles and M-79 grenade launchers more as a carpet of fire instead of line-of-sight weapons. The tactic worked, as the NVA stalled their advance, but again the cost was high. Vargas had started with 150 men, and he had about 60 remaining who were able to fight, including a squad pinned down and fighting for their lives.[9]

The enemy then again attempted to outflank Golf Company, and approximately twenty NVA charged toward Golf's 2nd Platoon, hurling grenades as they advanced.[10] Luckily for the Marines, Lieutenant Acly managed to get his mortars back on the target. He poured on the shells for fifteen minutes, dangerously close to his position. Weise had secured the perimeter with indirect fire from all sources and was able to bracket his perimeter as necessary. Simultaneously, the NVA had been shelling the battalion CP while trying to kill Golf and Foxtrot companies.

Weise had great faith in the battalion CP radio-net operator, Sgt. Charles W. Bollinger, who managed to handle the large amount of incoming traffic and disseminate the necessary data to all the company commanders (including Weise) regardless of how hectic, fluid, and confusing the situation became. Communications is arguably the most important asset in an ongoing battle, and Weise knew he would be reliably informed.[11] Weise also had the reliable and stalwart Sgt. Maj. John M. "Big John" Malnar handling the forward CP group. Malnar, a World War II and Korean War veteran, was the tactical commander responsible for the order of march, maintaining discipline, and gathering and passing on information regarding the constantly changing tactical situation.[12]

Echo Company had to move in, and we did so by crossing the creek, placing the tall Marines, including Jones, in the water to pass the shorter ones, along with the gear and weapons, to the link-up area with the battalion. As soon as Jones's 3rd Platoon, in the lead, and Rogers's squad, at point, spotted the NVA on the opposite bank of the river, they opened fire. They received nothing in response, so I ordered a cease fire. They were to get to their destination, not pick fights along the way.[13] We had to link up with BLT 1/3 and Golf Company 2/4.

By that time, we would be able to coordinate all the protective and supportive fires in order to get moving. The movement at this time made sense, as it provided some reasonable cover under darkness, and it worked. I called the lieutenants in, gave them their orders, and the order of march. We would work it two up, one back, and I would travel in front of the reserve platoon with the company CP.

So at 5 a.m., we fixed bayonets and began moving with two platoons. Jones was on the right, and 1st Lt. Gregory V. Sims was on the left, to the

Throwing the Gauntlet
—Lance Cpl. Steve Wilson

On May 2, following a day and night of no sleep, getting into the battle (a battle in itself), the platoon was stepping off at 0500, half in the perimeter and half in the paddy when the word came over the net: "Now fix bayonets!" The sound of steel on steel was not the most prevalent noise, but that of eyeballs clicking. We had watched the A-4s drop their loads on Dai Do and the green tracer rounds return fire during the jets' ascent.

This was not going to be a walk in the park, and we knew it. But with the order to fix bayonets, clicking eyeballs was the sound, as the word passed down the line, and was experienced by each and every Marine of 3rd Platoon. I saw it and felt it as the change occurred. [Livingston's] leadership over the course of seven months and some hellish battles had sharpened us. This command took us to another fighting level, and he was determined to let us know what the job before us was. We were prepared physically as best as possible and mentally at the very edge. The gauntlet had been thrown.[14]

north. Sims, a Georgia boy like me, was later shot in the stomach and medevaced (he later served in Marine Barracks in Hawaii with Sergeant Major Otto).* I must say that was really something to hear all those young fellows, 150 something of them, clicking bayonets. All down the line, you could hear these clicks. They were for real.

At this point, Weise had not given me a specific task, other than to locate the units in trouble. How I did that was up to me, so I had my security and patrols placed out, not knowing if we were going to be attacked that evening. I needed to get the weapons cleaned and the troops fed, and I needed to get prepared for whatever was coming

---

* I think Sims is now an architect in Atlanta. I hope that this book will be the catalyst for many of our Marines who are still around to contact me. I really do have an interest in them.

"When we flew [our Huey] over the field that morning above the Marines, I looked out. I could not believe what I was looking at. Lines of these men had fixed bayonets and were advancing into the enemy, who was still firing! I thought about how that had probably not been done since WW I; something out of the past."[15]
—Door Gunner Wally Nunn

our way. In fact, I do not think I received my orders until 3 a.m. on May 2, the next day. That was when Weise called me up and said that he wanted me to attack and, in doing so, join forces with Golf Company. He wanted me to kick off the attack at 5 a.m.

We were following the artillery, mortars, smoke, willy pete—anything we could throw at them from every direction possible. We were also very aware of the need to coordinate our fire and maneuvers, as well our calls for the supportive arms, to ensure that we did not hit Golf Company, because they were at the edge of the village. We were soon taking a significant amount of small-arms fire, particularly RPGs. The NVA loved using them, and they must have had an unlimited number, because they fired hundreds of them. It was unbelievable. I could not believe that no one took a direct hit with an RPG, given the massive barrage that raining in on us, but I do not believe anyone was hit directly. We were soon able to get very close.

My rear echelon started taking sporadic fire from Dong Lai, from the few NVA located in the hamlet to the north, so the rear echelon returned fire. I called in 60mm WP and HE on the hamlet, and as the enemy took cover, the 1st and 2nd platoons moved past the killing ground to join 3rd Platoon along the creek bank, where they established a hasty defensive perimeter. A few Marines had been hit, and Sgt. Elbert E. Cox Jr. had been killed with a head shot.[16]

The Marines of 1/3 and the amtracs came under intense fire as they pushed toward An Lac, and Golf 2/4 under Vargas was cut off and surrounded. Bravo Company was unable to evacuate casualties due to the number of wounded and dead. The NVA had maneuvered between Bravo and Golf companies. The aircraft could not land unless the LZ

Typical Livingston Fashion
—Brig. Gen. William Weise

Echo's overland movement from the bridge on Highway 1 to An Lac was not exactly a romp in the sun. Small groups of enemy and forward observers occupied many points along the Echo route of march. Captain Jim Livingston knew that he was badly needed at Dai Do. A natural fighter, he overcame his inclination to stomp on the enemy positions that harassed and tried to delay him.

He returned fire only when absolutely necessary, skirted enemy strong points, and moved to An Lac as quickly as possible. His last obstacle was a nearly unfordable, fairly swift stream about five and a half feet deep. Captain Jim solved that problem in typical Livingston fashion. He had a half dozen of his tallest Marines strip down, plant themselves in the deepest part of the stream, and pass the shorter, heavy laden Marines hand to hand through the shallow water. Not very fancy and not found in any field manual, but the "Livingston stream crossing" expedient worked. I recommend it to anyone in a similar situation. Incidentally, although soaked themselves, the Echo Marines kept their weapons and ammunition dry. That was Livingston's style—rarely fancy, but always effective.[17]

was secured, and then the wounded had to be collected rapidly and triage implemented. To do this, a check fire halting supporting arms had to be initiated. This check fire would allow for a safe LZ to be established on the southern bank of the Bo Dieu, protecting the birds from friendly fire. But it would also allow the NVA to break cover and continue their attack at the same time, unless an effective base of interlocking and suppressive fire was established. (During the battle, I was not aware of U.S. Army involvement to any extent, since significant army air assets did not operate in the Dai Do area until after May 3. But they were busy at An Lac and operating farther north, where the

NVA had also stalled the 2nd ARVN Regiment and the Gimlets were engaged against the enemy themselves.)

Even though Echo had arrived and established security at An Lac to affect a proper helo medevac platform to Mai Xa Chanh West, there was much to do. Fortunately, as Fritz Warren noted, "295 Marines would be evacuated, with [only] 81 losing their lives."[18] Luckily, we arrived at An Lac at 5:30 p.m. First Lieutenant Clyde W. Mutter, his recon platoon, and I led a few missions across the rice paddies and helped Bravo fall back safely to An Lac. We received word that Hotel and Foxtrot managed to get secured in Dong Huan. Quite by chance, we had just saved these men's lives, not to mention raising their morale. Golf Company was a different matter.

Unknown to us at that time, the NVA had prepared heavily defended fighting positions, including a few tunnels and alternate concealed routes, using the terrain as a force multiplier. Hundreds were hiding and could not be seen until we were right on top of them. It was believed afterward that the ARVN units and civilians (although possibly against their will) had assisted in preparing these positions. Weise believed this to be true, and I would have to agree.

BLT 2/4 was in a good position logistically, having been properly supplied with ammunition. "I'd rather have ammo than food, because you can't hurl a c-ration can at the gooks," was a common phrase among soldiers and Marines. Vargas and his Golf Company had relocated a hundred meters to the rear, where the men started to dig in as they began to lose daylight. Vargas knew that to attempt a crossing of the open terrain in the face of such heavy fire would have been senseless. Golf was surrounded, but they had the cloak of on-call, indirect support, and with illumination rounds, they would be able to observe enemy movement. Vargas entrenched his men and withstood many enemy assaults attempting to overrun his position. Golf and Vargas did a magnificent job, and they would be able to hold on till morning.[19]

Golf was still being hit and probed; we could hear it. Marines scored random kills as the enemy became visible. Many fired at shadows, forcing Vargas to initiate fire discipline. He needed to ensure he had enough ammo in case of a full attack. The one comfort Vargas had was the news that my company was nearby, and I rapidly assessed the situation for what it was.

The Marines had entered the attack in a piecemeal fashion—a reconnaissance unit, then a company, followed by another company, and so on, until they became bogged down. I knew that the NVA were not simply going to sit and shell us into submission; they would not have committed such resources if they did not have the intention of sweeping us back into the sea and occupying the entire province. The casualties at this time were twenty-four KIA and forty-four WIA, and BLT 2/4 had killed ninety-one enemy troops and captured two more.

The night of May 1 was not totally peaceful, as the NVA maintained a steady rate of indirect and machine-gun fire into Bravo Company, and Weise gave permission for 2nd Lt. Thomas R. Keppen (TAD, temporary additional duty, from 1/3, later killed on July 7, 1968) to pull back if all casualties were accounted for. The dead would have to be

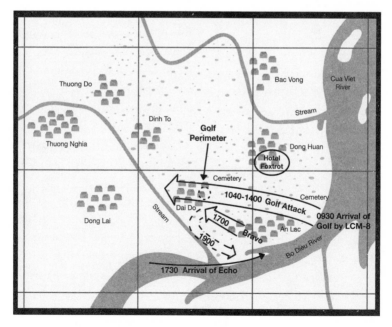

Attacks by Golf and Bravo companies, return of Echo Company, on May 1, 1968. *William Weise*

recovered later.[20] In fact, Bravo Marines saw forty to fifty enemy sappers crawling towards them, and the Marines fired them up, destroying their attempt.[21] Bravo was having to really pull itself together, and they used this time to reorganize.

When I finally managed to link with Bravo Company, I spoke to Keppen and the remaining noncommissioned officers, as well as some of the men in Alpha Company. The lieutenant had had about all he could handle, but was fairly responsive. I sort of took the fatherly approach. I spent a lot of time trying to get him calmed down, get him organized, and remind him that he was a leader and he had to take responsibility for his actions and the actions of his outfit. Those kids were in a state of near shock. They'd had the shit beat out of them, but I told them they had to get their stuff together because they might be back in this thing, and we might have to depend on them.

Meanwhile, Vargas had been previously resupplied with ammunition, but what he received was a cache of 90mm tank rounds for the M-48 tank cannons. Vargas voiced his displeasure over the screw up, and Weise ensured that the proper 5.56mm and 7.72mm ammo boxes, along with grenades, would be delivered. Weise assessed the condition: "There were always more targets than bullets in the Cua Viet area."[23]

> "Bravo Company was unable to penetrate Dai Do. It was stopped short by a withering hail of enemy fire, pinned down, and unable to move forward. As darkness fell, things looked grim indeed. Then Echo Company arrived, and the picture brightened."[22]
>
> —Brig. Gen. William Weise

The man in charge of the logistics was Capt. Lorraine L. Forehand, the battalion S-4 (logistics officer). He felt so bad about the screw up that he personally took the ammo to Vargas by boat up the dangerous creek. Vargas was impressed: "How the hell they ever got through there without getting shot, I'll never know."[24]

"Lane" Forehand was a very interesting guy. My first experience with Lane was not with 2/4. When I went over with 3/3 in 1963–64 as a young lieutenant, Lane was a company commander. He was a hell-raiser—liked his hooch unfortunately, as a lot of the guys did, but he liked to raise hell. One night he and a swabby got into a damned fight at the officers club at Camp Schwab in Okinawa. There was a steep cliff right below the club, and they came rolling down the hill, slugging it out! He was a hell-raiser, and at the end of the day he had a reputation, duly deserved in many cases, but he did a great job supporting the men in combat. He came from a very well-respected political family in Georgia, which I think was the Richard D. Russell family. Lane passed a long time ago, of cancer, I think. We all have very fond memories of him.

The enemy probes continued all through the night of May 1, and I know that Weise, like all of us, had no sleep that night. Planning the next day's operations, without really knowing where all the NVA were, must have been a daunting task.

By the time dawn broke on May 2, we had taken much enemy fire, but we did manage to enter the outskirts of the hamlet. It must have been pretty gut wrenching for the enemy to know that they had expended all that ammunition and rockets, just to see a company of Marines coming at them with fixed bayonets.

The 2/4 command structure and positions the morning of May 2, 1968, stood as follows: Echo 2/4 under me linked with Bravo 1/3 in An Lac under 2nd Lt. Thomas R. Keppen; Foxtrot 2/4 was commanded by Capt. James H. Butler in Dong Huan; Golf 2/4, under Capt. Jay Vargas, was still pinned down and surrounded in east Dai Do; Hotel 2/4, under 1st Lt. Alexander F. Prescott, was also located at Dong Huan. It was actually on May 2 at 12:23 a.m. that Weise issued the order for me to form an assault line under cover of darkness to link up with Vargas, and both units would then form an assault line.

I formed up Echo, and we departed at 5 a.m. for Dai Do, as Golf gave covering fire. As I stated, I led the reserve platoon. Then Vargas ordered Golf to attack the southern part of Dai Do from the rear. We still had the bayonets fixed, and we were heading into the action for real. It must have been quite a sight to the casual observer.

Simultaneously, according to the 3/21 after-action report, dated June 5, 1968:

> At 0755 hours twenty minute preparations were placed on Objective 1 (Lam Xuan East) and Objective 2 (Lam Xuan West) by two Marine artillery and one Marine 4.2 inch mortar battery. At 0800 hours, Co. G on the right and Co. B on the left crossed the LD.[25]
>
> At 0813 hours, Co. A crossed the LD, following Co. C. Co. B quickly advanced to the graveyard vicinity [at grid coordinates] YD 275687 and established a position from which it could support Co. C's attack on Objective 1. At 0900 hours, artillery fire preparation began on Objective 3 (Nhi Ha). At 1055 hours, Co. C reported that Objective 1 had been swept and seized without enemy contact. The attack was resumed, and at 1155 hours Co. B reported approaching Objective 2. By 1210 hours, Objective 2 was secured, again without contact with the enemy.[26]

What this information meant (albeit it was unknown to me at the time) was that the NVA had pulled their troops (minus a few troops for harassing fire) out of the area as a lure, reinforcing the main assault building towards Dai Do, thus preparing the 3/21 operational area for artillery strikes once we had entered the kill zones. I would not be aware of any of the army's actions until Nolan had written his book, and later I was able to meet a few of the participants, such as Wally Nunn and Ken Johnson, among others.

I knew only the BLT 2/4 operational matrix, its limitations, and I had my orders. The plan was for Echo to lead the assault into Dai Do to assist Vargas's Golf Company, with Hotel Company following. And once all three companies had been consolidated, they would then continue the attack and retake Dai Do. Foxtrot Company would remain in reserve with Bravo 1/3, which had been given a rest due to significant casualties.

On May 2, army Lieutenant Colonel Snyder sent his Alpha, Bravo, and Charlie companies moving towards Nhi Ha, following the Marine artillery barrage. The 3/21st's Charlie Company (under the command of 1st Lieutenant Kohl) was the first to enter the village, covered by Alpha (under Captain Osborn, with 2nd Platoon under Lieutenant Smith and

3rd Platoon under Lieutenant Kimball) and Delta companies (with Delta held in reserve under Captain Humphries), where they were ambushed by the 4th Battalion, 270th NVA Regiment, suffering twelve KIA and fourteen WIA. Bravo Company (under Captain Corrigan) secured Lam Xuan just south of Nhi Ha.[27] Alpha, Charlie, and Delta Companies managed to halt the NVA advance, but they could not push the enemy out of the village. The Marines laid down grazing fire and then retreated under my order. They received no further response from the enemy.[28]

The army situation was different on May 2. According to the 3/21 after-action report:

> The enemy continued his stubborn resistance and the artillery fire on his bunkers was having little effect. At 1455 hours Co. D began to move to the area of contact and at 1525 hours Co. B began receiving enemy artillery and rocket fire from the north. By 1555 Co. B had 4 WIA, and at 1604 hours, Co. C reported that the elements were observed withdrawing. Friendly forces did not pursue because it was felt that this was a trap. This feeling was borne out as Co. C began to receive heavy fire again at 1630; 15 minutes later Co. C reported 4 KIA. Medical evacuation continued by USMC aircraft and Otter vehicles. A, C, and D rifle elements broke contact with the enemy and by 1800 hours had established a consolidated night logger site vicinity YD282705. Co. B remained at its position. Results of the action were: 9 US KIA, 14 US WIA, 3 US MIA, 15 NVA KIA.[29]

This data is supported by the comments of Jesse Brooks, who was with 4th Squad, 2nd Platoon, Charlie Company, 3/21 196th, and on the ground during this time:

> I was in country from 10 Feb. 1968 thru 01 Feb. 1969. I was with C 3/21 196th, 2nd plat., 4th squad. I was wounded around May 6th, not sure what day exactly. There were 9 men KIA on May 2nd, 1968 at Nhi Ha. We were on a battalion size sweep. We were to be support for the Marines in that AO. We worked thru the Ville, S & D. We

The Fighting was Furious
—Brig. Gen. William Weise

Before Echo Company reached its assault positions, the enemy opened up with heavy volumes of small arms and mortar fire. The two forward [assault] platoons received heavy casualties and lost forward momentum.

But Captain Livingston immediately committed his reserve platoon, personally leading it forward to penetrate the forward enemy defense, and moved well into Dai Do. Livingston then widened the penetration, attacking to the right and left. He brought forward the two platoons previously pinned down in the rice paddies and continued to attack. The fighting was furious.[30]

went on to cross the rice paddies to the wood line on other side. We were ambushed; they were all around and between us. They popped up from spider holes. We could not get good fields of fire as they were between our own men. We had to advance to the rear.[31]

My company, along with the reorganized companies, had their operations order from Weise, and we launched the assault just before dawn. As my men moved out, I noted that Bravo Company had a lot of bodies still on the battlefield, which we passed as we began the attack on Dai Do. It's a sad situation where you're firing and maneuvering past the bodies of your fellow Marines. As we continued moving forward, the fire only increased in volume and accuracy.

Meanwhile, I had to lead the 160 men collected for the mission out of An Lac initially without the benefit of masking fire or smoke. Moving over open terrain against an entrenched and fortified enemy was not considered a great plan, but I had to work with what was available. What the enemy did get was one round of willy pete, until the initial fire mission was cancelled at the battery command center due to the commanders' belief that ARVN troops were in the area. Another reason we had no masking fire or smoke was that the army artillery of Hotel 3/12 had run short of rounds.

Along with the previous day's Marine casualties, we found three NVA dead and a 12.7mm machine gun from the early morning engagement. We fought the palace guard at Dai Do. They were big guys with new uniforms, brand new weapons, and close cropped haircuts. They were quality troops. Vic Taylor pointed out that "there were over seven thousand of them."[32]

We had just started moving when a NVA soldier was seen in the perimeter, and he was quickly taken out by Lance Cpl. Phillip L. Cornwell and his M-60, as other Marines fired M-16s.[33] Then, as the company moved forward again, two more NVA were spotted, and they were apparently surrendering. They were sent to the rear, where they joined two other NVA who had surrendered to Hotel Company. The intelligence gathered was important. Weise was told that the men were part of twelve companies in Dai Do, part of the 52nd Regiment of the NVA 320th Division. After that information was obtained from the prisoners of war (POWs), they were taken downriver.[34]

We had just started the fight.

CHAPTER 6

Where Hell Was as Far as the Eye Could See

I would rather die a free man than live a life of subservience to another.
—Ethan Allen

THE DISTANCE BETWEEN AN Lac and Dai Do was five hundred meters of killing ground, and when the first NVA rounds came in, Gunnery Sgt. Roscoe Chandler and I hit the deck as the lead elements reached within two hundred meters of the hamlet. The NVA were patient and from their entrenched positions opened fire with everything, directing RPGs at anything resembling a radio antenna.

As Chandler and I hit the deck in the cemetery, the burial mounds, which were basically graves within the rice paddies, provided the only cover and concealment. We had all these radio antennae, so everyone knew where the command post was. They knew where the commanding officer was due to all those target indicators. We had the platoon, company, and even the battalion TAC. The burial mound that was the only protection for the entire CP, including for Chandler and me, was blown apart by eighteen successive rocket hits. The graves were basically disappearing in front of us and all around as they took direct hits. One RPG hit the burial mound right in front of me, almost coming all the way through. I do not know how in the hell we all survived that.

My 2nd Platoon was on the left flank, and 3rd Platoon was on the right. The two lead platoons became bogged down, and we had a lot

Lt. Vic Taylor Wasn't Supposed to be There
—Brig. Gen. William Weise

Not many people know this about Taylor, and he certainly would never tell. . . . When the battle started on April 30, 1968, he was aboard the USS *Iwo Jima* recovering from wounds [received] during a previous battle (Task Force Kilo). Vic heard the medevac choppers landing on the flight deck and hurried to learn what was going on. All of the initial Marine casualties were from Hotel Company, suffered during the afternoon assault on Dong Huan. Vic never hesitated. He scrounged a rifle, flak jacket, helmet, and ammo, and jumped aboard one of the Ugly Angels H-34 helicopters returning to pick up more casualties. Vic, of course, never asked permission, as he knew it would be denied.[1]

of Marines killed. The first casualty was a friendly fire incident when a Marine ran ahead of his group. The bullet went through his flak jacket and ignited the rounds in his bandoleer. Then, once stripped of his gear, the Marine was again hit in the stomach by the NVA, receiving a flesh wound, and he retreated back to his squad.[2]

My Echo Company was slowed in the advance, and Captain Vargas moved his forty-six remaining Marines to assist us. Vargas was minus a company gunny, but he had the air liaison officer, 1st Lt. Judson D. Hilton, who had been with the unit since the day before.[3] Hilton later gathered a squad of leaderless Marines and covered the tactical fallback of Golf Company. His Marines heard an enemy mortar and took fire from well-concealed enemy soldiers, who were, in some instances, only a few feet away and could not be seen.

Casualties began to mount.

I had been coordinating the movement and directing fire when I happened upon several dead NVA in spider holes and saw Taylor was

The Fortifications were Unbelievable
—Lt. Col. Vic Taylor

The elaborate positions our Marines were forced to attack—the hundreds of meters of neck-deep bunkers, fighting holes, gun pits, and connecting trenches so cleverly woven into the hedgerows, buildings, and thickets—were constructed over the previous weeks by the full-time efforts of a local Viet Cong (VC) support battalion. The Army of the Republic of Vietnam (ARVN) unit responsible for the ground made no effort to interfere with the VC efforts or even to report them. Not surprisingly, the VC commander's brother-in-law was an officer in the ARVN unit.

The fortifications were unbelievable, and the NVA soldiers were popping in and out, up and down, shooting from all the holes. Fields of fire overlapped. To get at one bunker, you had to take the fire from another. By teams and pairs the Marines would throw grenades, then flank the bunker and fire up the trench. It was not our first time out. As usual, the enemy was almost invisible until we got right on top of them. Some broke and ran—most died in place. We took hits but got the rhythm and kept moving.[4]

taking fire from well-concealed enemy in the hooches and bamboo tree line. The tall grass also held its horrors. Grenade launchers and machine guns concentrated their fire on these hot points as the remainder of Echo moved forward, with Golf on the right flank in our one o'clock position, converging together to squeeze the pocket of enemy troops in the middle.

There were many Marines whose individual actions allowed Echo to make progress, such as Pfc. Marshall J. Serna, who killed several NVA soldiers, rescued several wounded Marines, went back to his M-60, killed a few more enemy troops, burned out the barrel, and then retrieved another machine gun. He advanced on a trench, firing his weapon when he was wounded by a grenade thrown from an enemy soldier in a spider hole. Ignoring his serious leg wound and the loss of blood, he managed to sight in and finally kill the NVA soldier who wounded him, before he lost consciousness. He would receive

An Orange, a Bullet, and a Bronze Star
—Lance Cpl. Frank Valdez

Our company was guarding the bridge at Dong Ha when the action first began. A beautiful spread of food had just been delivered to us, including juicy steaks and fresh fruit, when word came from HQ that we needed to force march over to Dai Do to reinforce the rest of the battalion. As we passed the stack of fruit, I grabbed an orange and put it in the cargo pocket of my utilities. In all the excitement, I quickly forgot about the orange.

I will tell you that during the course of the battle I never saw Captain Livingston take a backward step, and he seemingly never flinched, though I know that cannot be true. When I saw *Apocalypse Now*, I could have sworn that the character portrayed by Robert Duval could very well have been based on Captain Livingston.

After we had linked up with Hotel Company at Dinh To, the NVA opened up on us with small-arms fire, including machine guns, which kicked up the dust at our feet.

Both Captain Livingston and I hit the deck at the same time. As I continued lying there, Livingston stood up to reconnoiter the area. Just as he got upright, the enemy opened up again, hitting him in the thigh. At the same time, I felt a burning sensation in my lower leg, and my trouser leg was smoking. I slapped my leg, and said, "I'm hit!" I thought, "I'm out of here!" But, no such luck—just a couple of holes in my pants, no wound. We were able to get all the wounded and dead off the field of battle, and only then would Captain Livingston allow us to put him on a skimmer boat for evacuation.

the Silver Star and a second Purple Heart.[5] His actions allowed a platoon to sweep into the right flank of the village and establish a base of covering fire.

A while later, as I was resting and gathering my thoughts and wits, I remembered the orange I had put in my utility pocket the day before. I thought an orange sounded real good and took it out, expecting a nice, juicy piece of fruit. It was looking worse for the wear, and when I split it open, there, in the middle was a bullet! To the best of my reasoning, the bullet had gone through Captain Livingston's leg, traveled up the leg of my trousers, and, fully spent, lodged in my orange. I kept that bullet for twenty-five years, hoping to give it to Captain Livingston.

When I found out that he was to be the guest speaker at a [Marine] birthday ball in Ventura, California, I contacted the ball organizers and told them the bullet in the orange story. They sent someone a hundred miles to my house to pick up the bullet. They had the bullet mounted on a plaque, and I had the honor of presenting it to Major General Livingston at the ball. As I finished telling the story, I said, "And so, General Livingston, I believe you owe me an orange." He then tossed me an orange that had been given to him before my speech without explanation.

The last official thing the general did before he retired was to present me with a Bronze Star for actions at Dai Do. (He seems to think I saved his life.) In fact, he did a surprise presentation during his retirement ceremony. It seems he had recommended me for the Bronze Star twenty-seven years earlier, and did not know I had never received it until he and my wife, Becky, were talking. They both conspired to keep the presentation from me and did a great job of it. The general says to me quite often that every time he turned around during the battle, there I was. I tell him: "Yes sir, I was holding onto your leg, trying to stop you!"[6]

My men had brought up a forward air control (FAC) team on the fourth assault under Lt. James T. Ferland, but all three men on the team were wounded by an RPG. Ferland was wounded in one eye and could not see out of the other. He, Pfc. William McDade, and Lance Cpl. Jerry Hester were escorted to the road at An Lac.[7] Ferland returned to 2/4 within a week, being very lucky.[8] Even after clearing out over thirty bunkers and defensive positions up to this time, the fight was not over.

I had just been hit by grenades in my right leg, while my RTO, Frank Valdez, was even more severely wounded by the blasts. I was fortunate that the femoral artery had not been severed, yet despite my wounds, with assistance, we still somehow coordinated the collection and extraction of Echo's casualties: ten dead and sixty wounded. They were quickly moved to the riverbank triage and placed aboard boats to be safely moved to the helicopter LZ. During the process, a squad led by Cpl. Nicholas R. Cardona arrived, and Cardona took over as my company RTO. Cardona would be the only man from his entire squad who had not been wounded.[9]

During this period, I assessed the situation, organized the remaining Marines, and made an on-the-spot command decision: I decided to launch my reserve platoon. We got up and headed straight into the enemy fire, and then proceeded to drive right up the middle and through the entrenched NVA lines. I was following the tested and tried edict of penetrating and then widening the hole. We had practiced these types of small-unit maneuvers, and we were good at it. However, air support was available to the battalion to some degree, and I commenced the fourth assault against Dai Do.

We were piling it on there, and we were using weapons organic to the company, the M-79s, LAWs (light antitank weapons), rocket launchers, mortars—the whole bag. We were using anything we could find that would shoot, and then it was high-diddle-diddle, right up the middle, right across that same paddy again. I had been returning fire whenever a target presented itself, until my .45-caliber M-3 grease gun jammed. I was then handed a trusty M-14, which I maintained in each squad for sniper duty. It was survival of the fittest at that point. There were multiple targets; it was a matter of who you wanted to get involved with. I was banging away at a few of them. I do not know how many I hit. I was shooting, and people were dropping.

This was when we found ourselves in a built-up bunker complex, and the fighting at various times was furious and even hand to hand—really close quarters. We had sixteen men killed as we moved in and attacked those positions. We completed the penetration and began to roll them up, taking one position after another, forcing back the enemy that we did not kill. Some of the reports claimed we killed between five hundred and

> "Several times Echo Marines gained the flank of trench lines and placed killing enfilade fire on large numbers of NVA soldiers who remained to die in their positions. . . . Golf Company broke out of its perimeter to assist Echo Company clear Dai Do. Finally, after several hours of heavy fighting and heavy casualties, Dai Do was secured."[10]
>
> —Brig. Gen. William Weise

six hundred in this sweep alone. Of this, I am not sure, but I do know we eventually killed around three thousand to four thousand during the entire mission. I also know that there was later a mass grave where about two thousand enemy KIA were buried with the help of an engineering unit after we pulled out. That was just one such mass grave.

I have been given various numbers of the enemy I killed personally, around twenty-five or so. To be honest, I have no idea how many I killed. I really never thought much about it, as there were plenty to go around, and nobody was counting. There was nothing classic about it; it was just a matter of fire and maneuver. Marines just do what Marines do.

By 9 a.m., Golf and I radioed to Weise that Dai Do was secured, and by 9:14 a.m., Echo and Golf had pushed the NVA north out of Dai Do.[11] No sooner had I handed the radio handset back to Cardona than the NVA, still located in Dinh To, launched a fifteen-minute artillery barrage, lasting from 9:15 to 9:30, from the north to mask their retreat.[12]

It did come to our attention that Colonel Hull had tried to get the 2nd ARVN to cover our western flank. Even though we had secured Dai Do after four assaults, we were soon headed north to Dinh To, as the ARVN captured Dong Lai and Thong Nghia.

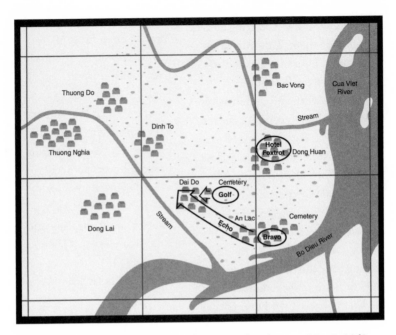

Echo Company attacks Dai Do, Golf Company breakout on May 2, 1968.
William Weise

Lieutenants Prescott and Boyle had led their platoons, using any available cover to advance undetected. After they had covered the five hundred meters to Dinh To and paused, they began taking fire. Marines went down, wounded, although the enemy could not be located. Vic Taylor's RTO was hit as rounds snapped through the tall grass. Taylor rushed through his men, locating the seriously wounded, and ordered other Marines to get the wounded back to safety. Soon there were too many wounded to advance farther. They were pinned down. The NVA had all corners and avenues of approach zeroed in with squad weapons. The kill zone was complete.

Some of the Marines discovered enemy snipers in trees as other NVA fired from huts and tree lines, as well as entrenched positions. Taylor also had other problems; many of their rifles were inoperable due to extended use and little time or the proper gear to clean them. Many Marines were wishing they had an AK-47 or a good solid M-14. Hotel was in bad shape.

Our under-strength battalion had managed to keep the NVA from crossing the Bo Dieu River, at least from the standpoint of establishing launching points, while the brown-water navy secured the waterways and shot up anything resembling a floating threat. What the NVA had done was successfully probe. They launched sporadic indirect fire and infantry attacks, withdrew and pulled the Marines in, to test their strength and resolve. Killing Marines naturally reduced American combat assets. The NVA hoped that it would, in fact, demoralize us so that we would be psychologically impaired and thus unable to retake Dai Do, let alone stem any subsequent attacks the NVA launched. History shows that was a bad decision. The officers took charge, when officers fell, their NCOs stepped up and handled the situations.

> "Captain Livingston and I were in visual contact most of the fight, and I never once saw him take cover or step backward. Instead, he moved among his troops, encouraging, threatening, comforting, urging, pushing them to virtually super-human feats."[13]
> —Lt. Col. Vic Taylor

Just prior to my arrival, Lieutenant Prescott had informed Weise of Hotel's condition; the NVA were so close that any indirect or air support would come dangerously close to the Marines. Weise surmised the situation, knowing that the company, which started out the size of two platoons, would soon cease to exist. He told Prescott that I was coming, and Prescott then yelled from his position down the line that "Echo is coming."[14] That was when Prescott fell wounded from a hidden shot from across the river. After passing full command over to Taylor, Prescott was taken to the wounded collection point.

Taylor and the company moved out just before 10 a.m. Taylor said of his men: "Some were standing watch, some readied equipment, many slept or lounged, but all were quiet. No nervous jabbering, no false bravado, no whining, no melodramatics—they were professionals. Most were teenagers, many with far less than a year away from home, but they were seasoned by months of fighting with a determined enemy. Despite their youth, despite their short time in the Corps, they

Where Does the Corps Get Men Like Taylor?
—Brig. Gen. William Weise

[Taylor] arrived at Dong Huan in time to help mopping up and reconsolidation. Captain Jim Williams, an outstanding company commander and combat leader, had been seriously wounded during the Dong Huan assault and had been medevaced. Lieutenant Scotty Prescott assumed command of the battered, but still feisty, Hotel Company. Two days later, Scotty would also be wounded and medevaced, passing command to 2nd Lt. Vic Taylor in the midst of a horrendous firefight. Young Vic Taylor was more than equal to the task, and a number of Marines are alive today because of his bravery and superb leadership. Vic did all this while he was AWOL from sickbay! God, where does the Corps get men like him?[15]

were as willing and serious—as professional—as anyone who ever wore a uniform. I was proud to be among them."[16]

Vargas and I could have written the same words about our own men. All of us commanders knew that many of our men were either dead or wounded, and those fit to fight were waiting to once again engage an enemy determined to kill them. Yet they unhesitatingly followed their orders and got the job done. Such was and is a United States Marine. When you are involved in an operation like this, you are doing everything for your buddies and for their welfare. You do not want to let your buddies down. I was responsible for the mission. I had to live with the results. A fellow Marine's life could depend upon my actions, and I would have to live the rest of my life with my decisions.

The casualties came in from every angle and direction. I was not near 1st Lt. Dave Jones when he apparently stood up and was hit by a mortar round that landed right behind him. His flak jacket was shredded, and his legs and his arms and buttocks were peppered with shrapnel. The diagnosis by his RTO, Lance Cpl. Steve Wilson, was simple: "You're legs are messed up, you need to get out of here."[17] Jones's first squad leader, Sgt. James W. Rogers, became a platoon leader.

Luckily, Dai Do was secured for the most part. The situation was hardly under control, but the Marines had not yielded ground. Vic Taylor and I worked together, but we faced an uphill battle. Taylor had assessed the advantages and disadvantages of the opposing forces, and listed these for our enemy's advantages:

1. Their unprecedented numbers on the battlefield.
2. The immensity and complexity of their fortifications.
3. Their uncommon aggressiveness and tenacity.
4. The incredible amount of firepower they brought to the points of contact.
5. [The NVA 320th Division] leadership by veterans with ten or more years of combat experience.

Against that list, our Marines' advantages might seem slim, but never underestimate the power of *esprit de corps*:

The men in their teens and early twenties. They followed and led, fought and endured, with loyalty and a soldierly steadfastness that inspired and sometimes humbled we who were privileged to lead them.

Our Marines' disadvantages were clear:

1. The elaborate fortifications that our Marines were forced to attack—the hundreds of meters of neck-deep bunkers, fighting holes, gun pits, and connecting trenches so cleverly woven into the hedgerows, buildings, and thickets . . . were constructed over the previous weeks by the full-time efforts of a local Viet Cong support battalion. The ARVN unit responsible for the ground made no effort to interfere with the VC efforts, or to even report them.
2. The combined strength of 2/4's five rifle companies was less than 700 men.[18]

A Moment of Levity in Hell
—Specialist Wally Nunn and
Warrant Officer Ken Johnson

From the start of the battle, the CO of 4th Marines, Colonel Hull, had great concern about air mobility. He requested that the army provide helicopter support for resupply, extraction, insertion, and medevac. The 174th AHC provided that air mobility for the entire battle [supporting 3/21]. There were three Dolphin 'slicks' and crews that accomplished this.[19]

During a rare lull in their support missions, the 174th AHC Dolphin crew of #910 (WO [1st Class Ken] Johnson, WO [1st Class Henry "Marty"] Wifholm, [Spc. 4th Class Frank] Dailey, and [Spc. 4th Class Wally] Nunn) landed aside a clearing by the Cua Viet River to conserve fuel. They shut down the aircraft, and two of the bored crew members (Nunn and Dailey) conspired to throw Wifholm into the river. "He kept bitchin' about how hot it was, and that he'd jump in that river for two cents. With my back to Marty, I gave them the nod for the go ahead," [recalls] Ken Johnson.

Upon coming out of the water, Wifholm took his clothes off to dry. As the hysterical bunch (with a half-naked wet Wifholm) neared the aircraft, a call came over the radio for needed helicopter support for the Marines. Johnson says, "It seemed that they had a unit which had taken a short burst from an Air Force

And we had more than personnel losses to deal with. Weise summarized the other losses we faced:

Equipment casualties were also high. Our last two tanks had to be dragged off the battlefield, and less than half our amtracs were operating. Many machine guns and mortars had to be replaced. Worst of all, most of the M-16 rifles in fighter. They had some badly wounded, so we did what we were there to do and went after it." They all boarded the aircraft immediately and were airborne, with Wifholm sans his clothing except for his shorts, boots and helmet. After they had dropped off the wounded, they got a priority call that the commander for 3rd Marines, Col. Milton A. Hull, needed a lift.

Ken Johnson tells us, "We had to refuel first. We landed nose-to-nose with a Marine CH-46 at the POL point. We got to laughing at the look on their pilots' faces. Wifholm said he wanted to get dressed, but we were in a hurry. I tried to make 'delay' excuses, but you don't keep the O-6 [Colonel Hull] waiting."

Upon picking up Hull (in freshly starched fatigues), the colonel spied Wifholm's lack of clothing and [asked, "What the hell is going on here?" He was told the chopper had just conducted an emergency evacuation of a bunch of his wounded Marines and Wifholm hadn't had time to get dressed. Hull then] stated (with his trademark cigar between his teeth), "I always knew you army aviators were a bunch of queers." Upon reaching their destination, Hull told them to land angled away from "his soldiers" and remain in the aircraft and get the hell out ASAP, to avoid his fellow Marines and counterparts from seeing them. Johnson also adds, "We laughed so hard, because we knew if we 'went down' and the NVA came upon us, they would see Marty and run."[20]

the rifle companies had malfunctioned and were discarded in favor of captured AK-47 assault rifles. In fact, when I visited Golf Company, I saw only one M-16 rifle. It was carried by Captain Vargas, the company commander. The only other functioning M-16 I saw that afternoon was carried by me. Clearly, the Marines felt their rifles had let them down! Personnel and equipment problems notwithstanding, we had a job to do, and we did it.[21]

Nowhere to Go But Forward
—Lance Cpl. Steve Wilson

It was 3rd Platoon that stepped out into that rice paddy to lead the company across into Dai Do on that fateful day. Dave was the fifth man, and I was the sixth of about thirty reinforced with weapons. By the time we reached the first trench line there were [only] thirteen of us left fighting, and two of us were wounded. I took shrapnel in the hand, but that was insignificant compared to those being caught in the open paddy hail of rockets and AKs. There was nowhere to go, but to thrust into the fight.

Until this past spring's return to Vietnam [in 2008] with "the two generals" (and Dave as my roommate), the skipper had not realized just how far our progression as 3rd Platoon had successfully progressed. We eliminated two T-formed trench lines and two bunkered mortars—everything in our path—prior to being hit. I have no idea how many we eliminated, but we maintained the attack and were linking with Golf when the blast got us both on the other side of the ville. My rank was lance corporal on that day, and I would be promoted to corporal by Capt. Jim Livingston some five days later while he was bedridden aboard the USS *Iwo Jima*.[22]

Meanwhile, at the wounded collection point, Prescott's previously paralyzed legs had come back to life. The bullet had struck his left canteen, flattened against his web gear, pushed a stud into his back, and bruised his spine. It then hit the right canteen and never even broke the skin, but knocked him into the dirt at over two thousand feet per second. He was back in the fight. And the fight had really just begun at this point. Soldiers, sailors, and Marines were in for a lot more punishment. We were also prepared to hand it out tenfold.

CHAPTER 7

Dropping the Hammer

Whenever possible, take the fight to the enemy.

—General Heinz Guderian

THE NVA HAD SLAMMED into Echo Company head on as our Marines swept Dai Do and Dinh To, while two elements of the enemy were running parallel to the riverbank on one side and around the village on the other to outflank us. Echo/Hotel only had one clear avenue: a tactical retreat. Lieutenant Taylor ordered the wounded dragged back to safety in a bounding tactical withdrawal. Then Taylor realized they had enemy to the rear. Marines laid down covering fire, as the enemy soldiers were visible in their attack. The first counterattack had begun.

The surviving NVA were withdrawing, although there were not a lot of them. Vargas and I were under no illusions regarding the tactic. The enemy was not retreating; they were probably regrouping. Once the village of Dai Do was secured through a final sweep, security was posted, the wounded were collected, the dead were bagged, and all but the most effective walking wounded were sent to the rear. Gear and weapons, both ours and theirs, were collected, and everything was stockpiled. Nothing was left for the enemy, and nothing went to waste. At 9:55 a.m., permission was received to send Foxtrot's 2nd Platoon from My Loc to join the main body.[1]

Weise was still not satisfied. He wanted the remainder of Echo and Golf to move on to Dinh To within the hour; as long as there were enemy soldiers in solid positions, there was the risk of continued indirect fire and a counterattack.[2] So Vargas and I, both suffering multiple wounds and with mounting casualties in our companies, received the order to continue the advance through Dinh To, along with Hotel Company, which was only seventy-five to eighty men strong, under 2nd Lt. Vic Taylor, positioned at Dong Huan. These Marines were holding on with their last breath, and the enemy was not letting up.

Vargas and I were both seasoned enough to know that one never allows the enemy to fall back and catch his breath; you choke the life out of him, hitting him hard and often until he has collapsed. For the rest of that morning Echo, Golf, and Hotel continued the advance on the entrenched enemy under heavy supporting arms and air strikes.[3] At this time, Weise joined Golf Company with Sergeant Major Malnar.

The great problem, as I have said before, was the well-constructed A-frame bunkers. These were strong enough to drive a tank over. In addition, many of the smaller positions were dug out under trees, where the enemy had boarded themselves up, roots and all. You really had to be within ten to fifteen feet before you could really see these bunkers, and, most of the time, the enemy would wait until we were that close before they would open fire. This was why all the kids killed in my company were taken out with head shots from these positions. However, Marines hit the positions, took casualties, inflicted even more, and neutralized them. To quote a famous Marine, "Anything else is half-assing and not typical of Marines."

Nevertheless, I was not as much wanting a fight, as wanting to see a fight thrust upon us won, with minimal friendly casualties and the maximum of dead enemy littering the field. There is a great psychological component to seeing a lot more of your dead than the enemy's, and I wanted that image to be seared into our enemies' heads.

> "I was impressed at his [Livingston's] anxiousness for combat, and he sort of had a smile on his face, like the combat he had been waiting for had at long last arrived, and he wasn't going to miss it for the world. He was itching for a fight, and he got it."[4]
>
> —2nd Lt. Jack E. Deichmann

I had completed assisting with evacuating the badly wounded, an effort coordinated with my XO, Dave Jones, who was still bleeding himself. Echo was also down to forty-five men at one point, but listening to the radio traffic, I called in to say, "[T]his is Echo Six. I'm going to help Hotel. They are really fixin' to get into trouble. I'll go get 'em."[5]

I took my remaining Marines and drove straight towards Dinh To as fast as possible, closing on Hotel's rear. Echo ran right on top of a platoon of NVA in hiding. Earlier, at 10:40 a.m., I had approached Taylor with a platoon-sized element as bullets struck the ground around him. I suppose I was oblivious to the enemy fire snapping around me, as I was sort of busy directing my men into position to shore up Hotel's tenuous defensive line. I then gave the order to go, and the Marines of both companies fixed bayonets, checked ammo, and struck out, led by Taylor and me.

Marines with jammed or empty weapons gathered anything they could find on the battlefield, from friend or foe, to continue the assault. As they did so, the NVA was maneuvering to outflank Echo and Hotel. By 1:40 p.m., the NVA took the initiative and launched another attack. The probes were over, and the enemy was coming back in force.

> "Such was Livingston's reputation. Even the riflemen in other companies knew him as a skilled, effective combat leader—a master craftsman at closing with and destroying the enemy."[6]
>
> —Brig. Gen. William Weise

Taylor saw that NVA camouflaged in leaves and branches were between twenty and fifty meters away in the brush. Taylor emptied his Colt .45 automatic as another Marine hurled one grenade after another as fast as he could. As the enemy broke cover, Pfc. Vincent A. Scafidi killed most of them crossing his line of sight, running an entire belt of 7.62mm ammo through his M-60 machine gun. He would later receive the Silver Star.[7]

Simultaneously, Cpl. Richard R. Britton was engaged in close combat, killing four NVA who attacked him in concert. He shot one with his Colt .45 and another with his M-16; another he bayoneted in the throat, and the last man he killed with his issued K-Bar knife. Britton suffered a slashing wound to the inside left thigh for his effort; then a grenade landed near him, and it was over. He passed out from his wounds.[8]

This was what our boys were up against.

Finally, Weise decided to have 1/3 and the 1st Amtracs flank his battalion in a "hammer and anvil" support operation. Foxtrot Company was ordered to the southern sector of Dai Do once the 2nd Platoon arrived to assist Golf and Vargas in the attack.[9] Prescott and Hotel were ordered to pass through Golf and Echo and press forward, reaching Dinh To at 1 p.m. I took the thirty or so Marines who were able to fight and moved north myself, and Hotel was counterattacked. Vargas was severely outnumbered and outgunned. I knew this, and radioed that I was on the way.

The army's 3/21 was also running into trouble, as stated in its after-action report:

> At 1250 hours, Co. C was well into Objective 3 [Nhi Ha] when they began to receive sniper fire from dug in enemy elements at 30 meters. At 1255 Co. B reported receiving automatic weapons and M-79 fire. At the same time Co. C reported that they had 10 friendly casualties. Fire had grown in intensity and in some cases contacts were made as close as 15 meters. At 1300 hours Co. A committed two platoons to Co. C's right (northern) flank to counter enemy movement in that area. Co. D was alerted to be prepared to reinforce Co. C. By 1330 hours the enemy fire included heavy machine guns and RPG rocket launchers. Co. B reported 1 WIA from sniper fire at 1400 hours.[10]

Weise needed the wounded and dead evacuated, and fresh troops inserted. However, so did the army's 3/21 on May 2; its after-action report continues: "At 1408 hours, Dolphin 248, the 3-21 Inf C&C [command and control] aircraft evacuated the casualties from Co. B and at 1430 hours, the Otters [aircraft] departed the Bn CP to evacuate Co. C's casualties. At 1451 Air Force and Marine Corps FACs were over the area of the contact, directing artillery."[11]

At 1:22 p.m., Echo and Hotel reported that they had secured Dinh To to the north, while ARVN units reported securing the village from the west. At 1:40, the enemy launched a counterattack from the north, and by 2:30, both companies were heavily involved in a major NVA assault. It was at this time that reports came into Weise (also known to Major Warren) saying both Vargas and I had been wounded and Echo and Hotel had sustained heavy casualties.[12]

Despite many of us being wounded (with me being hit twice), and despite being almost overrun and still taking heavy casualties, I noticed that we affected a successful retrograde maneuver with both companies. We were able to consolidate our forces, reorganize, resupply, evacuate the wounded, and prepare for the next evolution.[13]

The battle was far from over. Weise also knew that General Tompkins's forces were probably stretched far too thin to allow him to send relief without weakening his line along other points. Weise also knew that the NVA would probably follow the path of least resistance and attack the ARVN forces in Quang Tri City in an attempt to outflank the Marines as a whole. Having the South Vietnamese cover the approach to our flanks did not make most of us company commanders (or Weise) feel very comfortable.[14]

What Vargas and I did not know just prior to all of this was that Weise had been ordered by Colonel Hull all along to push harder and deeper. Weise had explained to his regimental commander that he did not have the manpower to accomplish the mission; he needed reinforcements. Hull was apparently sympathetic, but he had to answer to his superior, Major General Tompkins, who had not personally seen the battlefield and was not able to personally visualize the situation.

At 3:50 p.m., Golf and Foxtrot launched their attack, sweeping north, and the enemy fire increased in volume, intensity, and lethality.[15] Golf and Vargas were to push forward until they received enemy fire, then they would lay a base of fire, allowing Foxtrot to continue the advance. By 4:45, it was a fight to the death, and for fifty minutes, one of the fiercest firefights in modern history erupted. Marines pressed forward under direct and indirect enemy fire, as well as friendly artillery, mortars, and air strikes.[16]

My platoon also engaged, but then I was wounded again, through both legs, and could not walk. Golf was down to forty Marines, but still had four officers. Foxtrot was in better shape with eighty men in fighting shape, but just east of Dinh To, they became bogged down by heavy enemy artillery and automatic weapons fire. Bravo 1/3 was still in An Lac.

Weise had ordered Vargas to halt Golf Company until Foxtrot caught up, although Vargas was unaware that his rear support was not following. As they neared, they took heavy fire from the front and left flank at 5 p.m. At first Weise thought it was the ARVN mechanized support unit he had been promised: "[W]e saw a large number over there to the left, and we didn't realize that they were NVA and not ARVN that were on the move until we realized that we saw no APCs. Ten or fifteen minutes we looked at those guys."[17]

That was when Weise called in artillery on his own position, "danger close" between his men and the enemy. Enemy fire increased its tempo. An RPG killed Malnar, and Weise was seriously wounded by an AK-47 round. Golf had managed to halt the enemy advance and push through Dinh To, and the Marines were able to pick off many enemy soldiers advancing from the rear. As Weise stated: "[E]very Marine who was able to shoot, including wounded who could handle a weapon, fired, and the fighting was violent and close." Weise managed to organize a withdrawal, the healthy dragging the wounded. Golf managed to fight back to the relative safety of Foxtrot's tenuous position as Dinh To, where Major Warren had taken charge.[18]

The army was having its own troubles, as by May 2, A, B, and C companies of 3/21 in Nhi Ha had been heavily engaged, and the call came in for the 174th AHC to affect a medevac mission and render any and all assistance. The sky was full of a combination of friendly air strikes and artillery and naval gunfire, or "masking fire," to cover the Americans on the ground. Ken Johnson decided to fly Dolphin #910 in under the friendly fire, danger close, in order to exploit the NVA's confusion and evacuate the wounded while the enemies' heads were kept down.

For his actions, Johnson deserved the Medal of Honor, based upon the award criteria, and I hope that it is given to him in the future. His entire crew, including Nunn, should be decorated *ex post facto*, and Nunn's actions would at the very least warrant the Distinguished Service Cross.

The crew members in the other two 174th AHC helicopters were: commander WO1 Hank Tews, pilot unknown, crew chief SP4 Sam Davis, and door gunner Pfc. Allen Weamer (#864) and commander

Flying Under Friendly Fire
—Specialist Wally Nunn and Warrant Officer Ken Johnson

[According to Wally Nunn,] "Practically the whole [of Alpha] company had been either killed or wounded. They were annihilated! However, 'fast movers' were dropping 'drag bombs' just over the casualties to destroy the NVA that had them flanked. As we approached, Johnson and Wifholm were on the fire control net. They were getting trajectory reports from the arty, tac air and naval counter battery. Johnson (who deserved a Medal of Honor) flew in *under* the onslaught of incoming! The only thing is that Ken ordered me out on the skids to look up and see how low we were *below* the bombing!"

Ken Johnson adds, "Actually, we advised the FAC and pilots that we were coming in under them and it was not a mistake. We didn't want them to pull up if they saw us passing under them. I think they thought I was crazy, but it was a tactic that worked, because the bad guys were either ducking for cover or shooting at the jets instead of us!"

Nunn continues, "Then about 75 meters out from the flank, I spied a bunker and through the hole of it, [and] I could see the faces of the NVA. I yelled at the pilots, 'There they are! I am going to take them under fire!' Johnson called back: 'Don't shoot. For some reason they ain't shooting at us. Let's do our job and go get the wounded!' "[19]

unknown, pilot unknown, crew chief SP5 Carl McCoy, and door gunner unknown (#281). According to Nunn, "Both #864 and #281 were shot all to hell, [but there were] no injuries."[20] Helicopter #864 was shot down by an enemy tank during the daring mission. It should also be noted that these brave men all volunteered for these support missions! These men saved numerous army and Marine lives at the risk of their own.

Taking a Prisoner
—Specialist Wally Nunn and Warrant Officer Ken Johnson

On Friday, May 3, 1968, a Marine Crusader that was making a bombing run on the village of Nhi Ha was hit by enemy fire and did not pull up. No one saw a parachute either. However, U.S. personnel with a nearby ARVN unit spotted (with binoculars) a lone figure walking around east of the battlefield. A FAC in the air above then confirmed the sighting.

Ken Johnson and his crew chimed in on the radio, saying, "We're coming in low and hot, so direct us up." The FAC "Birddog" guided the 174th AHC slick from their fifteen-foot altitude and then a hop over some trees. [Johnson and the helicopter crew] immediately spotted an olive drab figure wandering aimlessly in a rice paddy. He appeared unarmed. When the aircraft approached, the man just stopped and looked up.

Johnson reported on the radio, "We got the pilot in sight. We're going to pick him up." Approaching very fast, Johnson saw the man's black hair and misfit fatigues. He yelled, "It's a dink, that's a goddamned dink!" As he pulled up and out, he yelled, "It's not the pilot! It's a hard-core NVA, and we are going to engage him!"

The Marines (monitoring the Army net) said, "Don't shoot him. We want to take him prisoner."

Johnson replied, "What the hell do you guys expect us to do out here? We've got our butts hanging out! We're going to kill

Meanwhile, on the ground, Lance Cpl. Jim O'Neill and his sniper rifle removed twenty-four NVA from the equation.[21] Then he went back into the fight again. As soon as he killed one of several heavy machine-gun crews, others would take their place and die for the effort. He fired 120 rounds in fifteen minutes. O'Neill kept the heavy guns off of the retreating Echo and Hotel Marines, allowing them to get the wounded to safety, to him!" The Marines then responded with a direct order not to shoot and to take him prisoner.

[Wall Nunn adds,] "We just circled around. I thought for sure it was a trap. I called over the intercom to Johnson, telling him that the Marines were crazy. I can have an 'accident' here, you know. Ken told me again to hold fire. An ARVN unit was about twenty minutes away. We thought about letting them come get him, but that would give the enemy time to surround us. Johnson told me to look the NVA over real good, because we were going in.

"I said, 'This is fucking nuts! No shit!' We landed, and I jumped out with my M-16 and screamed [at the NVA solider] 'Get the fuck on [the helicopter]!' I assumed I was probably going to have to shoot him anyway, but he was real scared and jumped right in. I held my .38 to his head all the way back to the 3/21st CP, but he was noticeably trembling from the helicopter ride and hanging on for dear life.

"When we got to the CP he was still 'gripped,' so I jerked him hard and threw him out. A Marine captain pulled some identification off of him out of one of his pockets. In another pouch pocket was a Chicom grenade! Johnson lifted his helmet visor and dropped his jaw. I, in the meantime, almost had my 'accident' I spoke about earlier." [According to Nunn, the POW was a former school teacher, conscripted as a medic, who had deserted and wanted to surrender. The final analysis after his interrogation was that he knew nothing of value.][22]

consolidate, and to regroup. The NVA finally realized their problem and began targeting O'Neill en masse. O'Neill entered Golf Company's CP and apprised them of the enemy heavy guns. He would receive the Bronze Star with V device, which was well deserved.[23]

Echo and Hotel managed to pull back, and as the distance between them and the enemy increased, the air and indirect support came in to mask their effort. I was having to manage several nightmares: evacuating the dead and wounded, dealing with being outnumbered and outflanked, and organizing the men into something resembling a cohesive unit so as to not lose anyone in the confusion.

I did not feel calm and collected, either at Dai Do or Dinh To, but I do remember that I was completely focused on accomplishing my mission. To do that, we had to kill a lot more of the NVA than they did of us, and we were well prepared for that reality. Once you lock your mind on something as serious as life and death, such as this situation, there are very few things in this world that can distract you. Giving up the ground taken thus far was not an option.

> "Captain Livingston seemed to be everywhere at once. His coolness and calmness are what kept a lot of us from panicking. Things did not look good at all, but he kept our spirits up and kept us determined that we were going to beat them."[24]
>
> —Sgt. James W. Rogers

During this period there was increasing air activity from all branches. The pilot of an F-8 Crusader, Capt. Stephen W. Clark, was killed in a crash, his jet brought down by concentrated NVA machine-gun and rifle fire— that was how close he was to the ground while trying to save his fellow Marines.[25]

Clark's behavior seemed to belie the realities on the ground. The confusion and "fog of war" often isolated men and kept them from witnessing adjacent actions. In addition, the NVA had increased their volume of fire at certain points, and with shells falling from both sides, helicopter operations were more suicide than sound military judgment. The lack of direct air support regarding gunship and on-location medevac in the Dai Do area was not unusual given the amount of fire from indirect sources, small arms, and rockets. That real chopper support would not come to the battle until May 3 and afterward.

Many times I had led my men into the first few dozen of the approximately one hundred fortified enemy positions, killing the enemy and moving swiftly to the next position. We continued this activity until I went down again with another serious wound, when a 12.7mm

We Must Have Had Air Support
—1st Lt. Dave R. Jones

To be honest, I don't remember what kind of air support we had during Dai Do. I know it must have been there, but it has totally escaped me. I do know that we often did have close air support and that each branch of the service had a different style. As I recall, the air force stayed much higher than either the Marines or the navy. I don't remember seeing air force jets swooping down across the battlefield. The navy flew low, but it came across your front (from right to left, or from left to right).

The Marines flew some missions like the navy, but they would also fly over the battlefield from over our shoulders (back to front). Obviously that was the most risky for friendly troops, but also very effective. But, as I said, I can't remember what kind of air support we had during Dai Do.[26]

machine-gun round hit my right thigh. The bone cracked, and bone fragments, muscle, and skin blew out of the exit wound; I was again covered in blood. Anyone who saw the event would have probably thought I was dead, sooner if not later.

That left 2nd Lt. Michael L. Cecil in effective operational command for the movement. Once I told my RTO (also wounded by shrapnel) to have Cecil take command, he began to crawl with his M-14, continuing to fire at the enemy he could see, making every round count, covering the withdrawal of his Marines under Cecil. Cecil was a brand new young lieutenant just beginning to learn the process, but he was an energetic officer. Unlike the majority of the other officers, who had the benefit of participating in previous operations in Quang Tri Province leading up to Dai Do, gathering knowledge and experience, he was thrown right into the big show. When I told him he had the company as I was being taken away, I could tell that it was not something that he had ever anticipated. However, as any good Marine officer, fresh or not, would, he said, "Aye, aye, sir" and took command, ready to do his job.

I was unable to extricate myself alone, but that was not my intent. My Marines' safety was what drove me, and the boys knew it. Seeing their skipper down and knowing I would probably not make it, two Marines came and grabbed me, neither one flinching under the fire snapping around them. They saved me.[27]

Ironically, word had spread regarding my situation, and a herd of Marines who had just left the very firefight tearing them to pieces were gathering to go back into it again to get me. Within a few minutes, Lieutenant Taylor was shot in the mouth, but he still linked up with Lieutenant Boyle and Lance Cpl. James L. Barela. All three went back for an M-60 that had been left behind when they were confronted by a dozen NVA. Taylor decided to let them have the gun, because they were closer. They managed to get back along the river to the 60mm mortar section.

As I was carried into the hastily established perimeter, I ordered all other casualties to be seen to first, from triage to medevac, and even if I lost consciousness, my order would not be disobeyed.[28] As the Marines carried me to safety, we were met by Major Warren, who had moved the Bravo CP to the vicinity of Dai Do when word came that I had been shot.[29]

Sergeant Jim Rogers was with the group of Marines who wanted to leave the battlefield with me. Warren appealed to Rogers to take Echo Company back to Dai Do, so as not to put other Marines at risk. Rogers, then acting as a platoon leader, successfully led Echo back to the battle area and formed a defensive position.[29] Echo Company, with assistance of Hotel, had destroyed approximately one hundred fortified enemy positions and killed well over five hundred NVA.

By that time, Golf Company had been ordered to secure the opposite riverbank to prevent the enemy from establishing a strong position, especially with regard to setting up mortars. Many of the men hit the water and tried to board the shallow draft boats. One boat overturned, and men hit the water, but climbed back on board and finally made it to their appointed location.

During the process, the boats stopped and loaded up wounded, who were stripped of all gear and weapons in order to lighten the load and thus enable more Marines to be moved at one time. Meanwhile, as the navy boats were uploading casualties, I was on the radio with Weise, despite being wounded a total of three times, bleeding heavily, and unable to walk. Somehow I was still conscious and lucid, and after a brief conversation, I told my battalion commander that I would stay and continue doing my job. Weise told me to go and they would be fine.

I was loaded onto a boat, sent to the main triage station, and prepared for the medevac. As much as I wanted to, I was unable to resist the order from my superior officer. Really, I could not even move, and what bothered me terribly was that I knew that Vargas and his men were still in deep trouble. I had a lot on my mind. Within a few hours, I was able to limp on a cane, observing the growing line of dead Marines lining the riverbank. I was appalled to see the press corps and a television crew removing ponchos from the faces of dead Marines to get their money shots. Seeing them do that started my lifelong disdain

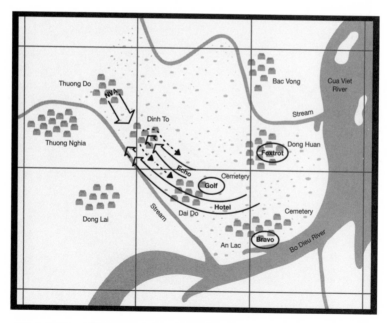

Attack by Hotel Company, rescue by Echo Company, enemy counterattack, and withdrawal to Dai Do on May 2, 1968. *William Weise*

of the media. To be honest, that really jerked my jaws. I've never been so jacked in my entire life!

While I was in a state of limbo, Weise had just ordered another attack against Dinh To. Lieutenant Cecil took over Echo Company as the new skipper and carried on until the operation was over.

Although I was out of the fight, it would rage on. Bravo, Golf, and Hotel still had their trial by ordeal to endure. Weise said, "My first concern was helping Bravo Company out of its predicament. Its second company commander and most of its key personnel were wounded during the late afternoon attack to relieve pressure on Golf Company."[31]

That concern was not insignificant, since the ARVN unit had withdrawn without notifying the Marines that they were leaving the party, adding to my view that the ARVN were in bed with the NVA. Upon their withdrawal, the NVA troops managed to slip in behind Weise's men, and his Marines soon began taking small-arms fire from the previously protected rear. Then the Marines were hit with a frontal

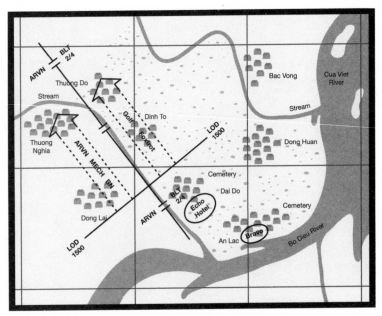

Planned attack by BLT 2/4 and ARVN Mechanized Battalion on May 2, 1968. *William Weise*

Time to Pull Back
—Brig. Gen. William Weise

Realizing that Echo and Hotel could not hold their position in Dinh To, I told both company commanders to pull back to Dai Do. At this point Captain Livingston was hit in the leg by machine-gun fire. Unable to move, he would not permit himself to be dragged to the rear until he was certain that all other wounded were evacuated. He then ordered the able-bodied Marines to pull back, fearing that they would be overrun protecting him. But the Marines refused to leave their leader and pulled him to safety.[32]

assault, as well as simultaneous flank attacks. According to Weise, "Things were not looking good at all. . . . Things were getting worse."[33]

Every Marine, including RTOs, were involved in the fight; Weise "called in artillery so close the shrapnel was landing among [his men]" along with naval gunfire and helicopter gunships.[34] Sergeant Major Malnar was killed by a rocket, and there were other losses. But the enemy attack was stopped. Weise ordered Vargas to withdraw, and Vargas did so, bringing all his wounded with him by executing a brilliant fire and maneuver.

It was reported at 5:40 p.m. that Weise had been wounded (he would later receive the Navy Cross), and his companies were being overrun by "waves of NVA attacking south."[35] The dead and wounded could not all be retrieved immediately due to the heavy volume of enemy fire. That recovery would have to wait. Weise arrived at the triage point, and as stated by Major Warren, "When Weise passed me on the stretcher, he passed the BLT on to me. Weise's RTO, Sergeant Bollinger, who was badly wounded, made a fist with his good hand and said to me, 'No more PT,' as I was the individual who led the CP group on daily PT runs. I organized the remaining Marines into a defensive position. There were approximately twenty-five Marines left in each of the rifle companies. Major Charles W.

We Were All by Ourselves
—Brig. Gen. William Weise

We had just entered Thuong Do. The "friendly" ARVN armored battalion had abandoned our left flank without our knowledge. Foxtrot Company was pinned down and unable to move. I and my small command group were moving forward in the attack with Golf Company, under Capt. Jay R. Vargas. Golf had only forty Marines left after three days of heavy fighting. We started to receive heavy enemy fire from our left and right flanks and sporadic fire from the rear.

At that point, enemy fire from the front intensified, and the NVA began a frontal assault against Vargas's forward platoon, which was only about twenty yards in front of us. (I had previously moved my command group up abreast of Captain Vargas's command group, and we joined them in an abandoned enemy trench when the enemy assault began.) I told Vargas to pull his forward platoon back and set up a hasty defense, which he did with great difficulty because by that time friend and foe were intermingled.

It was sheer chaos—hand-to-hand combat, all types of small arms, enemy and friendly artillery, rocket and mortar fire so close that the shrapnel tore into our positions. Every Marine in both command groups fired his weapon, threw grenades, helped the wounded, and killed enemy soldiers within a few yards of our position. A Golf Company radio operator beside me was bleeding profusely from a wound in the upper left arm. I helped him take off his radio and stop the bleeding. I used his radio to

Knapp (the XO) relieved me later that evening."[39]

At 6:30 p.m., sixty Marines from the base camp at Mai Xa Chanh were sent to assist the four rifle companies. By sundown, the Marines were formed into a defensive perimeter in the southern area of Dai Do. A flare report our situation, as both of my radio operators were seriously wounded, their radios destroyed. Throughout this wild pandemonium, the Marines performed superbly and the enemy assault was slowed down long enough to conduct a withdrawal bringing all the wounded back to Dai Do.[36]

Vargas was everywhere, giving orders to small groups of Marines, helping move wounded, and occasionally firing his rifle. His presence, inspirational leadership, personal actions, and total disregard for his own safety averted complete disaster and turned an impossible situation into an orderly withdrawal.[37]

Just after I ordered Vargas to withdraw, I was hit on the left side by what I later found out was an AK-47 round. At first I didn't realize the wound was serious and continued firing my weapon and directing various actions. As we started back, I found that I couldn't climb out of the trench and needed help to do so. It was then that Captain Vargas came to my aid and half carried, half dragged me back far enough to be out of immediate small-arms fire from the front. I'm not exactly sure how far he carried and pulled me. I do vaguely remember he had to leave me several times to go back and direct the withdrawal, making sure all wounded were evacuated.

In the process, he carried/dragged other wounded to relative safety. Captain Vargas turned me over to other Marines, who carried me back to an LVT [landing vehicle tracked] and to Major Warren. The LV carried me to the riverbank and a skimmer boat, which carried me to the triage point at Mai Xa Chanh. I was subsequently medevaced to the medical ward of the USS *Iwo Jima*.[38]

aircraft and all supporting arms were ordered in to illuminate the area and remain on call to prevent a nocturnal enemy penetration. With exception to a few enemy probes along the perimeter, the rest of the evening passed relatively without incident. During this time, the battalion executive,

Major Knapp, who had been holding the fort for the battalion rear headquarters aboard the USS *Iwo Jima*, assumed command of 2/4.[40]

Weise, Vargas, and Golf Company had managed the seemingly impossible. They had stopped a vastly superior force, in effect blocking that force's movement forward and containing it, allowing the enemy the choice of remaining and dying in place, or breaking out and taking their chances. This seemed to be a fairly accurate description of all the Marine units: holding the line and doing their jobs. By the end of the afternoon on May 2, 1968, each company averaged approximately forty Marines and one commissioned officer. Each of these "companies" was basically the size of a reinforced platoons. Dai Do proper that day had cost the 3rd Marines 40 KIA and 111 WIA, while 380 NVA had been killed.[41]

It was noted that aerial observers had located groups of the enemy retreating towards Thuong Do during the night of May 2–3, and at daylight, air strikes were called in to interdict their retreat. Later on May 3, BLT 1/3 took over operation control of Dai Do from BLT 2/4. This exchange briefly placed Vargas and Golf, along with Hotel, under the command of Colonel Jarvis, which allowed our men to collect the dead Marines from the May 1–3 fight. This mission was completed by 7:35 p.m., and by 9 p.m., both companies were relocated at Mai Xa Chanh.[42]

In addition to the bravery exhibited by my men, Weise, Vargas, and others on May 2, 1st Lt. Judd Hilton had his own legend in the making. According to Weise:

> First Lieutenant Hilton, our FAC, also played a key role in the successful withdrawal. He organized a squad of eight or nine Marines, which laid down a withering hail of fire to the flanks and front as we pulled back. He fired an M-79 grenade launcher until he ran out of ammunition. Then he fired various enemy weapons he had picked up along the way. He also talked in several helicopter gunships that fired their rockets right into the midst of attacking enemy only twenty yards from his position, and he helped move the wounded. Judd Hilton, our duty aviator, fought as well as any infantryman on the battlefield. Many Marines owe their lives to that courageous officer.[43]

My participation in the Battle of Dai Do, or perhaps more accurately called the Battle of Dong Ha, according to the 3rd Marine Division records, was over. The battle and the surrounding firefights would last until May 15, involving Marines not only from 2/4 and 3/3, but also 1/9, 3/9, and 1/26. They would also include the army's 2/21st/196th, the army's 2nd and 3rd Battalions, the 5th Cavalry Regiment, the 1st Cavalry Division (Airmobile), and the 1st ARVN Division.

These involvements alone illustrate the broad scope of the enemy operation. This was perhaps the greatest large-scale offensive of the war short of Tet. The numbers of men and the units they threw at us meant there was a sincere determination to overrun the entire province. By first removing 2/4, and then the remainder of 3rd Marine Division, they would have had a much easier time of rolling up all of Quang Tri Province.

For the rest of May 2 through the next day, May 3, the fighting for Dai Do was basically over, although control of the entire sector was still in question. The final casualty count is taken from Keith Nolan's remarkable work: The 3rd Marine Division suffered 233 KIA, 821 WIA, and 1 MIA. The navy lost 15 KIA and 22 WIA. The ARVN counts were 42 KIA and 124 WIA, and the NVA admitted losses of 2,366 KIA and 43 POWs in American hands.[44]

If not for the assistance and bravery of the army and Marine helicopter crews working the area north and west, and the battalion surgeons at Mai Xa Chanh West, namely Lt. Frederick P. Lillis and Lt. Runas Powers, as well as the individual Marines and corpsmen, many more lives would have been lost. All these specialists came together to save men under terrible conditions.[45] As for me, personally, I was very proud of my Marines.

However, one of the more distressing factors was the knowledge that several Marines who were killed during the battle had been found with their hands tied behind their backs. This report was from Col. Charles V. Jarman, CO of 1/3, and mentioned in *U.S Marines in Vietnam*.[46] It would appear that the NVA executed their prisoners as we took control of the battle. These executions were unacceptable and a clear violation of the laws of war under both conventions of The Hague 1907 and

Geneva 1949, and no one in Washington did a damned thing about it during the later peace talks. The Communist murderers, in this battle and many others, were never held accountable for their illegal actions.

Much may be reiterated regarding the difference between the army's and Marines' uses of rotary-wing aviation. Army crews were not under the same strict rules of operation as Marines and were able to take greater risks at hot LZs under fire, as demonstrated by Ken Johnson, Sam Davis, and Wally Nunn; Marines were forced to husband their limited assets and not permitted to "freelance" over the field of battle. The army method did not require check fires from friendly indirect fire support; hence, the fluid nature of the ground battle could continue uninterrupted. This factor was mentioned by Colonel Hull, who apparently admired the army aviators.

Despite the army aviation presence in the sector, they were not readily available for use by 2/4, as stated by Weise:

No helicopters landed in the Dai Do battle area during the battle. We did not request helicopters for medevacs because it would have required us to lift the supporting arms while they were in the area. We could not afford to do that. Around-the-clock use of artillery, naval gunfire, and close air support were critical. In addition, the enemy fire was so heavy that the helicopters would probably have been shot down. However, after the main part of the battle was over, late on May 2, 1968, a Marine helicopter from HMM-362, the Ugly Angels, made a daring rescue of Pfc. Boss.[47]

The 3rd Battalion, 196th Light Infantry Brigade, under Lieutenant Colonel Snyder, had landed at the LZ near Lam Xuan East at 8 a.m., May 1, occupying both the east and west villages, and then continued to Ni Ha. They ran into an ambush, losing nine KIA, four MIA, and fifteen WIA. Although I was totally unaware of these developments, this information does assist us in seeing the broader picture. Their efforts definitely distracted at least some of the enemy, giving us a little breathing space.

CHAPTER 8

Closing the Noose: An Assessment

Allowing an enemy unit to escape and regroup is unthinkable.
—Waffen SS Brigadefuehrer Otto Kumm

THE BATTLE WOULD RAGE for another week at various locations before the next major engagements, but I would not be part of those operations. The long road to recovery was ahead of me. Vargas and I would both eventually receive the Medal of Honor for our actions, but to be completely honest, I really did not feel that my actions warranted such a distinction. There were dozens of Marines who exhibited great bravery in the face of almost certain death. I know, because I saw these men, their actions. Those were the real heroes. I watched them kill, watched them save their buddies, and watched many of them die and even more become wounded. One must experience this first hand to appreciate the toll it takes on a commander.

I must say that the battle would not have been as successful, in my opinion, without the massive effort and bravery of Vargas and Golf Company. This is not to diminish the actions of all our Marines. However, Golf was in a unique situation. Their casualties, difficulties in maneuvering, limited numbers of men, inconsistent and erratic fire support, and the lack of intelligence on the enemy in general forced Vargas to make intuitive decisions. Going with the gut feeling is often a very viable way of problem solving. The instincts are honed by experience, and confidence is instilled by progressive success. Jay Vargas had it all. Weise wrote: "Captain Vargas knew his men well, and they knew and respected him for his outstanding competence as a combat leader and his compassion. I knew that I could depend on him and Golf Company."[1]

Weise also explained the actions of Golf during the withdrawal, including how Vargas's actions earned him the nation's highest honor: "As we withdrew toward Dai Do, we met stragglers and small groups from Foxtrot Company. Captain Vargas quickly organized them to support the withdrawal and move the wounded. Those wounded who were able fired their weapons. We fell back behind a curtain of supporting arms and our own small-arms fire. Raw courage and the performance of individual Marines, inspired by leaders like Vargas and Hilton, made the withdrawal possible."[2]

Everything was Different at Dai Do
—1st Lt. Dave R. Jones

My perceptions of the enemy changed dramatically during Dai Do. We had never had a fight like that before, at least not while I was there. We could see the enemy, and for many of our Marines, that was the first time they had actually been able to see their targets. We had had a somewhat similar experience on March 18, but at Dai Do, the NVA force was much larger, much more entrenched, and had many more supporting arms. At Dai Do, the NVA stayed and fought unlike any other time I was in RVN. I daresay that nobody else can claim to have been directly between two Medal of Honor winners at the time they both earned their awards. Jay Vargas was almost to my immediate right and, of course, Jim Livingston was almost on my immediate left until I was wounded and evacuated.[3]

Back on the *Iwo Jima* word had spread of the early casualties, and the walking wounded were asked to return to the field. Captain Robert Mastrion, two days on his back, took two canes, secured a Colt. .45 ACP, located his gear and boots, joined others who were also bandaged and bloodied, and climbed into the waiting aircraft. He was going back in and would be active again on May 3. Right behind him was a platoon of volunteers, including officers and additional walking wounded.

The area around Dai Do would not be secured until almost a week later. The exact size of the enemy force would not be known until many years later, when Weise would speak with the former NVA commanding general. The Marines had faced a division supported by several VC companies.

At the end of the day, we kept the Cua Viet River from being sealed, which would have cut off all the supplies for all trace areas and would have been a strategic defeat for U.S. forces, probably bigger than Hue City. If the river had been sealed, all those American units up in there would have to be withdrawn or air supplied. Or we would have had to try and supply them by coming up from Route 1 through Quang Tri, Hue, up in that area, and with what was going on in that area, it would have been a strategic isolation. And probably Dong Ha would have fallen, and that would have really been a strategic defeat.

In my opinion, the thing that enabled us to complete the mission and successfully extricate the dead and wounded, given that we were not very organized, was that the enemy would attack up to a point and then they seemed to break contact. Once they gained a tactical advantage, because of the attrition we had undergone, the fact that I was hit, and the fact that we began to pull back, they did not pursue the way a Marine would have. Instead, they sort of broke contact, failing to follow through on their attacks, and they did not pursue us to the extent I thought they would. I don't think they realized the significant tactical advantage they had there for a while; they had been hit so hard they did not realize how hard we had been hit. I don't think that there was any tactical thinking beyond the level of where the contact was taking place. They were obviously not getting the kind of information they needed to make good tactical decisions at the higher level.

Part of this analysis is supported by standard North Vietnamese doctrine, which was true for all Communist military organizations the world over. Decision making depended upon rank, while rank and decision-making capability was determined by political reliability. Junior officers, noncommissioned officers, and enlisted men, while considered militarily reliable, were not considered completely politically reliable. The prevailing attitude was that the lower the rank, the lower the intellect, and the more susceptible to enemy propaganda and the lure of decadent capitalism. Thus, removal of the officer structure and command element ensured confusion within the enemy ranks. It sounds illogical to an educated mind, but given the basic precepts and dogma of Communism, it makes perfect sense that they would trust very few people. And that doctrine bit them in the ass on the battlefield.

It could be said that Corporal O'Neill's actions as a sniper probably removed most of the immediate decision-making capabilities within an entire battalion. This forced the NVA to fall back, regroup, and wait for an officer to issue an order, whether that officer was cognizant of the situation or not. This possibility cannot be ignored, and the basic indecision inherent to Communist military organizations was probably our greatest ally.

This ridiculous mindset carried over into military training, where the political officer (PO) was just as important as the commanding officer; the military never left home without one of the former. Often Communist organizations' COs would have their tactical decisions overridden and plans changed by the POs, who may or may not have been militarily competent. The image of success and the power of the Communist Party was given greater consideration than the actual victory, a phenomenon not unknown to some United States leaders in our history.

The NVA military structure did not allow for much in the way of independent thought. Communism had proven since the days of Josef Stalin that he who thinks for himself is not thinking of the party, so initiative at the lower ranks was not fostered. Sheep are to be led, not instructed in leadership.

The American military has always been organized differently. Each man was trained and expected to take command at the next pay grade or beyond. This is even truer of the United States Marines, Army Airborne and Rangers, Special Forces, and Navy SEALs, which are the accepted elite of American fighting men. This organization is the primary reason for nearly every American victory in Vietnam. Following orders was critical, but independent thinking and analysis of conditions and situations, fostered by *esprit de corps* and honed by relentless training, have proven to be sound. In the Marines, it is standard operating procedure. Under Weise, it was religious doctrine. Under the Communists, it was an unknown quantity.

The Marine company commander, normally a captain (known as the skipper) knows that his XO, traditionally a first lieutenant, is competent and able to take command should the skipper be removed from the equation. Likewise, the XO knows that the company first sergeant or company gunnery sergeant (usually the two most experienced men in most Marine units) can, in the absence of any platoon leaders, take command of that company. Each platoon leader knows that, as a Marine, the platoon sergeant will take command of his men should the platoon leader be removed. The platoon sergeant knows that his senior squad leader will pick up the pace should the mantle of command fall upon him. At no time is a Marine unit leaderless.

This is the great strength of the Marines: leadership by example and tradition, with competence through training. Corporals leading platoons and sergeants leading companies are not rare occurrences in Marine Corps history. The result is over two hundred years of unparalleled success forged by fire, and our Marines in Vietnam exemplified these traits. They were soon to add even further to that glory, and BLT 2/4 would receive a Navy Unit Commendation for the ordeal at Dong Ha.

Of my many accomplishments, I must say that I was most proud of the opportunity to take a reinforced company of 180 Marines and hit the NVA 320th Division, numbering about 10,000, in concert with the 2nd Battalion, 4th Marines. We were outnumbered about thirty-five to one or more, and by the time we linked up with Hotel Company, which was being overwhelmed at Dinh To, I had 34 or so men left out of the original 180. We lost a lot of good Marines there. Lieutenant Prescott had assumed command of Hotel, but when we arrived, both companies

The Fog of War
—Brig. Gen. William Weise

The day before the battle the entire ARVN force moved from the area to be contested . . . to engage an enemy that was supposedly making an attack on a village along Route 1. This movement required 3rd Marine Division to deplete BLT 2/4 assets by moving Company E to the bridge North of Dong Ha. I cannot begin to describe the confusion, which was the epitome of what we call the "fog of war."

. . . But none of the Marines or Sailors who fought had a full understanding of the larger picture. The action was so fast and furious there was no time for detailed five paragraph orders. It was a matter of reacting immediately to one desperate situation after another with inadequate assets and little intelligence. Our success was due to the extraordinary performance of the individual Marines and by leaders like Jim Livingston.[4]

had decided that attacking immediately was better than rallying and reorganizing, given the enemy's strength and positioning.

We had everything thrown at us—rockets, machine guns, you name it. Then the fight became hand-to-hand, nasty business. I had been wounded by .50 caliber and shrapnel, but still managed to execute an orderly extraction of the dead and wounded. It was not because I was superhuman or a super Marine. It was because I was a highly trained Marine officer, simple as that. There is no magic formula. My ability comes with proper training and the positive reinforcement of rigorous and relentless discipline. In my opinion, there is no substitute for competence, and there is no better litmus test for the character and mettle of a man than in the Marines. Even though I could not stand after being hit so many times, I was able to continue on with the help of a number of great Marines. Our *esprit de corps* would allow for no other course of action.

In his own book, Weise noted "the absolute lack of effective coordination and execution on the afternoon of 2 May and precarious position that BLT 2/4 was put in (by the) silent withdrawal from the battlefield by the ARVN unit," writing:

> An Lac, Dong Huan, Dai Do, Dinh To (and Thuong Do) were the responsibility of the 2nd ARVN Regiment prior to the beginning of this engagement. It is inconceivable... that the 320th NVA (Division) troops could have been so well dug in, mutually supporting bunkers, communication, (trench) lines, and infrastructure without having (worked on the positions) over a period of days and probably weeks. It would have been nigh impossible for the ARVN not to have gotten wind of this activity, as these areas were occupied by ARVN family members and... camp followers.[5]

Weise has a plausible argument—one I have supported and perhaps most (if not all) of the officers involved supported as well. What made this engagement unique was not so much the lack of detailed intelligence about the actual enemy threat. Instead, what made this battle such an important tactical illustration and strategic platform for further study by Marine officers is the reality that, once the size and strength of the threat was discerned, Weise and his company commanders took the initiative and pushed ahead, despite the overwhelming superiority of the threat. Knowing the strength of their enemy, the NVA were probably not expecting a direct confrontation by an offensive-minded Marine unit. The audacious action and threat we presented must have taken them quite by surprise.

Again, citing Weise:

> Despite numerous problems and possible treason, BLT 2/4 accomplished its mission. A superior enemy force was driven from the river banks, and the Cua Viet and Bo Dieu Rivers were opened to traffic. How badly was the 320th NVA Division hurt? I'm not sure, but much of its fighting effectiveness was destroyed. Major General Raymond Davis, who became commanding general, 3rd Marine Division, after the Battle of Dai Do, stated that the defeat of the 320th Division

during August through September 1968 was hastened by the punishment it took during April and May. Other U.S. and ARVN units fought against the 320th prior to, and after Dai Do, but I'm certain that BLT 2/4 played a major role in its final defeat.[6]

In preparing this book, I had requested that all of the officers who could be contacted to contribute their opinions regarding the pros and cons of our mission. This is as much an exercise in post-battle analysis as it is a learning tool, the successes and mistakes of which present and future leaders may learn from.

Dave Jones supplied the following assessment:

> I am probably one of the last people who should be evaluating or assessing what happened at Dai Do. I was a young lieutenant who was not planning to make a career out of the Marine Corps. On the other hand, I was always serious about my job as an infantry officer because I learned very early that my decisions affected lives. That was, and still is, a humbling and consuming feeling.
>
> Preparation was probably the key to our success at Dai Do. [We] constantly train[ed] to be physically strong. However, I believe that what the *physical* training really did was to make us *mentally* strong. We thought we could go anywhere and do anything. And that, I think, is what got the survivors through Dai Do.
>
> Many men did not make it, and after returning to and walking that battleground in the spring of 2008, forty years after the original battle, I can see why. My platoon of probably less than fifty men, and our company of around 150 men, had the responsibility for crossing over 500 meters of open rice paddies in the face of literally thousands of regular North Vietnamese soldiers and heavy supporting arms. A huge number of our men did not survive the crossing of that paddy, but our platoon and our company accomplished its job. We never considered the alternative to victory because we were mentally tough.
>
> And I believe that trust was another factor in our success. Fortunately, the troops trusted and followed their leaders without questioning or batting an eye. And junior officers trusted and

followed their superior officers. Orders were given often and quickly, and obeyed immediately. Perhaps the most important component of that trust included the trust every Marine had for each other. We all knew that someone would be there to help us when we needed it and to take care of us if something bad happened.

Finally, commitment played a major role in our success. The troops were committed to victory, and in my modest opinion, every one of them that day was a hero. One of my regrets is that so many who acted with valor were never appropriately recognized. I saw so many acts of courage by unidentifiable heroes. Crossing that rice paddy required that every Marine trust his leader, trust his fellow Marines, and remain committed to the beliefs that make Marines different. I know that I was in the company of courageous men who will never be forgotten.

Did anything go wrong? I am sure it did, because when bullets are flying, chaos is common. But adrenaline can neutralize much of that confusion, and it did that day. All I know for sure was that the men I led did everything they were told to do and more. Their actions led to a successful end to the battle, and there is no question in my mind that their actions also saved my life.[7]

Major George "Fritz" Warren provided these analytical comments:

1. Insure that the BLT (I use BLT throughout, as 2/4 was task organized into a BLT) aid station, with its complement of two surgeons and associated corpsmen, are located away from the immediate battle area, so that medevac helicopters could safely land to evacuate the WIA and KIA.
2. Do not call medevacs into the battle area. The BLT had learned from constant combat situations over the past two months that calling in a medevac resulted in a stopping of supporting arms while the helicopter was doing the medevac, and the loss of this fire power could be catastrophic to the ongoing battle. Additionally, the helicopter was put at risk, as were its crew and any passengers.
3. Be skeptical about relying on host country national forces, unless you have your own liaison officer with such organizations. Also, be

careful of placing such forces in tactically important positions in the defense plan.

4. Take all possible actions to commit a unit, with all of its organic and attached personnel and equipment, as a unified, cohesive unit and not on a piecemeal basis. BLT 2/4 was committed on a piecemeal basis throughout this battle, and the commander had to make the most from the assets available.

5. When a commander is engaged with the enemy, higher headquarters should evaluate all his requests for additional combat firepower and make every effort to provide the appropriate assets. Bill Weise constantly requested additional firepower (tanks, 106mm Ontos, priority of close air support) to no avail. Finally, on the last day of the battle, BLT 2/4 was given priority of close air support, but never received additional tanks or Ontos, which would have provided the BLT commander with combat power that could have proved decisive over the three-day battle.

6. Division should have been more skeptical about the commitment of its reserve force (Task Force Robbie—a motorized/mechanized force) when requested by the host country national forces (2nd ARVN Regiment), since this decision left the division command post undefended.

7. The aggressive and constant combat-arms and physical-conditioning program of the BLT units paid handsome dividends during the fierce and exhausting three days of constant combat at Dai Do. The old saw "the harder we work the luckier we become" was certainly true for BLT 2/4, and this philosophy was employed due to Generals Weise and Livingston.

8. On the last day of the battle, the battalion commander (Weise) was briefed by the regimental commander on the details of a joint BLT 2/4–ARVN assault of the enemy positions. The absence of a liaison officer from either the division or the regiment led to considerable confusion as to the location and actions taken by the ARVN unit. As a result, BLT 2/4 suffered heavy casualties from the exposed flank that was supposed to be covered by the ARVN unit. (On this note, see number 3 above.)

9. The two-way flow of intelligence information could have prevented the surprise nature of the NVA attack. Division should have been able to prepare the BLT 2/4 commander (Weise) with warning orders and briefings about the departure of the ARVN unit to his left and the commitment of the division reserve (Task Force Robbie), which was ambushed going to the aid of the ARVN unit, leaving the division compound exposed. Neither the division nor the regiment provided such information to the battalion commander.

10. The S-4 needs to be prepared to conduct an aggressive resupply of ammunition, food, and water while KIA and WIA are being evacuated from the battle area. The battalion commander needs to provide the S-4 with personnel assets to carry out the resupply mission in both daylight and in darkness. At Dai Do, Capt. Lane Forehand used the recon platoon, under the command of Bill Muter, to carry out this resupply function in an outstanding manner.[8]

These comments by Warren are very much on target and are invaluable lessons that were, in fact, learned, but should never be forgotten. These lessons are especially critical in today's conflicts where multinational forces operate together, as well as in conjunction with perhaps less than reliable indigenous forces. A firm hand on the wheel keeps the mission on track.

The analysis of this combined operation would not be complete without the critical and very poignant comments from my old battalion commander and great friend Brig. Gen. William Weise. Above all others involved, he provides the most in-depth analysis and operational knowledge of the problems that were experienced at his level, both during and after the fact:

1. Complete lack of usable intelligence hampered 2/4 throughout the battle. We were tasked to clear an area outside our assigned TAOR without any idea of the enemy situation. The only enemy information of any value was obtained by BLT 2/4 units in close

contact with a superior enemy force after the battle was joined. The lack of usable intelligence from higher echelons forced us to react to one desperate situation after another.

2. Seeming indifference of the 3rd Marine Division commander to repeated requests for additional support once the battle was joined. The battle was fought about two and half kilometers from the division CP at Dong Ha Combat Base (DHCB). The sounds and smoke from the battle were clearly audible and visible at DHCB for three days. Yet neither the commanding general nor any member of his staff visited Dai Do during the battle. The regimental commander, Col. Milton Hull, and his operations officer, Maj. Dennis Murphy, on the other hand, visited two or three times and were close enough to the action to dodge enemy supporting arms on those occasions. On one occasion, during Colonel Hull's visit, my radio operator and runner shot an enemy soldier carrying a machine gun about fifty meters from our position.

3. Having to piecemeal BLT 2/4 units and Bravo Company, 1st Battalion, 3rd Marines, into the battle and never having enough assets to fully exploit temporary success.

4. Failure of the M-16 rifle. The M-16 A1 rifle would jam whenever even a small amount of sand or dirt got into the receiver. The only solution was to field strip and clean the rifle. It is virtually impossible to keep dirt out of the receiver during a firefight in which Marines are hitting the ground, rolling over, diving for cover, etc. As a result, Vietnam-era Marine riflemen lost confidence in "the Marine's best friend," his rifle. Battle-tested Marines scrounged M-14s and enemy weapons, especially at Dai Do. I've addressed this problem more thoroughly in my September 1987 *Marine Corps Gazette* article. Colonel Kevin Conry, who commanded 2/4 in 1990 and 1991 during Desert Shield/Desert Storm, told me that his Marines had similar problems of the M-16 A1 jamming frequently from sand in the receiver. To date (from reports I have read), Marines in Afghanistan and Iraq still have this problem with their M-16 rifle despite its many modifications in recent decades.

5. Apparent inflexibility and lack of ingenuity of the 3rd Marine

Division commanding general (who missed the opportunity to trap and destroy the 320th NVA Division). Once the division reserve (Task Force Robbie) was ambushed and bloodied, 3rd Marine Division seemed to sit on its hands insofar as the battle at Dai Do was concerned. The chance to trap the 320th NVA by inserting units north of Thuong Do was lost due to inaction. Where would these friendly units come from when all maneuver units were tied down on "McNamara's dye-marker" positions or otherwise committed? One way would be to request additional units from XXIV Corps (which the commander eventually did, but too late to be of consequence). Another way would be to commit three of the four rifle companies and a command element from several dye-marker positions and helo lift them into positions from which they could block and/or attack the enemy from its rear.

6. Poor fire support coordination (at the division level) between artillery/naval gunfire and air support. Division Fire Support Coordination Center (FSCC) immediately checked (suspended) artillery and naval gunfire support when medevacs entered any battle area to preclude helicopters from being struck by friendly fire. This was not necessary. All that safety required was to insure that the helicopter flight path was an appropriate distance from the gun target line(s). This should have been easy to coordinate between the division FSCC and direct air support center (DASC). Checking fire during the battle would have been disastrous for 2/4, so we moved our casualties by stretcher, amphibian tractors, and otters to the riverbank at An Lac. From there, they were carried by small skimmer boats about five and a half kilometers to a helicopter evacuation point at Mai Xa Chanh.

7. Inadequate air support during first two days. This inadequacy was due to the cumbersome U.S. Air Force method of controlling and allotting air support. Note: in March 1968, the U.S. Air Force was given control of Marine air by MACV [Military Assistance Command, Vietnam] in the mistaken belief that better efficiency in the allocation of air assets would result. When it was available, air support did an excellent job.

8. The massive use and timely availability of artillery and naval gunfire were critical throughout the battle.
9. The superb performance of the Marines and sailors at all levels was the key factor in 2/4's success.
10. The intensive operations and frequent enemy contact prior to Dai Do toughened and sharpened 2/4.
11. The scheduled and ad hoc training conducted prior to Dai Do, despite heavy operational commitments, helped Marines gain confidence and made them more effective in combat.[9]

I have been asked that if a larger troop commitment had been projected into the Dong Ha/Dai Do region in time, or even if troop numbers had been increased throughout Vietnam in general, could the NVA have been completely destroyed in the province, thus altering or even delaying the final collapse in 1975?

In response to that, I do not think troop commitment had any significance; we did not pursue the tactical advantage of going north. We sat around and allowed ourselves to get shot at for all those years, and we never developed our strategic and tactical advantage and moved north. We could not go across the Ben Hai River; this was forbidden. We had all these rules of engagement; we could not level the strategic advantages against the hard targets where the supplies were coming from.

In 1968 we were hit, but we hit back even harder. It took the NVA until 1973 to get enough strength to try anything of any significance. They had to regroup and were not able to go on the battlefield again until 1973. That was almost a five-year hiatus. In 1973 we had Hanoi on its ass, and the war was basically won. Then it was backed off again. We were still piddling around; we lost the advantage with the public, with the American people, and the press helped create that disadvantage.

The politics of the day must be addressed and included, simply because all wars, especially the Vietnam conflict, may be fought by the military on the ground, but larger strategic decisions are made by politicians. The media in that day and age, while rather infantile in its technology in comparison to the technology of today, was strong enough

At War During Trying Times
—Lt. Col. George "Fritz" Warren

I will say that the political environment back in the States affected all of us in one way or another, and any account describing the performance of Marines in combat during the latter years of the Vietnam War that does not discuss this environment will lack some of the richness of the commitment of those who served their country during these trying times.

During my tour with 2/4, both Robert Kennedy and Martin Luther King Jr. were gunned down in my country. I remember very vividly standing on the side of a hill, thinking about how strange it was that I was serving my country, fighting for the rights of a people that I did not really know, halfway around the world, while back home free men were not able to express their views without being shot dead. I still feel resentful that when our young Marines returned home after their tour, many bearing the scars of war, they were despised, spit upon, and called killers of innocent people by citizens in their own country. I am not sure how much of these feelings would be appropriate in Jim Livingston's book, but the political environment of the times was relevant to the sacrifices of those of us who served our country in Vietnam.[10]

to influence politicians, who in turn mandated methods of action ten thousand miles away from where the action was. That was a media war as much as it was a battle of bullets and bombs.

About the division of Marine assets, especially the dispersion of 2/4 assets, now-retired Brigadier General Weise has said: "The assignment of BLT [2/4] attachments to other organizations may have seemed a more efficient use of assets to somebody, but it was clearly a mistake. Any greater efficiency gained came at the cost of reduced battalion effectiveness, and lives were lost because of inadequate or unresponsive support in critical situations."[11]

One may ask, why did the NVA want to overrun Dong Ha, Dai Do, An Lac, and the surrounding region so badly? The answer is that isolating these areas along the rivers would have cut American forces off from supplies, allowed the enemy to interdict and control the critical river traffic, and possibly even establish a more firm foothold for launching more intense attacks upon the south in the near future.

Weise wrote his own opinion: "After having failed at Khe Sanh and Hue during the 1968 Tet Offensive, what could be a greater propaganda victory than destroying and temporarily occupying the largest Marine base in northern I Corps? Another possibility exists. The NVA may have intended to seize the provincial capital city of Quang Tri, only ten kilometers south of the Bo Dieu River. Such a bold stroke would have been possible if the 320th NVA Division had not been stopped on the north bank of the Bo Dieu."[12]

I could not agree more.

CHAPTER 9

Final Analysis

Veterans are the most precious jewels in our nation's treasury.
—Colonel Jay R. Vargas

WHEN ASKED TO COMPARE the basic differences between army versus Marine concepts and applications of battle, this is what I say: The Marines fought while totally nondependent on supporting arms. The army depended very much on supporting arms and oftentimes would not engage the way the Marines would. As a consequence, we may have had more casualties, but at the end of the day, the way we fought was totally without supporting arms, without helicopters, and without moving around and going to firebases—an enclave sort of attitude. Except for some of their special units, the army, by and large, did not have the amount of field time that Marines had.

When asked how I felt about being awarded the nation's highest honor for valor, the answer was quite simple. I felt very humbled to be so supported by my battalion commander, then–Lt. Col. Bill Weise. Later, after about two years, I was ordered to the White House to receive the medal. At the time I was at Fort Benning as an instructor at the U.S. Army Infantry School. It must be said and has been said by many recipients, and I know this to be true: no one wears this medal alone. I like to think that all of us fighting together held the line, that we all supported each other. Everyone has fear. It is how you manage that fear, control it, and turn that fear into a positive action that matters. All of us have our opinions of our fellow Marines based upon their actions, personalities, etc. I have to say that these men I served with, top to bottom, were the finest human beings I have ever known.

My RTO, Lance Cpl. Frank Valdez, returned the sentiment:

> I had the opportunity to see the skipper in many different situations. A couple of observations: The skipper led from the front, at all times. I don't mean just during combat situations, but by his example. He believed in maintaining a disciplined unit, and that included PT and haircuts, even in the field. As a nineteen-year-old lance corporal, at the time, I didn't truly appreciate the importance. I now know that by looking like Marines, we felt like Marines, and as a result, we fought like Marines. In all my interactions with the skipper, I cannot recall a time when he yelled or screamed at his troops. He didn't need to. His bearing and that Georgian drawl spoke volumes. Here was a leader of Marines, at his finest.[1]

There are a lot of memories and faces of your comrades, the men who never lived to see their story told and for whom we wear this award. I do not think any of us consider ourselves real heroes because we survived, if that makes any sense. We wear the awards for those Marines and sailors who did not make it home. Those are the people we honor, and it is a sacred and honored privilege to wear the award in their names. I know Jay Vargas feels the same way. Receiving it is a great distinction, but also humbling, because somewhere along the way, other good fellows died, and we are the witnesses to their actions and bravery. We are the holders of their history and legacy.

In his article about his men at Dai Do, Brigadier General Weise wrote: "I was privileged to command those magnificent Marines and sailors, who stopped the well equipped 320th in its tracks on the north bank of the Bo Dieu River and drove it back toward the Demilitarized Zone. I believe that we conducted a successful spoiling attack that prevented the much larger NVA unit from launching a ground assault on the Marine combat/service support base at Dong Ha, headquarters 3rd Marine Division (Forward)."[2]

In the post-war analysis of these events, certain new information, previously unrecorded, has come to light. Thanks to Brigadier General Weise, we now have another perspective on Dai Do and the losses suffered by 2/4. In addition, a letter to Weise from Col. R. D. Camp Jr., USMC (ret.), offers a first-person perspective of what was going on at the division CP during the Battle of Dai Do:

May 18, 2004

Dear General Weise:

As I mentioned, I would like to give you another view of Dai Do. At the time of the action, I was General Davis' Aide—who was assigned as the Deputy, Provisional Corps Vietnam (later 24 Corps) based at Phu Bai. I don't remember the exact date, but it was probably around the 2nd or 3rd of May, when Generals Davis and Rosen (C.G. Prov. Corps) visited 3rd MarDiv. As we flew into Dong Ha, I distinctly remember seeing air strikes and artillery fire in what I learned later was the area of Dai Do. During this first visit, General Tompkins briefed both general officers, in broad terms, about the fight and pointed out the location on a big map tacked to the wall of his office. I vaguely remember him saying that the fight started when a Navy supply LCU was fired upon as it navigated a bend in the Cua Viet River a few clicks north of Dong Ha.

Davis and Rosen closely followed the brief and asked questions, which indicated their interest. At the end of the brief, the entire party returned to the helicopters and departed. The next day we returned for another brief and observed the same conditions as the first day—wisps of dirty smoke from air strikes and artillery shells. Thompson gave the same abbreviated brief, except this time the two guests seemed to ask more direct questions, which I took to be somewhat directive in nature. Of course as a young officer, I didn't completely understand the subtle interplay that was going on between an Army general and the C.G. of a Marine Division. I believe General Davis was caught in the middle, trying to maintain a neutral stance.

On the third day I was surprised to learn that we were again flying to Dong Ha. General Rosen's Aide, an Army major, seemed particularly serious as we arranged the flight. I vaguely remember the two generals closeted in Rosen's office for some time before heading to the helo pad. I observed the same conditions around Dai Do as before. After landing, the generals headed off to Tompkins.

However, Rosen's Aide pulled me aside and shook his head, meaning we were excluded from the brief. As we stood outside . . . he leaned toward me and, in a very conspirator-like whisper, told me, "If Tompkins wasn't a Marine general, Rosen would relieve him!" I was so taken aback that I didn't know what to say, because even at my junior level, I knew the battle was being badly handled by the division, so I kept quiet.

I thought the information was so controversial that I never discussed it with General Davis, nor did he ever openly express any fault with General Tompkins' performance. As you know, a short time later Davis took command and drastically changed the division's scheme of maneuver—but that's another story.

I do remember visiting 2/4's field headquarters sometime after the battle. Your S-3 gave the brief—and my one memory of that day was his account of the individual and collective bravery of the Marines. He described a line of fallen Marines littering an open field. The last man stretched out in an NVA machine gun nest with his bayoneted rifle impaling the gunner. The hair on my arms stood up—and I'm not too ashamed to admit, tears coursed down my cheeks.

Again, I enjoyed our brief chat—and I look forward to seeing you again in the future.

Warm Regards,
and of course,
Semper Fi,
R. D. Camp, Jr.
Colonel USMC (ret)[3]

This letter from Colonel Camp provides the missing link regarding the lack of immediate and proper response to the actions detailed at Dai Do. Although his observations are from his own unique perspective, they may explain the massive losses incurred. The following is a response email from Weise to Camp:

> May 25, 2004
> Dick:
>
> I too enjoyed our brief encounter . . . your letter arrived yesterday. Thank you very much. For years I believed 3rd MarDiv let 2/4 down, terribly. If we had gotten help from other ground units and earlier priority for air support, a lot more Marines would be around today telling their grandchildren about that battle. I also believe that we could have annihilated the 320th NVA Division and saved General Davis a lot of trouble, as well as a number of casualties after he assumed command of 3rd Mar Div. I remember the *Gazette* article you and General Davis (what a great leader) wrote about destroying the 320th during the summer and fall of 1968.[4]

The division command's apathy about supporting 2/4 when assistance was needed most was perhaps not intentional. The battle did increase in momentum rapidly and was a continuing metamorphosis, always evolving and changing. If we did not have accurate on-site intelligence reports, then logic would dictate that we had nothing but running commentary to send up the S-2 chain of command. Even if this is the actual explanation, more should have been done to assist those men fighting for their lives. Then again, hindsight is golden.

As a postscript, although this book is researching and analyzing the events of the battle, it is understood that war is not a perfect science. Confusion, noise, lack of or changing intelligence, ever-changing circumstances, delayed or disrupted communications, as well as the ever-present fog of war contributed to the losses. What is also evident in the analysis four decades after the events in question is the professionalism and bravery displayed by American and a limited number of North Vietnamese troops.

The same confusion can be said to have affected the aviation assets employed, especially during the medevac situation as experienced by Captain Forehand. He witnessed a pilot withdraw without taking wounded on board because the pilot was afraid of drawing fire, which he eventually did, and Forehand was so upset at the pilot that he fired his own M-16 into the fleeing chopper.[5] Although this was a unique circumstance, it emphasizes the fact that fear unchecked is a disaster in the making.

The Battle of Dai Do and the surrounding region has remained a virtually unknown piece of American history. This is quite unfortunate, given that that terrible week in 1968 was arguably one of the most important events during the entire American involvement in Vietnam, if not *the* most important. Although the losses were tragic, the American lives that were lost and shattered were not without a positive outcome. Had the men of 2/4 and their supporting units (including the U.S. Army and ARVN that remained) not held their ground and routed the enemy, it is certain that tens of thousands more allied lives would have been lost in retaking that lost territory as the war continued. There would no doubt have been an American counterattack to retake Quang Tri Province had it fallen. The enemy would have had even more time to dig in; to reinforce, strengthen, and expand their defenses; and improved their ability to launch more concentrated attacks to the south. The Vietnam Memorial would most definitely have additional panels inscribed with the names of those Americans tasked with the mission of recovering the area. The Marines, sailors, and soldiers involved performed a miracle of modern combat arms, and the nation owes them a great debt.

It must be mentioned that the world press, especially the news organizations, tended to underplay (if report at all) any great successes achieved by American forces and their allies. In his book *Reporting Vietnam: Media and Military at War*, William M. Hammond, observes: "The official agencies that handled the press in Vietnam during the early years had little control over what those reporters wrote . . . As for the American news media, much of what they published on the subject reflected their nation's preoccupation with Communism and the Cold War."[6] The "defeats make news" mentality that prevailed in Vietnam still exists today. Unlike during World War II and before, good news from the war front is not considered sensational enough to sell newspapers or achieve high television ratings. Therefore, the virtually unknown engagement at Dai Do during the first week of May 1968 was a direct product of intellectual dishonesty and abject, financially driven apathy on the part of the media. Veterans of Iraq and Afghanistan are learning all too well that the same apathy exists today.

The men at Dai Do, Dong Ha, and Dinh To fell into obscurity, their actions forgotten by all but the few who fought and survived, until various books and other publications emerged, such as Keith Nolan's book *The Magnificent Bastards: The Joint Army-Marine Defense of Dong Ha, 1968* and the article written by Bill Weise for the *Marine Corps Gazette*.

In the final analysis of the battle in general, 2/4's actions in particular, and the numbers involved and the running timeline of the engagement, the results were remarkable. The battalion had overrun and occupied or destroyed over one hundred bunkers and prepared positions, and most, apparently, were taken out by Echo Company. I was actually far more concerned with containing my ever-shrinking unit into a cohesive defensive posture, while launching attacks and counterattacks as soon as situations presented themselves. The greatest satisfaction I have, apart from our winning the battle proper, was that our successful efforts saved Golf Company and Vargas from certain death, just as Vargas's rapid thinking and lucid decision making salvaged his unit. The other officers and men also played their part admirably. That, for me, is the best memory I take away from the event.

I think it is very important to state that only years later, when many of us went back to Vietnam and revisited the old battleground in the Cua Viet, Dai Do, and Dong Ha region, did it really become apparent to me how desperate the situation had been for the enemy. I spoke with a NVA leader, and I spoke with the former VC chief in the area, and they explained why they had been so staunch in their defense.

The reason the NVA were fighting so fiercely was the fact that we were right there on top of the command structure, which was only about a hundred yards from the edge of the village. I have been able in retrospect to analyze the battle events, reevaluating the terrain and learning interesting things from my former enemy. Our effort was threatening to force them out into the exposed rice paddy, where the indirect fire and air assets would have had at them. They were boxed in with no place to go. This was Custer's last stand for both of us. They explained why they had been throwing wave after wave at us, complete with the kitchen sink, hitting us with everything they had left at least three times in massive do-or-die assaults. That was where the close-quarters combat really took place. Their attacks were the last acts of a group of brave and very desperate men.

After meeting and speaking with my former enemies, I also found it interesting that, with the exception already noted, none of them seemed to have really been aware of our disposition, illustrating that the classic fog of war cuts both ways. They were apparently having some tactical as well as strategic issues, especially tactical, given what they were faced with as far as options.

The actions of 2/4 under Weise, as well as those efforts by Vargas and other company commanders, halted what would have been a hammer blow against the province. Weise's command and control of a very chaotic situation can only be described as incredible. Given the lack of constant intelligence, nullified communications, and reduced forces, to achieve such a victory against such overwhelming odds has seldom been realized in military history.

Another memory I have is from May 2; after spending two hours on the bank of the Cua Viet at the wounded collection point and triage, I was flown aboard the *Iwo Jima*, where the bulk of the wounded were collected. The wounded at the river and aboard the ship included Bill Weise, Capt. Jim Williams (CO of Hotel Company), and many Marines who were much more seriously wounded than I was—many with body and head wounds.

Within another two hours on board ship, I went into surgery to repair the wounds, especially the mangled legs. The surgeons placed one in a cast. After two more days, following a case-by-case evaluation procedure based upon troop availability and the severity of the wounded's injuries, the wounded were sent to various other medical facilities.

Upon being stabilized, I was transported to Da Nang, where I was loaded with many other wounded, mostly amputees, aboard a C-141

Starlifter. I think I was the only guy on board who was not an amputee. We were flown to Clark Air Force Base in the Philippine Islands, where some of the young wives of service members would come and give the wounded men drinks. Afterward, an aircraft took the men to Guam, where the air force wives also showed the men great hospitality and compassion. Finally, the aircraft landed in Honolulu, Hawaii. As we were offloaded, the deputy commanding general of the Fleet Marine Force, Pacific (FMF-Pac) pinned Purple Hearts on the men, including me. Most of the men and I were then moved to Tripler Army Hospital.

I was almost immediately sent into the first of what would be several surgeries over the next couple of weeks. Soon I was visited by my wife, Sara. My recovery following the required surgeries was slow and followed by physical therapy. I was allowed out of the hospital, and Sara was shown how to change the dressing and keep the wounds clean, especially the severe thigh wound. That wound had a plug placed in it, due to its size, and it continued to drain. After another three weeks, Sara returned stateside. With a couple of months left on my tour, I was sent to Camp Hanson, Okinawa, while still on crutches. While there I was assigned to the 9th Marine Amphibious Brigade as the staff secretary, along with Capt. James Vargas, who was *aide-de-camp* and also recovering from his wounds.

During this period, Jay Vargas and I knew that Bill Weise had recommended both of us for the Navy Cross for gallantry and heroism under fire. What we did not know was that the recommendations had been upgraded to the Medal of Honor. Both of us were informed that we would not be returning to Vietnam any time soon. They were afraid of us going back and getting hammered again.

Upon completing my tour in Asia and returning to full duty, I rotated back the States to attend the Amphibious Warfare School at Quantico, Virginia. Upon completion, my next assignment was as the assistant Marine Corps representative at the United States Army Infantry School at Fort Benning, Georgia. I would remain back in my native Georgia for two and a half years.

In 1970, while at Fort Benning I received news that would change my life forever. Sara and I made the trip to Washington, D.C., at the request of President Richard M. Nixon, where other honored members of the armed forces received the nation's highest award for valor. I have to confess, it was a humbling experience.

We were assigned a Marine captain as an escort and provided with stellar hotel accommodations for the entire family, including my father, mother, brother, and sister-in-law. We also took our baby daughter, Kimberly, with us. We were escorted into the East (Blue) Room for the awards ceremony, where President Nixon greeted all the families and service members. All the services were represented, and Gen. Lewis Walt was the senior Marine representative.

I thought Nixon appeared to be a warm person, which was my first impression. Perhaps as a young captain I was overcome by the entire event itself and what was transpiring. He reached out to the families of all the recipients. He even tried to take Kimberly from the arms of my wife, who was holding her as the ceremony transpired, but Kimberly would have absolutely nothing to do with him. He tried to hold her, and she just totally refused President Nixon.

So that was one of the subtler funnies we all recalled from the ceremony. We had a fine tour of the White House. We were treated and hosted well—very professionally—and everything went as you would anticipate. It was certainly a defining event. I was in stellar company, and the Medal of Honor was awarded to the following personnel in this order:

Lieutenant Colonel Charles C. Rogers, U.S. Army

Captain Paul W. Bucha, U.S. Army

Captain Ronald E. Ray, U.S. Army

Sergeant Allen J. Lynch, U.S. Army

Specialist Four Frank A. Herda, U.S. Army

Major M. Sando [Jay] Vargas, U.S. Marine Corps

Captain James E. Livingston, U.S. Marine Corps

Lieutenant Commander Thomas O. Kelley, U.S. Navy

Lieutenant (Junior Grade) Joseph R. Kerrey, U.S. Naval Reserve

Donald E. Ballard, Hospital Corpsman Third Class, U.S. Navy

Captain James P. Fleming, U.S. Air Force

Sergeant John L. Levitow, U.S. Air Force

Following the ceremony and the return to normal life, I found myself assigned as Director of Division Schools for the 1st Marine Division at Camp Pendleton, California. After that tour, I became the S-3 for 3rd Battalion, 7th Marines.

The war in Vietnam continued to rage, and the political climate in both Vietnam and the United States was in a constant state of negative evolution. The military fought its enemy in the field, as well as a hostile and jaundiced media back home. American military victories were back-page news, while political antiwar rallies and domestic anarchy became the headlines.

The situation in Vietnam was changing for the worse, despite the avalanche of American troops and a string of one-sided victories in our favor. I was to return to Vietnam, but in a very different and unaccustomed capacity. I would be one of the few military men entrusted to help salvage American assets as the war wound down, thus becoming an eyewitness to a debacle that was created by the American media, which supported errors in judgment by politicians who fostered a decade of flawed policies and who placed restrictions and incomprehensible rules of engagement upon American and coalition forces, thus nullifying years of military success.

The bell would soon toll, and the U.S. military in general and the Marines in particular would be expected to perform a major miracle of logistics, politics, and military precision. Once again when politicians failed, the Marines would be called upon to do the near impossible.

CHAPTER 10

Operation Frequent Wind: Prepping for Evac

War is an ugly thing, but not the ugliest of things; the decayed and degraded state of moral and patriotic feelings which thinks nothing worth a war, is much worse. . . . A man who has nothing which he is willing to fight for, nothing which he cares more about than he does about his own personal safety, is a miserable creature, who has no chance of being free . . .

—John Stuart Mill

THE COMMUNISTS IN THE north had been severely beaten since the Tet Offensive. In fact, the North Vietnamese and their Viet Cong allies never won a substantial battle after Tet. Given the evidentiary prowess, determination, and leadership of the U.S. military, how did we fail? Or did we fail at all? Militarily, the United States defeated the NVA and Viet Cong time and again. However, the various U.S. political administrations failed to adequately support a total war strategy necessary for ultimate victory. President Lyndon B. Johnson made glaring errors in judgment, and Richard M. Nixon picked up the pieces and attempted to refloat a sinking ship.

After more than a decade of direct American involvement, worldwide and domestic criticism and internal discord fostered by a biased liberal media and propelled by the various social movements eventually eroded the political will necessary for complete success in Vietnam. The United States Congress was less than friendly towards the Department of Defense, and politicians bankrolled their elections with payouts from supporters who led the antiwar movement. What most of these political and financial echelons failed to see was the larger picture. The Communists were determined to ultimately overrun all of Southeast Asia, and they had been fostering proxy wars in Asia since the 1950s and in Africa since the 1960s.

The politically wavering and militarily incompetent Lyndon B. Johnson administration had, by all definitions, snatched political defeat from the jaws of military victory. Almost sixty thousand Americans and many more allied nationals, including South Vietnamese, South Koreans, Australians, and Thais, had perished supporting a nation that was unable or unwilling to defend itself. Nixon's "Vietnamization policy" was emplaced to allow American ground forces to eventually withdraw, thereby allowing the South Vietnamese to continue their fight with American materiel support. Continued American support became imperative following the Paris Peace Accords of 1973. This program was also a complete failure. All the weapons in the world will not help a force that has no will or courage to fight.

South Vietnamese politicians in Saigon demanded the resignation of President Nguyen Van Thieu, hoping to emplace a candidate that Hanoi would find more politically reliable.[1] This overt action created a ripple effect throughout the South Vietnamese civilian and military population. If the South Vietnamese government lost its political will and acquiesced to the north, and America was deemphasizing its involvement, then what chance did their military have? The oak tree of defeat grows from the smallest acorn of indifference, or in this case, incompetence.

The South Vietnamese government had failed their greatest ally, the United States, as well as its own people. Likewise, our government, through its myopic vision of global harmony, decided to abandon a friend, leaving South Vietnam to deal with the Communist onslaught with half-trained, under-motivated troops and politically unreliable leadership. What the average person (including the average American) does not understand is that these decisions and betrayals were not the responsibility of or due to the actions of the U.S. military. In fact, the military in the field was never even consulted, only informed of these decisions afterwards and expected to save the day. The United States Marines became Saigon's emergency 911 call.

The actions of the 18th ARVN Division, along with indigenous support personnel, against NVA General Van Tien Dung's 232nd Tactical Force in the Battle for Xuan Loc, in Long Khanh Province, forced the Communists into a change of policy.[2] By April 16, 1975, South Vietnamese forces had stalled the NVA advance forty miles northeast of Saigon and the airbase at Bien Hoa.[3] People with connections, money, and motivation boarded civil aircraft leaving Tan Son Nhut Airport.[4] Everyone knew what was coming. On April 20, ARVN Brigadier General Le Minh Dao was ordered to withdraw his 18th Division, 1st Airborne Brigade, and support personnel to Ba Ria. The house of cards had just collapsed.

The following day, President Thieu, a true coward of the first order, resigned and flew with his family to Taiwan. His vice president, Tran Van Huong, took power and only lasted one week in office. The NVA and General Dung had surrounded Saigon by April 27, and on April 28 General Duong Van Minh was named president on the heels of the departed Huong.[5] By that date, the situation was as follows: the 232nd Tactical Force contained Highway 4 on the Long An Front; the 3rd NVA Corps contained Route 1 on the Cu Chi Front; the 1st NVA Corps controlled Highway 13 on the Binh Duong Front; the 2nd NVA Corps dominated the QL-15 Front, focused upon Long Thanh and Ba Ria.[6] Saigon was completely surrounded.

Subsequently, the political and the military situation in the country deteriorated rapidly. The U.S. Embassy and the U.S. Defense Attaché Office (DAO) Compound, located near Tan Son Nhut Airport, were ordered reinforced, and the Special Planning Group, formed to plan an evacuation, took the lead in anticipation of indigenous personnel overwhelming the fortifications in the panic that was sure to come. The security threat could not be overestimated.[7] The military situation in Saigon following the Communist offensive effectively forced President

Gerald R. Ford's hand.[8] Ford had three great responsibilities:

1. To evacuate American civilian, military, and CIA assets without alarming the indigenous population to the point of panic and riot.

2. To protect and/or destroy all sensitive documents.

3. To protect America's image during Operation Frequent Wind.

United States military assets in support of the operations included the following, cited in appendix J of the 1990 book *U.S. Marines in Vietnam: The Bitter End, 1973–1975*, by Maj. George R. Dunham and Col. David A. Quinlan, USMC:[9]

<u>Navy 7th Fleet</u>

2 aircraft carriers with 125 fighters and 33 support aircraft and 12 anti-submarine helicopters; 17 amphibious assault ships; 14 destroyer escorts; 11 supply/replenishment ships.

<u>Marines</u>

1 Marine Amphibious Brigade (sea based forces with 1 Battalion Landing Team including the Security Evacuation Force); 3 BLTs (land-based forces); 63 troop transport helicopters, 8 helicopter gun ships, and 6 command and control helicopters.

<u>Air Force</u>

193 fighters, 112 support aircraft, and 69 passenger-transport aircraft.

Performing the first function fell upon two primary sectors: the ground-force commanders and the air-asset commanders. Major General Carl W. Hoffman, the III Marine Expeditionary Force (MEF) commander, replaced the 1st Battalion, 4th Marines (whose headquarters was the USS *Dubuque*, LPD-8). I was aboard the USS *Blue Ridge* with elements of 1st Battalion, 4th Marines, having been assigned there by Maj. Gen. Kenneth Houghton, commanding general of 3rd Marine Division. He knew me from the 1st Marine Division, where I had been assigned as the operations officer for 3rd Battalion, 7th Marines.

Therefore, I was with a new security detachment on April 17, 1975. BLT 1/4 had been serving as the Amphibious Evacuation Republic of Vietnam Support Group, part of the Amphibious Evacuation Security Force that included 9th and 12th Marine Regiments, 3rd Engineer

Battalion, 7th Communications Battalion, 3rd Tank Battalion, and the 1st Amphibious Tractor Battalion. Durham and Quinlan explain in *U.S. Marines in Vietnam*, "Men from these units formed two 72 man detachments, comprised of a 12 man head-quarters detachment and three 20 man sections."[10]

It was clear the ARVN forces would not be able to further delay, let alone stop, the NVA at Xuan Loc. Because the United States had downsized its forces following the agreement signed in Paris in 1973, there was not a lot that we could do either defensively or, especially, offensively. The die was cast. What the military had gained through their sacrifices, the politicians had thrown away, and the dead meant nothing to them.

There was also concern with regard to the two remaining American consulates at Bien Hoa[11] and Can Tho.[12] Communist capture of those locations, along with personnel and sensitive documents and communications gear, would have proven disastrous. Consul General Richard Peters, seeing the inevitable outcome, ordered Gunnery Sgt. Robert W. Schlager to have his Marines assist the consulate staffs in the evacuation procedures.[13] Sergeant Ronald E. Duffy, Sgt. James M. Felber, Cpl. Carlos R. Arraigna, Cpl. Gary N. Lindholm, and Lance Cpl. Dean M. Kinzie rapidly did so.[14] The consulate staff, under Peters and the Marine detachment, arrived in Saigon on April 24. As of April 29 the consulate at Can Tho was still operating under Consul General Francis McNamara.[15]

U.S. ships were strategically placed offshore to support the pending evacuation; Marines were trained and prepared for insertion as a security blocking force, and intelligence officers updated briefs on the situation. Many of the Marines offshore had just been stationed in Okinawa two weeks before, and many were inexperienced, but well trained. To quote the late Col. Aaron Bank: "I would rather have ten well trained, highly motivated green recruits than a hundred seasoned cowards."[16] I firmly believed in the same philosophy, and it had proven to be true many times. In this event, it was to be no different.

We had been receiving boatloads of South Vietnamese refugees sailing out to the fleet. Practically anything that would float had people clinging to it. These people were hoping for the opportunity to get the hell out before the Communists rolled in and started killing or "reeducating" everyone. We had a specially task organized group, hand picked, consisting of engineers, military police, intelligence types, and interpreters, screening these people before they came aboard the ships, ferreting out anyone who may have been carrying weapons or been a Communist sympathizer, a VC member, or even a spy. Finding a spy or enemy sympathizer was not beyond the realm of possibility. We pulled a lot of people off the coast, and they had to pass through a clearance system on shore. The evacuation was, I believe, the largest in recorded history, given the numbers of those who tried to get offshore. I think that only the evacuation of Dunkirk in May 1940, with over three hundred thousand Allied soldiers, topped this operation with regard to the actual number of people effectively evacuated by sea.

We even had a South Korean boat, an old landing ship (LST), that was flown over to assist with the evacuation; it went dead in the water while loaded with people. It did not have water, and people were dying, God rest their souls. I flew over the ship in a helicopter, but we obviously could not land that Huey on that LST with all those people. We would not have accomplished anything and probably would have been killed ourselves.

The Marine Security Guard (MSG) detachment was under Maj. James Kean,[17] (who was stationed in Hong Kong) along with Master Sgt. John Valdez as his non-commissioned officer in charge (NCOIC).[18] Major General Houghton, commander of 3rd Marine Division, placed the 9th Marines operations officer, Maj. David A. Quinlan (coauthor of *U.S. Marines in Vietnam: The Bitter End, 1973–1975)* as commander of these smaller units.[19]

I was a major and on my third tour in Vietnam, and I was the operations officer for Regimental Landing Team 4, commanded by then Col. Alfred M. Gray (later a general and commandant of the Marine Corps).[20] Gray's time on the ground was limited; however, he was very effective during his time in the DAO. As stated earlier, men evaluate their commanding officers, and Ken Crouse, a lance corporal at the time, working the embassy rooftop during the evacuation, said this regarding Gray: "I was a 0311 with 1/4 the prior year and was there when Colonel Gray assumed command of the 4th Marines. The months I had left on Okinawa under his command were a stark contrast to the months under previous commanders. Not that there was anything wrong with them; it's just that with Colonel Gray in command, you always know where to find him: in the field with his Marines."[21] I agree with that assessment. General Gray was always a Marine's Marine, and I am proud and honored to have served under him in 4th Marines in a short period in the 2nd Marine Division.

As stated previously, Saigon was not the only point of NVA contention. The entire country was being overrun, and Americans and their support personnel were all trying to get to the security of the U.S. compound. There was no way for the U.S. commanders to predict with accuracy when the final wave would overtake Saigon. As Anthony A. Wood said, "Our concern in Saigon was that you cannot predict the rate of collapse, and the city was so large and the population so intense at this point that we thought that we would only have at best twelve hours after we began to complete our actions."[22]

By April 21, departure flights were operating on a half-hour schedule from Tan Son Nhut. In addition, the navy ran the "Da Nang-Saigon ferry" to the USNS *Sergeant Kimbro* on April 28. The next day there was a rocket attack against Tan Son Nhut Airport, killing Marine Cpl. Charles McMahon, Jr., and Lance Cpl. Darwin D. Judge. These young Marines were the first two KIAs of Operation Frequent Wind.[23] They were, ironically, the last two ground casualties of the Vietnam War. Following this attack, many ARVN pilots were ordered to take their aircraft to Thailand, and in the process, they jettisoned auxiliary fuel tanks and bombs, littering the runway and thus making portions of the runway unusable.[24]

One very interesting fact was when some of the South Vietnamese pilots took off and went "Chu Hoi," flying around and actually bombing Tan Son Nhut, I was very close to where that bombing took place. That was very close to the old control tower, and these pilots pickled the bombs right on the airstrip. This happened before the evacuation had even been called.

This damage became problematic, as days earlier the order had been given for all American civilians to depart Saigon. The CIA was already in gear following the orders of Station Chief Thomas Polgar. Staff Sgt.

Boyette S. "Steve" Hasty described the situation: "At that time, we didn't know that they [the CIA] were pulling their own bug out, and we were a little bit worried about them, but it finally dawned on us that they were not coming back."[25] In fact, approximately eighteen CIA men, along with McNamara, had climbed into an LCM (landing craft mechanized) headed towards the fleet.[26] Polgar even admitted that "we were a defeated army."[27]

The damage to the airstrip was one of the major reasons U.S. ambassador Graham Anderson Martin was convinced to abandon a fixed-wing evacuation and focus upon a rotary-wing solution.[28] Martin was a man under immense pressure. He had lost a son in Vietnam, and he was losing his embassy. At 10:51 a.m., on April 29, 1975, Ambassador Martin hung up his secure phone; he had just spoken with U.S. Secretary of State Henry Kissinger. There would be no more politics or diplomacy; the situation was in the hands of the military from that point forward. Operation Frequent Wind's Option IV was ordered to be executed, and I was handed the message from an army officer.[29]

On Tuesday, April 29, the first Air America helicopters landed on the deck of the USS *Vancouver* (LPD-2) with the first of many waves of evacuees.[30] On April 30, South Vietnam officially surrendered. The NVA never lost a single man or fired a shot in anger to take Saigon. A decade of sacrifice had been thrown away. However, there was a lot going on up to that point.

President Ford knew he had the best men possible to complete the evacuation mission. His problem was the algebraic X factor, the unknown that always haunts any commander. Even the best laid plans often fall to the wayside in the face of adversity. This is when damage control becomes the operational paradigm, and the value of a commander's contingency planning becomes evident. However, once Ambassador Martin and his staff were secured and the military firmly in control, the atmosphere changed.

I was assigned as RLT-4 operations officer under Colonel Gray as all of this was unfolding. In my opinion, Gray could not have made a better series of decisions. What was needed was an intelligent, cool, and tactical thinker. The deteriorating situation left no room for error.

The RLT S-4, Maj. John L. Murray, organized the complicated airlift plan as I perfected my own plan for reinforcing the DAO compound, which was seriously understaffed and had been housing between two hundred and six hundred Vietnamese nationals on a daily basis.[31]

I had to get Gray on the phone to discuss the numerous options before making a final decision. We had options, such as bringing out just the Marines and other Americans, or also evacuating nearly a million Vietnamese using the peninsula at Vung Tau. When I was handed the execute message by an unknown army officer, all I heard was, "You got it, Major," and then I was in charge of pulling this entire nightmare together. Well, that forced my hand. I managed to get Gray on the "deep throat" phone on the *Blue Ridge* and said that we needed two companies with a recon unit and a battalion command group—or whomever he wished to bring. That was the immediate requirement.

He sent two rifle companies from 2/4, which seemed ironic given my history with the "Magnificent Bastards" on my previous tour. Gray and Gen. Richard E. Carey came in by two separate Hueys, and Carey established a command and control center in order to coordinate all units and keep track of all movements, which proved to be almost fruitless. Gray was busy doing a masterful job, as was his way. He walked around the perimeter and gave his flak vest to a Marine, encouraging the troops, making sure they had the proper gear, showing his presence in a very professional manner. But that was just his way; being in the field with the troops, not behind a desk, was the way he commanded. This was the epitome of a proper leadership posture.

It may seem innocuous and almost standard operating procedure for a Marine leader to perform these actions, but you must remember that there were hundreds of thousands of people in Saigon—and no doubt South Vietnamese civilians just outside our perimeter. You would never know if there were VC or North Vietnamese in these groups. Many of them had weapons, and all of them had fear. Panic and small arms are a bad combination, and every Marine on that detail saw it first hand as they flew in. These people had only one driving ambition, and that was to get into the various American perimeters, such as the embassy and even the DAO compound, and get out.

Try and picture the situation from my perspective. You had tens of thousands of people trying to get out of the city—by air, water, any way they could. Then you had those people who wanted to evacuate, but they had to do so through our secure centers; hence the massive crowds. Then you had the Marines and soldiers organizing the departures, vetting the new arrivals, and on top of this you had armed men, whose affiliation was uncertain and subject to change with each gust of wind, within maximum effective range of our guys. Then, if this was not enough to keep you busy, you had perhaps a million NVA with tanks and towed artillery racing for the city, pushing the panic factor to extreme levels. Finally, after absorbing all of this, you had to plan the extraction of every single American military man and civilian before the roof fell in.

This was one of the key lessons that evolved from Operation Frequent Wind: the concept of compositing. This process unfolded while all units (three Marine Amphibious Units) were at sea and we had security detachments the ground. Numerous liaison trips by personnel aboard *Blue Ridge* using Air America helicopters resolved many issues, but not all of them. I was effectively cut off from anyone else, running my operation with less force than I probably needed, but with enough to get the job done if everything went according to plan. I was not worried about the NVA proper launching an attack against us. We were leaving, and they knew it. My concern was the panic that was certain to grip the remaining ARVN assets and civilians.

The army officer and I had coordinated a plan, and the ongoing operation was placed in motion. Part of the plan was to provide the image of order and good discipline among the American force to counter the rising pandemonium in the streets outside in the city proper. At night, the 9th MAB and DAO hustled to increase the momentum of the mission without raising any outside concerns. The last thing we needed was panic.[32] I also recommended to Carey that we move the 2/4 recon platoon over to the embassy to assist holding the wall. This recommendation was executed.

One part of the mission that I think should be explained was that a few days earlier we had entered the embassy grounds and cut down the trees to effect landing zones, in the anticipation that we would have to move a lot of people in a hurry. It may amaze readers to know that we actually had some people working there who could not understand, nor did they appreciate, why we were cutting those trees down. Now, anyone who knows me will say that I do not like stupidity, I do not like repeating myself, and I do not like those who have no clue what is transpiring questioning my authority or any proper authority. You would not believe how ridiculous it was trying to explain our actions with the clock running out. We had to prepare the LZs, that was part of the operational plan, and it was not negotiable.

Also part of the mission was a platoon of Marines from the USS *Hancock* arriving in civilian clothes on April 25, following a message sent by DAO to Washington on April 21. The platoon, led by 1st Lt. Bruce P. Thompson-Bowers of Company C, 1st Battalion, 9th Marines, was to act as the security force.[33] On April 25, Maj. David E. Cox, the Advance Air Element air liaison officer, held a readiness briefing with the commanding general of 9th MAB and Regimental Landing Team 4 (RLT-4) on the *Blue Ridge*.[34]

At this point I was very pleased with the actions and efforts by all parties given the scope and depth of the operation. Potential LZs were located and prepared with security, wind socks, mapping, and landing markings, including visual approach path indicators and reflective markers.[35] In addition, thirteen rooftops had been designated as LZs for the evacuation of Americans. Following the *Blue Ridge* briefing, it was decided by General Carey that operations would be conducted at night to minimize visual observation by the citizens and thus reduce the anticipated panic that would ensue. Upon Major Cox's return, each LZ was specially and distinctly marked with "footprints" for clarity.

Twelve CH-53 Sea Stallions operated in waves during limited visibility, during which time I had my hands full controlling the ground-security operation with eighteen Marines in the DAO compound.[36] There were three established communications facilities using high, very high, and ultra-high frequency transmitters/receivers.[37] The situation was deteriorating so rapidly that on April 27 Vice Adm. George P. Steele upgraded the 9th MAB's alert status from six hours to one hour—just one hour to be ready to move everything and everyone.

Given the rising tempo, I maintained constant contact with my air liaison counterpart at the Alamo, the nickname given to the 9th MAB headquarters. On April 28, Maj. Morris W. Lutes, the executive officer for Provisional Marine Aircraft Group 39 (ProvMAG-39), and I boarded an Air America helicopter headed for the DAO compound.[38] These flights and their coordination were critical; the 1973 Paris Peace Accords had limited the U.S. military presence to fifty combat personnel in country. Choppers could not drop off Marines or soldiers in large numbers and go beyond that maximum. They had to only send air crew or stay on board.[39] Ambassador Martin addressed this concern with Maj. Gen. Homer D. Smith Jr. (U.S. Army); thus, every arrival had to report to the compound by midnight.[40] Ironically, Lutes and I were bumped off our helicopter by a Vietnamese general and a U.S Army colonel, and we were forced to remain at the headquarters overnight. During this time, I was able to speak with Colonel Gray, updating him on the situation in the DAO.[41] As the Tan Son Nhut airfield was adjacent to the DAO, the timetable for evacuation was constantly being updated due to ongoing operational requirements, intelligence, and available air assets. At 8 p.m. on April 28, the order was given that the airfield was to resume fixed-wing evacuation operations at 9 a.m. It was estimated that between fifty and sixty C-130 sorties would be required to evacuate at least ten thousand people. This plan was soon scrapped; helicopters were the only viable option.[42]

Around this time the CIA was bringing in their helicopters, and they really wanted to get the hell out. They loaded up on the helos and flew out to the ships; you will see this in some of the old archive footage. They did not even shut down the helicopter engines, but jumped out with the rotors still turning.

The security force and air crews were expected to surpass the fifty-combat-personnel restriction dictated by the Paris Peace accords. Lutes and I finally landed at Tan Son Nhut for a meeting with the DAO evacuation planners. They had limited time to complete a full reconnaissance of the DAO, the Air America compound, the embassy, and Newport Pier.[44]

The Power of a Mob
—Capt. Anthony A. Wood

There was a lot of shooting going on. Most of it in the air, but you couldn't tell. We had a bus flipped over by a mob. You don't know the power of a mob until you see a bus picked up and thrown over. Eventually the mob picked up my jeep and threw it over so we had to get off and find our way to a bus. The last convoy came in at about five o'clock in the afternoon. I was with it. It was a very slow convoy that had taken a long time to get in. The last bus had been shot up.[43]

Another situation developing was the efforts of Capt. Anthony A. Wood, nicknamed "Wagon Master," who had preplanned routes for buses and other vehicles in order to ex-filtrate Americans, including the often reluctant and undeserving media.[45] So tense was the situation that two ARVN factions actually broke out into a fratricidal firefight, pinning Americans, who had been loaded onto buses, in the crossfire. Wood managed to have Lt. Col. William E. McKinstry convince the ARVN commander to allow the buses to pass through into the compound gates. Wood performed a remarkable feat by gathering the vehicles and personnel as the situation deteriorated and crowds openly attacked vehicles.

One of the daunting tasks facing the personnel in the embassy was the destruction of sensitive documents and all intelligence and communications gear not being utilized in the evacuation.[46] Explosives were set by Capt. Raymond J. McManus and Master Sergeant East on April 29 to complete the task.[47] This equipment and data could not fall into the hands of the North Vietnamese.

In addition to the implosion within Saigon's military and political infrastructure, the U.S. Marines and U.S. Air Force were experiencing their own failure to communicate. The problem was regarding the coordination of assets under both Rear Adm. Donald E. Whitmire, head of Commander, Amphibious Task Force 76 (CTF-76), and Lt. Gen. John J. Burns, commander of United States Special Advisory Group (USSAG) 7th Air Force. Burns applied the term *L-hour*, or lift-off hour, to mean when a helicopter was launched for a sortie.[48] However, to Marine pilots, the term *L-hour* meant the time a helicopter would land in a sortie, in this case the evacuation zone.[49] This juxtaposed and contrary method of interservice definition would become problematic, to say the least.

My men were the final defensive line for the evacuation of the DAO compound. Every decision by my superiors, whether they were right or wrong, would impact the mission and the defenders. Given the inherent pandemonium both within and outside Saigon, the rest of the Marines and I were being asked to perform a minor miracle. However, there were other problems, and many were not readily visible to the Marines on the ground.

I was there with a handful of Marines, hoping to accomplish the mission and stay alive doing it.

CHAPTER 11

Last Chopper Out

The interesting thing about war is that it always changes, but still remains the same.

—Generalleutnant Hans Baur

THE PLANNERS HAD CALCULATED that the flight time from the ships to the innermost LZ was thirty minutes, and vice versa. This did not allow for the time to load and unload passengers. My group was the farthest away near the besieged airport and, therefore, the most exposed. I had spoken to Colonel Gray about the April 29 rocket attack upon the airport and the resulting casualties. Also, in the DAO compound, Col. Wylie W. Taylor had informed Gen. Carey of the same information. RLT-4 was prepared.[1]

Beyond the DAO compound, confusion was resulting at the helicopter direction center aboard the USS *Okinawa* as the fleet of South Vietnamese helicopters attempted to land on the ship and offload their passengers. These actions choked the flight decks loaded with Marine helicopters on standby awaiting their take-off orders.[2] It seemed that the numbers of people trying to escape were endless.

In addition to the *Okinawa*, the other ships handling this heliborne operation were the *Hancock, Dubuque, Denver, Duluth, Mobile, Peoria,* and *Vancouver*, all stationed in the South China Sea.[3] The units involved were Lt. Col. James L. Bolton's Marine Heavy Helicopter Squadron 462 (HMH-462) and Lt. Col. Herbert M. Fix's HMH-463, and these

Helicopters were Everywhere
—Gunnery Sergeant Russell Thurman

[T]he sky filled with helicopters, and most of them weren't ours. They were Vietnamese flying every conceivable helicopter they could get their hands on. So there was a lot of drama going on. The sky was like black with helicopters. Needless to say, tensions were kind of high because those helicopters were trying to land on our ship [the Okinawa], the primary ship for taking refugees off and going back in."[4]

units were also supporting BLT 2/4.[5] These assets were located on the *Okinawa, Peoria,* and *Vancouver*. This high number of troops required twenty-three CH-53s.[6] This wave was augmented by ten U.S. Air Force helicopters from the carrier USS *Midway*.[7]

Unknown to me at that time, my problems kept increasing.

The plan was to insert Lt. Col. George P. Slade's 2/4 into the compound, and later, if necessary, insert BLT 1/9, under Lt. Col. Royce L. Bond, for auxiliary support and crowd control.[8] The confusion continued when General Burns's message to 9th MAB to "execute" the helicopter operation was received at 12:15 p.m., although it had been sent at 10:52 a.m. and delayed in transmission. According to *U.S. Marines in Vietnam: The Bitter End, 1973–1975*, Capt. William R. Melton, a company commander in 2/4, stated: "An unsubstantiated rumor circulating among the ship's company and the Marines on the *Okinawa* was that the message somehow had gotten lost in the *Blue Ridge's* message center."[9] This delay did not surprise me since the operational immediate messages had stacked up constantly during the operation.

Meanwhile, other officers and I were kept informed of the events constantly developing. This communication was critical, and also amazing, given that, as Gen. Homer Smith points out, "There was no television. You were down to radios. There were no newspapers, so the only words they got were through the grapevine."[10] In my humble opinion, the grapevine was not exactly the best source of real-time intelligence.

The more information we had, the better we could alter or supplement the planning. Since even the best laid plans change frequently in the face of the unknown, contingency planning becomes even more critical. The Marine Aircraft Group 36 (MAG-36), with Hueys, Cobras, and Sea Knights, joined ProvMAG-39 under the command of Col. Frank G. McLenon in support. The inclusion of these additional assets and the overlapping of sorties and responsibilities was an organizational nightmare under the best and most complacent of times, let alone during the collapse of a nation with the potential for civil war and riots. The command and control of all of these assets in such a confined air space was also daunting. I would equate organizing all these elements to juggling a dozen live grenades without pins in a firefight, while giving a briefing at the same time.

At 4 a.m. and later at 3:06 p.m. on April 29, 1975, NVA rockets hit Tan Son Nhut, just as the first helicopters touched down at the Alamo.[11] Marines from 2/4 disembarked and took their stations. There were 679 people awaiting inside the compound for the initial airlift. Twelve CH-53Ds from HMH-462 lifted off with their first loads. Upon reaching the sea, they were directed to the first ships available for reception, just as the outward-bound aircraft departed the fleet. The first refugees were unloaded on the *Okinawa* at 3:40 p.m.[12]

Unknown to many of us on the ground, President Ford had placed a moratorium on the evacuation. Lieutenant Colonel Harry Summers has noted:

> The only time I have ever been lied to on an operational matter was the evacuation of Saigon. When a foreign service officer who was an assistant to Graham Martin came down and looked us in the eye and lied to us, knowing it was a lie, that the evacuation was going to continue, that the helicopters were en route, that we should just stay there and wait for the helicopters to come, knowing that the president

> ## Anyone Not Evacuated Would Have Been Taken Captive
> ### —Capt. Anthony A. Wood
>
> We never really thought that the North Vietnamese were interested in harming Americans, because we were leaving the country and interfering or harming Americans would result in a suspension of the evacuation and the introduction of combat forces. Nor did we think that they really wanted to interfere with the thinning of the mission or the Vietnamese leaving the country because effectively, all future troublemakers, from the North Vietnamese point of view, were leaving the country. It was helpful to them. But we did think it was possible that they would seize the capital quickly, that we would not have completed the evacuation and a sizeable American community would remain captive.[13]

had cancelled the lift . . . something that is absolutely unforgivable . . . and only then later did we find out it had been cancelled, and were told to sneak off the landing zone, to leave people to their fate, and again, a very disgraceful performance.[14]

My area of responsibility with regard to the landings and takeoffs also saw heavy traffic. The LZ controllers' ability to communicate with the crew chiefs and guides was complicated by the inherent noise and rotor wash. Not only did these men have the great responsibility of making sure the aircraft were not overloaded, but they also had to maintain a running estimate on the remaining number of refugees and calculate how many more helo lifts would be required. Keeping an accurate count and load manifest was critical, as were the timing and accuracy of helicopter landings and takeoffs.

Despite these variable factors, the communications ensemble worked very well. In fact, it was due to prior planning with regard to the LZs that communications and security were in place to ensure the withdrawal would go smoothly. The DAO and U.S. embassy communications relay was supported by an airborne C-130 communications platform, called an ABCCC (Airborne Battlefield Command and Control Center), code named Cricket.[15] This system kept all involved abreast of the operation's flow, the numbers of evacuees taken, the number remaining, the status of the inbound and outbound helicopters, the arrival of the security force, and the status of the compound security.[16]

Another piece of information was the embassy reporting that it had over 2,000 people ready for evacuation. (Major James Kean, in charge of the Marine Security Guard, put the number at 2,500.)[17] This information was disturbing, since the roof of the embassy could hold one CH-46 and the parking lot LZ could accommodate one CH-53 at a time. General Carey then changed the plan; the *Hancock* launched most of its CH-46s at dusk, thus creating the longest and most grueling part of the operation. Also, Carey moved the recon platoon of 2/4 from the DAO to the embassy, where they joined 1st Lt. John J. Martinoli, the FAC for 1/9, as additional security supporting the MSG detachment.[18]

The NVA Had No Reason to Attack Saigon
—Lt. Col. Harry Summers

We knew they [the NVA] were there, but again, from my conversations in Hanoi, I had the feeling that they were not going to launch an all out attack on Saigon. It didn't make much sense, they didn't have to. I mean, the South Vietnamese Army was collapsing, there was no reason to destroy the very prize they'd been working to gain for the last thirty or so years, so I didn't think a direct assault on Saigon was in the making.[19]

At 10:05 p.m., DAO operational control shifted from the LZ control teams to 2/4, who were still on the ground as the security detachment. Indiscriminate mortar rounds began falling sporadically around the compound, but caused us no major concerns. These random explosions were the result of the North Vietnamese pushing into Saigon proper, which they would do the next day, April 30, 1975.

Meanwhile, outside the DAO and embassy, the crowd of indigenous personnel kept growing exponentially. Panic, like sulfur, has a unique odor, and it was heavy in the air. By 10:50 p.m., the Alamo and annex teams had been evacuated. According to Kean: "We had 2,500 evacuees already inside the compound. Then we had an Embassy staff of several hundred. This was roughly noon on the 29th when the emergency evacuation was given and there was a lag time. The helicopters started flying later in the afternoon and they were going to Tan Son Nhut."[20]

The last of the evacuees arrived on the *Okinawa* at 12:46 a.m. on April 30, 1975. However, the night was far from over. The DAO evacuation had lasted "nine hours and involved over fifty Marine Corps and Air Force helicopters," says *U.S. Marines in Vietnam: The Bitter End,*

We Did One Hell of a Job
—Gunnery Sergeant Russell Thurman

Pilots had to be rotated because of the number of hours that they had in the air. Some of these pilots were way over the safety mark, yet they continued to make those runs. . . . [T]he fact that the Marines kept their heads, I think is a real tribute to them. No one fired a shot. The fact that they flew the number of hours. . . . [W]e lost just one bird. It went into the water. There were no crashes. There were no disasters. . . . It was a very emotional time. It was like we did the right thing. We did one hell of a job . . . the largest helicopter evacuation in the world.[22]

1973–1975.[21] The DAO evacuation would set the stage for future noncombative operations in the USMC.

The embassy evacuation was a different matter. After learning that the rhythm and flow of the evacuation had tapered off, General Carey "decided to use platoons from BLT 1/9 as ground security forces in reserve."[23] Carey soon learned that Admiral Whitmire had halted all flights to the embassy, because of the length of flight operations (twelve hours for crews in most cases) and because incoming thunderstorms were reducing visibility, making it especially hard for pilots to see the properly marked LZs.[24] Whitmire had also been informed that the embassy was on fire; however, the fire was actually U.S. personnel burning documents and money.[25] By 10:50 p.m., Carey relinquished oversight of the evacuation process to Col. Alfred M. Gray.

I knew what every other Marine officer knew: by dawn Saigon would be in enemy hands. Hence, the momentum of the operation needed to be accelerated, not reduced, if anything. One of these reductions in momentum was the halting of the aforementioned helicopter

All the Pilots Deserved Medals
—Maj. James Kean

Everybody flying . . . should have been given some kind of medal because they had to come in and hover over the Embassy and helicopters really don't hover, they move around. Then they had to drop 70 feet. It's a vertical descent into this compound and then he would start stacking people on. Sitting target . . . and then there were a bunch of goons, we called them "cowboys" that were deserters and were armed and shooting at the helicopters. We could see the tracers from time to time. I would yell at Sergeant Valdez and he would send some Marines to find these guys and clean them out. I never did ask what they did, and I didn't care. But it stopped.[26]

flights due to maximum hours flown. Lieutenant General Louis H. Wilson, FMFPAC commander, was informed of this by the 7th Fleet commander. Wilson, in true Marine fashion, pulled rank, threatened charge sheets against anyone, flag officer or not, who hindered his Marine pilots as they were evacuating Marines.[27]

Valdez voiced the concern the Marines felt upon finally being evacuated: "[Once on board,] we could still see the chaos going on down there. Confusion in the embassy compound. By this time you could see North Vietnamese tanks on their way to the presidential palace. We [were] exhausted. Relieved . . . that they hadn't forgotten us, because for a moment we thought they'd really forgotten us."[28]

Had that action not been taken, there is great doubt that all the Marines still on the ground, including me, would have been saved. I was still there making sure all the adjacent locations were clear of Americans before releasing my men and myself for extraction.

Unfortunately for the remaining Saigon evacuees, the U.S. Air Force helicopters did not resume flight status after the twelve-hour session; they remained grounded with their air crews. It was up to the Marines to extract everyone else before they became guests of the NVA. "By 0215," says U.S. Marines in Vietnam: The Bitter End, 1973–1975, "one CH-46 and one CH-53 were landing at the Embassy every ten minutes."[29] Communication breakdowns continued. During the latter stages of this operation, Vietnamese men in the crowds began firing M1 Garand rifles at the helicopters.[30]

Major Kean and Master Gunnery Sergeant Valdez managed to disrupt the ad hoc sniping at the helicopters, thus reassuring the air crews in their constant and inherently dangerous business. The flights renewed their previous vigorous pace following General Wilson's direct action. The Marines flew the whole time. The air force would only fly eight hours and shut down because that was the time they would fly. They had CH-53s aboard the Hancock, and they put eight hours on them and cut them off. The Marines kept flying. These guys were strapped into the cockpit for sixteen to seventeen hours.

Once Ambassador Martin was on board his helicopter, the call was given that he was safe and on the way.[31] This information was perceived to mean that the evacuation was over, when, in fact, the Marines holding the fort at the embassy were still awaiting extraction. The oversight was finally corrected within two hours—a long two hours for a handful of Marines staring down tens of thousands of panic-stricken people pushed closer by an invading enemy army. Pandemonium had already erupted at the airport when ARVN personnel resorted to fighting and, in some cases, killing each other in their fight to be on board the evacuating aircraft.[32]

Meanwhile, the crowds at the embassy gate had started climbing over and pushing to enter the grounds, forcing the Marines to secure the area and withdraw as the last helicopters came in for the final extractions.

Although the time passed slowly, none of the Marines doubted that they would be rescued. It is a Marine tradition to leave no one behind, if at all possible. However, there were two exceptions. Through a misunderstanding in communications, the bodies of Cpl. Charles McMahon and Lance Cpl. Darwin Judge, who had been killed at the airport, were

Waiting for Our Chopper
—Maj. James Kean

The next to last bird left [with Ambassador Martin] and we told the crew chief, don't forget us.

There were 11 of us left . . . All of a sudden somebody came back and they discovered this crew chief got word to people that there's 11 guys sitting back there. We waited two and a half hours. We watched the sun come up. We watched Big Minh and his motorcade come down the street . . . And then was this lone Sea Knight comes out of the sun. The Marines all along said: "They're coming for us Maj.?" And I said: "Sure they're coming." I had no idea but I was wondering, where are they? . . . Steve Bauer set off a tear gas grenade. Of course we didn't have any gas masks so we gassed ourselves. It was a classic final act of Vietnam.[33]

Guarding the Embassy Gates
—Master Sgt. John Valdez

For a while we were opening the gates, but every time we did that masses of people kept pushing the gates and then we had to push them back out. At the end we just kept the gates closed and if somebody pointed out a Vietnamese that had to be evacuated, we would just jump on each other's shoulders, reach the top of the gate, and yank them inside the compound. We could no longer open the gates because we couldn't control them. We couldn't control the people any longer. Some people had jewelry, money. They tried bribing some of the Marines because the Marines were the ones that were doing security at the gate, but the Marines didn't take any bribes.[34]

left behind in the Seventh Day Adventist hospital, along with the casualties from a crashed C-5 Galaxy.[35] They were retrieved the following year through the efforts of Senator Edward M. Kennedy (D-Mass).[36]

I really thought that we had brought out those bodies of the two Marines who were killed, but there was a disconnect in the information that I had received. There was a lot of confusion then, as the night before Frequent Wind we were taking a lot of incoming from rockets. We were staying in trailers occupied by some of the staff from the DAO. Also, due to the peace accords, they had this group of observers from various nations, such as Poland and third world nations. They had their helicopters and living quarters, so it was a very strange arrangement.

Almost 5,000 people had been evacuated from the DAO compound under the guidance and leadership of Colonel Gray and me. An additional 978 U.S. citizens and 1,120 foreign nationals had been secured from the embassy.[37] The Marine Corps flew 1,054 flight hours and 682 sorties. One CH-46 pilot, Capt. Gerry Berry, logged eighteen and a half flight hours in a twenty-hour period.[38]

Operation Embassy Snatch
—Capt. Gerry Berry

In fact, my very first mission was called Embassy Snatch. . . . Nighttime is more difficult than daytime. We also had weather involved here. . . . We had two missions coming into Saigon. We were originally supposed to come in high because we were worried about the antiaircraft artillery and things like that. Up above a certain level you do not have to worry about that as much. . . . There's no radar separating all these helicopters flying around Saigon. . . . Every four or five hours you would have to shut down and check out your helicopter, like a ten minute stop. . . . I'd already made the call "Tiger, Tiger, Tiger" [Meaning "Ambassador Martin on board"].[39]

The Marines lost only two aircraft. The first an AH-1 Cobra piloted by Capt. John W. Bowman, Jr., and 1st Lt. David L. Androskaut, who ditched at sea during darkness after running out of fuel. Both men were recovered safely.[40] The other loss was a CH-46 Sea Knight, which crashed into the sea upon night approach to the *Hancock*. The bodies of the pilots, Capt. William C. Nystul and 1st Lt. Michael J. Shea, were not recovered, although the two enlisted crewmen survived.

Thus ended the largest and most sustained air evacuation by helicopter in history.

But the operation did not completely end with the final flights out of Saigon. Thousands of panic-stricken refugees loaded themselves into small boats and pushed out to sea, hoping for rescue. The four-day total, from start to finish, was over 40,000 persons rescued, with the April total numbering approximately 130,000.[41]

When we were getting ready to pull out, I had a platoon of Marines, about forty-five men, with myself and Al Gray, on a nighttime operation. We had already retrograded 2/4 out along with people at the embassy.

The Helicopter Crews were Heroes
—Master Sgt. John Valdez

Finally, the Embassy, along with U.S. Missions (DAO, USIS, USAID) and four American Consulates (Bien Hoa, Nha Trang, Can Tho, and Da Nang) were evacuated in April 1975; an event often associated with defeat and retreat. It is worth remembering, however, that the final hours of U.S. military involvement in South Vietnam were marked by acts of heroism. You have to love those helicopter pilots and their enlisted crews, they were magnificent. All Marines and other branches of service that participated in the evacuation were a true testimony to the saying—A Band of Brothers.[42]

The only thing I could do to enable the helo to get in and out was to take all the cars that had been left behind by the people at the DAO, place them in a big circle, and place a Marine in each car.

As we heard the helo coming, I contacted the pilot, and he responded. I told him to land in the middle of the lights. At this time, we were being rushed by South Vietnamese, particularly those civilians who had worked at headquarters, the post exchange (PX), and the club, and for the members at the DAO, the embassy, or what have you. They were all trying to get aboard that helicopter, as everyone understood by that point that it was all over. They were trying to rush me and the troops, and we did not want to harm them. We did not engage them, but shot at their feet, trying to hold them off and send them off. I managed to get the troops on the helicopter. Gray said that he was going to be the last man on board, so he could be secure in the knowledge that no one was left behind. I saluted him, saying, "Aye aye, sir," and got on board.

We had just loaded on and were just about ready to lift off when here came two guys out of nowhere, saying "Don't leave the two of us." I think it was either a captain and a warrant officer or a captain and a gunny, who had been left behind to activate the thermite, to destroy all the money, communications gear, what have you, that was left in the DAO. If memory serves, they had about 10,000 pounds of thermite packed all around this gear.

Well, they activated it and had just a few minutes to get out of there before it all went up and started burning big time. We managed to get them on, and somehow this helicopter, which was configured for twenty-something people and had over forty on board struggled. But it got off the ground. As we took off, there were thousands of people left behind. The South Vietnamese Army just quit, and the North Vietnamese were right outside the fence when we pulled out.

We had been told to develop an escape-and-evasion plan. Since I was in civilian clothes, I did not want to get caught by the North Vietnamese and have to affect that plan. We got out by the skin of our teeth, but we managed to get everyone out, except the two Marines who had been killed, McMahon and Judge. The embassy still had a couple of helicopters that were taking off. (As I was not there at that time, I cannot give any specific details first hand.)

We flew back to the *Okinawa*. We were all dead tired and had not slept since I do not know when. After landing, Maj. Ramsay Green, the S-3 (operations officer) of 2/4, took me down to his stateroom, where I cleaned up and went to sleep. We were headed to Subic Bay with all the people we had recovered, and when we arrived, we dispatched platoon-sized teams with lieutenants to sort through everything. We then reorganized everything according to specific capabilities. We remained in Subic until the USS *Mayaguez* incident; for that operation, we dispatched Ray Porter, the XO of 1/4, so they were the responders.

Approximately 730,000 personnel served in the U.S. Marine Corps from 1965 to 1975. Of that total, 500,000 served in Vietnam from Da Nang and the first large-scale deployments in 1965 to 1968, the year that saw the largest Marine involvement, with almost 86,000 Marines in country at any given time, and through the final pullout in 1975. The Corps suffered over 13,000 KIA and 88,630 WIA.

I left the DAO and Vietnam after a long, personal war. My previous desire to leave the Corps after a while and go into the civilian arena as an engineer waned. The Corps had become my life, although not in the way many may think. I was with a family, a brotherhood that had proven itself loyal to me. I would have felt disloyal not to have remained and served my country and Marines for as long as possible. Upon the withdrawal from Saigon, I became the operations officer for the 4th Marines under Col. Al Gray.

But we should not have pulled out of Vietnam at all. We had lost the strategic advantage based on what was happening in this country, not the war on the ground. In 1973 the NVA were on their asses again, whipped for the second time, bad. But we allowed them to build up again because we went into this Vietnamization program; sure, we trained the Vietnamese, but they didn't know how to fight without all of our support. We did not teach them to be real, independent infantrymen.

We ought to have thrown a big quality initiative into it. The one thing that we in the Marines did very well was the selection and assignment of our advisors. Choosing the best people for the job served many purposes, and unlike in the army, where such special assignments were considered career debilitating, in the Marines it could enhance a career. Only the best were chosen.

However, taking on a job you were suited for was not the way to get on the fast track for promotion. In the army, an officer had to get his six months in as a company commander, and hell, by the time a guy got acquainted with his company, he was being rotated, because he had his ticket punched by somebody, just like with the ribbons. The U.S. Army officers often simply did not spend enough time with their men, and by the time they finally learned their job, they were rotated. We in the Corps did not function in that manner. Our officers remained in the field with the men, learning and perfecting the job requirements and becoming damned good at the job.

The army was a different animal. They had a pack of ribbons for a company commander that had six months of success, with a Silver Star, Bronze Star, and a damned Army Commendation. When I was down at Fort Benning, they would get their Silver Stars through the guard mail. I mean, that was indicative of the culture. Therefore, we Marines dug our own foxhole.

Following that last tour of combat duty, I returned to Quantico and was then assigned to Marine Barracks in the United Kingdom. Following that service, I became commander of the 6th Marine Regiment. (That was where I met Colin Heaton, who served as a scout sniper in Surveillance and Target Acquisition Platoon [STA] in Headquarters Company, 1st Battalion, 6th Marines. This explains his great interest in chronicling my story. He said that I was a hard ass, but that I was a fair hard ass.) My last assignment was commander of the 4th Marine Division (Reinforced) and the last command was Marine Forces Reserve, which placed Sara and me in New Orleans.

When I'm asked my perspectives on the future of Vietnam, the normalization of its relations with the United States, and the impact of the war upon America today, well, I say that the military didn't lose that war. It was a strategic defeat because of the attitude in this country, but it turned out to be, for the military, a strategic win because the enemy knew we could kick their ass every day of the week. And later the Berlin Wall fell, and Communism imploded. I think Vietnamization has some positive aspects to it. I would rather have the Vietnamese being pulled our way, instead of being pulled in some other direction.

If Vietnam wants us to be their friend, good. I think that 80 percent of the people there were not alive during the Vietnam War. You have basically a whole new country. In ten or fifteen years, all the people who were associated with the war will be dead, so you're really dealing with a new Vietnam, and maybe we can scare them away from Communism. Or superimpose the Chinese model of Communism, and they will ultimately become a pretty free people. So we may win before it's over with. Capitalism always wins, and they like capitalism over there. Every kid has a computer, and they like their cell phones, TVs, and really love their motorcycles.

They were introduced enough to America during the war and subsequently through the travel of people going back, including Vietnamese who live in this country and invest a lot over there. So I do believe that capitalism is going to prevail again over there. They want a better life; they're out of the bush now. Like I said, 80 percent of the people do not know a damned thing about the Vietnam War, other than a few shattered churches and schools. They do not retain the same sense of identity for the past like we do. I mean, you should go around and look at their monuments, graves, and graveyards. They do a very poor job of keeping them up. Look at the river on the Ben Hai where a big freedom assembly took place after the war. The place now looks like a trash dump.

I have often reflected upon my many missions and actions. This is not to say that I ever regretted any of my decisions, given the circumstances at the time. However, I could not be human if I did not second guess my actions, analyze the results, and think about how I would perform such actions again if placed in the same circumstance and how I could perhaps do a better job. I think that reflection, even if one reflects upon a complete success, can lead to a more thorough planning model in the future. If we learn from our mistakes, that is called progress.

When we do not learn from our successes, we have a tendency to fall into a state of complacency. This I always refused to do, and I refused to allow my Marines to dwell in the comfort zone. No matter how well they performed, whether on a PT run or on a field exercise, I both praised a good job and hammered home the errors when mistakes were made. Regardless of how well the men did, there was always room for improvement, and hard training and attention to detail are the benchmarks of eventual success in all walks of life. I thought about Saigon in particular. Dai Do is a given. I feel comfortable in the knowledge that if I had to do these two missions all over again, I cannot really think of many things that I would do differently, given the same set of circumstances.

The Marines carried the day, and that is the simple truth. Thus, America ended its involvement in the longest continuous conflict in its history. After hundreds of thousands of Vietnamese, almost sixty thousand American, and even more allied dead, the final act was one of retreat. As thousands clambered to overrun the embassy, DAO, and airport to escape, the final evacuation of an ambassador and thousands of military and civilian personnel fell upon the shoulders of a very few and very proud Marines. I consider myself lucky, and I thank God that I was allowed to be one of them.

Left: Newly commissioned 2nd Lt. James E. Livingston. *James E. Livingston*
Right: First Lieutenant Dave Jones as a platoon leader in 1967. *Dave Jones*

Livingston on sea duty, 1967. *James E. Livingston*

BLT 2/4 situation briefing in a destroyed Buddist temple in the village of Mai Xa Chanh, March 1968. Brigadier General William Chip, commanding general (CG), 9th Marine Amphibious Force (seated center with helmet), briefing officer Capt. Richard Murphy, intelligence officer (S-2), BLT 2/4 (kneeling), Capt. James E. Livingston, CO, Echo 2/4 (seated far left), and various 9th MAB staff officers. *William Weise*

Left: Major General Rathvon McClure Tompkins, CG of 3rd Marine Division, March 1968. *William F. Weise* Right: Captain Livingston, exhausted after several days of fighting at Ving Quan Thuong during March 1968. "Jim Williams and I received Silver Stars. I was nicked by an AK-47 during the assault. This was really my first Purple Heart, but I was not concerned at the time; I just wanted to kill the NVA." *James E. Livingston*

Sergeant Major "Big John" Malnar (left) and Lt. Col. William F. Weise during Operation Night Owl. Malnar would be killed in action on May 2, 1968. *William Weise*

Marines of BLT 2/4 clearing the bank of the Cua Viet River, April 30, 1968. *William Weise*

Marines debarking from an H-34 helicopter, which was always an interesting way to get into a fight. *U.S. National Archives*

Lieutenant Colonel Weise was placed with the other wounded at the river for medical evacuation on May 2, 1968. *William Weise*

BLT 2/4 Marines loading on LCM-8 after the Battle of Dai Do on May 3, 1968. This was the way most Marines were evacuated. *William Weise*

Left: The open grave Livingston slept in during the Battle of Dai Do, May 2–3, 1968. *Steve Wilson* Right: Captain Lane Forehand, S-4 (intelligence) officer for BLT 2/4. *William Weise*

BLT 2/4 memorial service for the fallen, held on the USS *Iwo Jima*. *U.S. National Archives*

President Richard Nixon with Captain Livingston, wife Sara, daughter Kim, mother Ruth, and brother Donald at the White House, 1970.
James E. Livingston

Left: Livingston with his Medal of Honor. *James E. Livingston*
Right: Colonel Livingston as regimental CO of 6th Marines.
James E. Livingston

Livingston swearing in his daughter, Kim, at Annapolis in 1991.
James E. Livingston

President George Bush with Livingston. *James E. Livingston*

CHAPTER 12

The Philippines

The greatest thing about freedom is that you never realize how valuable a commodity it is until you have lost it. If nothing else, it is the most important thing in the world to fight and die for.

—Col. James. N. Rowe

THE HISTORY OF THE Communist influence within the many islands and provinces of the Philippine Islands dates back to the 1960s when the insurgency was in its infancy and the Maoist Communist Party was formed by Bernabe Buscayno (alias Commander Dante). The Communist Party of the Philippines (CPP) split in 1969, and the National People's Army (NPA) was formed as a result. Their ranks grew from about 2,000 in 1972 to over 26,000 by 1983.

The repressive regime of Ferdinand Marcos had given teeth to the Marxist call for a people's uprising. Peasants, political dissidents, and the disaffected were always the prime targets of Communist recruitment since the early days of the movement within the Soviet Union and later within China.

Marcos had made many enemies, and the support he received from the United States made the Communists think the United States kept him in power; hence, their suffering was caused by the United States. The NPA had targeted his supporters (among others) for years, earning it a place on the U.S. State Department's Foreign Terrorist Organizations list. There had been little in the way of national programs to stem the growth of the CPP and its offspring, the NPA. Like a cancer, the CPP spread across the nation. In 1983 it was determined that Communists controlled 2 to 3 percent of the villages within the country, and some 6,000 full-time guerrillas were harbored in these villages.

However, there were some successes, such as the killing of over a dozen terrorists in 1976–77, the arrests of Jose Maria Sison and Bernabe Buscayno in the 1970s, and the capture of the former CPP party chairman Rodolfo Salas and NPA chief Romulo Kintanar in 1988. Kintanar was allowed to escape shortly after his capture in 1988, and several soldiers were indicted for complicity. The arrest of Japanese Red Army leader Hiroshi Sensui, believed to be setting up a satellite terrorist base in Manila, was another success, and he was deported to Japan, where he had charges pending. At that time, the Communist strength was estimated to be at 24,000 to 26,000 personnel. This was a decline from the previous decade.

The removal of Marcos and the election of Corazon Aquino seemed to refute the Communist paradigm and knocked the CPP's planned reforms off their axis. In fact, Aquino's election with U.S. support had come as a shock to the NPA and CPP (which boycotted the February 1986 election), as her administration openly discussed massive reforms within the police and military, as well as amnesty negotiations with the guerrillas.

The new face of Philippine politics was what the nation needed, but the hard-line Communists were intent on destroying anything politically out of alignment with their warped ideology. Aquino and the Americans still had to go, despite estimates stating that the NPA support had dropped slightly, from approximately 25,000 to less than 20,000 personnel, following her election.

The NPA launched a massive program of terror and financial extortion, forcing the people and businesses to pay a special tax to fund the Communists. Those who refused were often killed, sometimes with their entire families. The threat of regional, let alone national, political instability was clear. The Philippine government did not have the resources with which to arm, staff, and pay their police and armed forces to effectively counter the terrorist threat; therefore, the U.S. government provided additional funding, including approximately $180,000,000 per year on average, as of 1983, for military and economic aid alone, and scheduled increases of around $481,000,000 per year in all types of funding by 1990–91. U.S. federal law prohibited the United States from funding the local police forces that were usually the first line of defense for foreign nationals against attack. Corruption was always a problem, and thwarting that took more than just money. It took initiative and dedication on the part of the very police and military who were being bribed and persuaded.

Under Celso Minguez—the founder of the Communist movement in the area of Bicol in Luzon Province—and other leaders scattered throughout the island country, the insurgents were getting bolder.

In February of 1987, the sixty-day cease fire, in which Aquino offered land, jobs, and pardons to guerrillas in an effort to diffuse the situation, ended, and the NPA again launched its program of terror, although it had been weakened by defections. Murders, mutilations, and tortures once again became the norm. Mass graves were discovered, and foreign businesses began to abandon the nation, causing higher unemployment rates. This was what the Communists wanted. Happy, healthy, employed, and relatively safe populations do not need revolutionaries. They have too much to lose. Therefore, if you do not have poverty, instability, and mayhem, you create it.

Aquino implemented a new counterinsurgency plan, which ordered military units and various supporting agencies to infiltrate and remove guerrillas from various regions, establish mobile security patrols to prevent their return, foster support for the government, and create local militia and police units to maintain law and order. What was also needed was a good hearts-and-minds campaign to bring the villagers, mostly uneducated and paranoid, into the comfort zone. If they trusted the government, success was assured. If they did not, then the entire operation was a waste of time and money.

The old plan under Marcos had placed cordons and embargos and launched random search-and-destroy operations, often without discrimination, thus alienating much of the population that should have been protected and cultivated for greater support. The great disparity between the very wealthy and the impoverished was the catalyst; if there had been a solid middle class, the Communists would have never had a chance. In 1987 the United States began deploying Special Operations teams within the country to help train and support the Filipino military.

From October 1988 to April 1989, I was a colonel and served as the senior Marine representative to the Joint U.S. Military Assistance Command in the Philippines, later serving alongside U.S. Army Special Forces advisor Col. James Nicholas Rowe of 1st Special Forces Group, the senior army representative. Sadly, within two weeks of my departure, Rowe was murdered in an ambush while in his vehicle on the way to the Joint U.S. Military Assistance Group (JUSMAG) in Manila, an incident still mired in controversy.

The American officers knew there was a delicate balance between necessary offensive American and Filipino military operations, and the Philippine government's need to project some measure of control over the internal discord. I found myself in a unique (although not unfamiliar) position of diplomat and warrior. The difficulties of balancing this military role as an advisor with the nuances of diplomatic delicacy cannot be underestimated.

During my tenure, U.S. forces operated within the country to augment the local and national Filipino forces. Intelligence gathering and hearts-and-minds operations, just as in Vietnam were the primary methods utilized. The reputation of two nations and the survival of the Philippines were at stake. The Filipino people had suffered in many ways. We were intent upon reducing, if not, in fact, ending that suffering, as well as securing and protecting American military and global economic assets.

The year 1988 saw the Filipino military launch large-scale air and ground assault missions in Mindoro, displacing the many mountain Mangyan tribes who had always wanted autonomy from Manila. One of the sparks was the comment made by Filipino Gen. Honesto Isleta during a March 2, 1987, BBC interview: "On the ground war, I would say that if only there would not be this sword of Damocles, of human rights, over our heads; and perhaps if we look at these NPAs as . . . foreigners . . . in our country, not as Filipinos, then we could go all out.

To heck with human rights."[1]

Christian missions were filled with the Mangyan people trying to escape the war zone, and March refugee estimates totaled 350 persons throughout Mindoro. Most of these people left their homes after being forewarned of the bombardments. Many of the Mangyans gave information on NPA strongholds and camps, making the military action more effective. The success of these operations forced a massive, Stalinist-style purge within the Communist ranks to root out perceived informers and traitors; paranoia had been instilled and was thus a great weapon of psychological warfare. The CPP and NPA were soon killing each other in a frightful fratricidal frenzy.

The major bases, such as Clark Air Force Base and Subic Bay, had been consistently hardened against terrorist assaults, following the murders of several American military personnel in 1987. This increased security at the bases was what brought me into working closely Col. James Nicholas "Nick" Rowe, who, after spending time as the commander of the 1st Special Operations Warfare Training Battalion at Fort Bragg, North Carolina, was assigned as the chief advisor of the U.S. Army's division of the JUSMAG in May 1987. The division's function was working in conjunction with the Central Intelligence Agency, assisting the Philippine military and intelligence organizations, as well as developing an infiltration system within the NPA.

The NPA had been responsible for dozens of murders and kidnappings of American military personnel, especially U.S. plants within the terrorist movement, including American civilians and foreign nationals living within the country over the previous decade. They had specialized in targeting business owners and missionaries. The threat escalated from the 1970s through the 1980s, reaching critical mass by the time I arrived.

Rowe had gathered credible information that the NPA was planning major operations, including assassinations of key Philippine and American military and security officials. Rowe also had credible information that the NPA had gathered data identifying CIA and other operatives in the country, creating a hit list. From the investigation since then, it appears that the Defense Intelligence Agency (DIA) and U.S. State Department's Intelligence and Research Bureau were duly informed, yet they ignored the warnings. In fact, the State Department had been monitoring NPA's counterintelligence efforts for about a year before Rowe's warnings, which were developed from information his own intelligence network had given to all departments in February 1989.

The most likely reason for the apathetic approach from the DIA and State Department was that pulling CIA operatives from their covert operations would raise a warning flag to the NPA that their plans had been uncovered. The CIA had effectively penetrated the ranks of the NPA since the early 1980s, although to what degree it had is still classified. Rowe had apparently even informed the CIA and DIA specifically that he himself was a target; he had a high profile because the story of his spectacular escape from Viet Cong captivity in 1968, after over five years of captivity, was well known. Rowe was a legend, and that made him a Communist target. In fact, Rowe's report to Washington stated that he was either number one or two on that assassination list.

It is believed by some sources (although they cannot be named due to national security issues and at their requests) that the Communists believed Rowe to be a CIA trainer and handler of agents responsible for infiltrating the NPA. This information has never been confirmed or denied officially. The great problem was that I was also a member of the mission, which placed me and other senior officers in danger. It is unconfirmed, but plausible and believable, that I was at the top of the death list. The Communists had openly declared that they had wanted to kill at least one high-profile Vietnam veteran, and we had two in country.

Other senior military commanders and I worked to inhibit the insurgency, which was (and still is) multifaceted. The Filipino government and population saw first hand the great effort exerted by the United States. Stemming the flow of anti-government action was not easy; however, it was being accomplished. The anti-government Communist influence up until the 1990s has subsequently been replaced by the fundamentalist Islamic movement in the region today.

Part of this blatant disregard for the safety of the human assets was ironic; six months before Rowe's death, the DIA had been receiving reports of Cuban assistance to the NPA in Luzon, and that the intent of this assistance was to locate and eliminate any and all CIA assets. If true, this information would have changed the entire dynamic of the counterinsurgency operations. This information, if corroborated, would also confirm the extreme personal danger all of the senior advisory staff were in.

It had been reported that Rowe was in Greece in 1987, working with Delta Force. There had been a credible report that Vietnamese agents had located him in Greece, and that he was targeted even then for assassination. Hence his extraction and reassignment to the Philippines. Former 5th Special Forces Group commander Col. Robert Mountel has stated that Rowe "was a target when he went over there because of his dealings with the North Vietnamese and his time as a prisoner. They had him on their list."[2] No U.S. agency will discuss this issue.

I had managed to coordinate many civil-defense and government-relief operations within the country, supported by the local police and military contingents. Well-fed, educated, employed, and relatively safe populations do not make or support revolutions. This was clearly understood, and establishing some semblance of stability and support for the people was at the core of perceived governmental legitimacy and success.

I understood this situation very well; it was the same as the situation in Vietnam. The geography had changed, but the problem had remained the same. During my tour of duty, terror attacks and economic destruction were greatly reduced in the major population centers, and even the hard-to-reach and -control rural areas were more peaceful. The regular presence of proper civil and military authority, trained and educated in the art of human handling, paid off handsomely.

The success could be measured, and once again this was a job I felt good about. However, as with any successful mission, there is also tragedy to some degree. As stated previously, within two weeks of my departure, Rowe was ambushed. His chauffer-driven staff car was riddled with bullets fired from hooded assailants in a small white car that pulled alongside his vehicle during a traffic stop in Manila on April 21, 1989. The .45-caliber handgun and M-16 fire riddled the vehicle, and Rowe was immediately killed by a headshot. The May 1989 issue of *U.S. Veteran News and Report* stated that Vietnamese Communists had placed a contract on Rowe and probably collaborated with the NPA on the killing. Two months after Rowe's death, Minguez and the NPA claimed responsibility, stating they "wished to send a message to the American people" by Rowe's murder. Minguez said, "We want to let them know that their [United States] government is making the Philippines another Vietnam." [3] What was not stated (and was perhaps unknown) was that Rowe was not alone on the death list. I had probably just escaped assassination and was completely unaware of it.

There were two arrests following the murder. Juanito Itaas and Donato Continente were identified as being in the vehicle by witnesses who apparently knew them. Continente was released from prison in 2005, after sixteen years. Itaas is still in prison at the national penitentiary in Muntinlupa, serving a life sentence.

Apparently, due to budgetary constraints and congressional cuts, the Defense Attaché System (DAS) had eliminated 72 percent of its vehicle budget, so it did not provide armored vehicles for the operatives in the country. The budget cuts eventually caused the removal of the entire DAS with the exception of a small crew that performed rudimentary tasks. This budget reduction may have cost Rowe his life. It certainly reduced the effectiveness of the intelligence-gathering operations.

By the end of 1989, over a hundred Filipino businessmen, security members, and government officials had been assassinated as well. This time period saw the rise of the Moro National Liberation Front (MNLF), a radical Islamic collective that continues to operate to this day. Our actions in working with the government, along with Rowe and others, proved that the terrorists could be dealt with on several levels. The military application is only as effective as the internal political success in handling the needs and desires of the population. Over time, the Filipino people have come to realize that their interests lie in mutual cooperation, as opposed to internal discord and sectarian and religious unrest.

It seemed that we had once again left an indelible mark of excellence in our wake, yet the future would prove that I, at least, was not yet finished with tackling massive problems.

CHAPTER 13

The Twilight Years

If you think being wounded is bad, try being stupid, or dead.
—Col. Gregory Boyington, USMC

AFTER I WAS PROMOTED to brigadier general on June 10, 1988, I had some interesting assignments. First, I was appointed Deputy Director for Operations at the National Military Command Center in Washington, D.C., or J-3. The only thing of any major consequence occurred when I was in the meeting with General Colin Powel, then chairman of the Joint Chiefs of Staff. We were sitting around the table as he was working out the plans with President George H. W. Bush for Operation Blue Spoon, (later renamed Operation Just Cause), which was the invasion of Panama in 1989. Shortly after that, I stayed around the Pentagon for a while and monitored that operation.

My next command, perhaps the most notable of these twilight years, was at the Marine Corps Air Ground Combat Center at Twentynine Palms, California. I worked on the Desert Warfare Training Program, a more intense and realistic training program for desert warfare, and we converted the Marine Corps from the M-60 main battle tank to the M-1 Abrams. You must keep in mind that at that time we were in the first phase of Operation Desert Shield, just prior to the ground war in 1991, which was Operation Desert Storm. This was where I was first introduced to the Marine Reserves, with which I had never had any previous relationship. I learned to appreciate and respect them immensely.

This assignment allowed me the opportunity to become instrumental in changing the way the Corps approached combat training. This episode of training Marines to go into Desert Storm is one of the highlights and most fond memories of my career. Twentynine Palms was one of those places that took a while to grow on you, but I grew to love the base and enjoyed the greater community outside the gate. They were great people.

Following this assignment, I commanded the 1st Marine Expeditionary Brigade at Kaneohe Bay, Hawaii. Sara had already gone over to the islands, and so that was an easy transition. The main job was bringing the brigade back to Hawaii from deployment in the Persian Gulf in 1991 and getting it reconstituted and organized. Colonel Wayne Rawlins was the regimental commander, and he had worked for me as my operations officer when I was G-3 (division operations officer) at 2nd Marine Division. He later worked for me when I was commanding officer of 6th Marines, where I had four battalions. Rawlins later became a major general and is an outstanding officer. He is one of the finest combat Marines I have known.

On July 8, 1991, I was promoted to major general. My final assignment on active duty as a new two-star general was taking command of the Marine Forces Reserve, which included the Marine Service Support Group, located in Kansas City, and the 4th Fleet Service Support Group and 4th Marine Air Wing, 4th Marine Division, all in New Orleans, Louisiana. I have to admit that I did not know a damned thing about the reserves, but I saluted and took my marching orders. Upon receiving this tasking, I also became one of the dominant forces in the restructuring of Marine Forces Reserve through October 1994, under the auspice of then-commandant of the Marine Corps, Gen. Carl Mundy.

We were able to put our reserves together and enhance our operational capability and readiness, and I was real tough on them. My objective was to bring them up to speed in every area, ensuring that, at a moment's notice, they were ready to go anywhere in the world when the regular active-duty Marines needed them for operational support. I think we were able to accomplish that task. I know that we developed an effective Marine air/ground team that was able to do whatever the commandant required of us, and of me, in order to augment and support the regular forces, whatever the requirements were. I think the reserves were able to do a great job in Desert Storm, but I think we were able to move them to the next level by this consolidation of forces. I think it was a very good strategic move on the part of Carl Mundy to bring that about, and the results speak for themselves, even if you look at today's current conflict.

I also continued my education beyond the bachelor of arts in civil engineering I'd received from Auburn. I completed the masters in security policy from the United States Air War College and a masters of management from Webster University. I have always believed that active-duty Marines should continue their education, whenever possible. This is very difficult for Marines in the combat-arms MOS (military occupational specialty), but we have the best educated group of Marines, and the best educated entire military as a whole, in the history of the world. I think that this emphasis on education speaks volumes about our military and says that we are able to attract educated and motivated individuals.

Following my retirement in 1995, I was appointed to the New Orleans Levee Board on March 5, 1997, by then-governor M. J. "Mike" Foster, by direction of the honorable Fox McKeithen, Louisiana secretary of state. My contributions included planning and updating the levees in the city and coordinating city and state organizations in conjunction with the federal government, including the Army Corps of Engineers.

While on the levee board, I tried to hold everyone accountable for their actions and their failures. I opened the books on them; I made them redo their budgets, as they were throwing money away, and I went through every dollar with them. We kept expenditures down, and I pissed off all the good old boys raking in the dough. So there was a lot of frustration coming my way, and I broke their bubble a little bit. I think my biggest frustration, in the end, was that we weren't able to come up with a technique to seal a fractured levee before my wife and I left New Orleans. I was always convinced—and told the Army Corps of Engineers and all the people there—that we should come up with a quick-response technique. I was concerned about terrorists being able to use just basic dynamite to fracture a levee and flood the whole city.

I suggested we utilize the National Guard helicopters next door, at the Lakefront Airport; they had UH-60 Blackhawks, and I was encouraging the National Guard to position large sandbags where the Blackhawks could pick them up and drop them in at a breach at a levee, which ultimately is what happened. It was very frustrating to me that we did not get in and finish that plan. I was leaving, but I pushed that plan to the wall. When I left, I did not reach back and ask "Did you do that?" But if they would have followed through on my suggestions and implemented some common sense, they would have been much quicker to respond to those two breaches in the levee that occurred during Hurricane Katrina. I think everyone has a piece of the blame here.

The City of New Orleans was probably uppermost to blame, because of the lack of leadership on the part of Mayor Ray Nagin, but the state was also very much to blame. The disaster resulted not from a lack of capabilities, assets, and money; at the end of the day, it was purely a lack of leadership that caused the disaster. People blamed the president and the federal government, but the right people have not been blamed or held accountable. Nagin, Louisiana governor Kathleen Blanco, and certain elements on the levee board leadership should have been held responsible and taken to task. There was an epidemic of corruption, complacency, and lack of common sense, and it cost lives, but they are not willing to admit that. These local politicians would rather blame the federal government than plan ahead and take personal and professional responsibility for their actions. Ironically, they blamed the same government that they expected to continue feeding them tax dollars.

Each and every one of those people in the city and state government should be held accountable, but they never will be. If they were held to the same standard as the leadership as those at Enron, they would all have been indicted on multiple charges, including negligent homicide. But those who placed these leaders in their positions, lined their own pockets, and even continue to keep these defective leaders in power will see to it that there is nothing more than consistent disinformation about the disaster events, while deflecting anything resembling responsibility from themselves. When people complain about Hurricane Katrina, they somehow always fail to address the millions of dollars the federal government gave the city in order to prevent such a disaster from happening and where all that money went. Strangely enough, that piece of information never seems to be relevant, and those who could answer that question are always out of town or out of answers. They certainly will not return telephone calls. They should at the very least be out of a job, if not incarcerated.

I have always liked being busy, so I also served New Orleans in many voluntary capacities over the years. I tried to help bring some organization, logic, and discipline to the police department while part of the newly founded New Orleans Police Foundation (now the New Orleans Police and Justice Foundation). Needing competent assistance, I brought in Col. Terry Ebbert, a Navy Cross Marine from Vietnam, as well as John Cassabon, a great guy, to help. Although the crime rate in New Orleans was just absolutely horrendous—annual homicide rates peaked in 1994 at 421, the highest per capita in the nation—and the police force was having all kinds of difficulties, Cassabon and Ebbert brought quality leadership to the foundation. As Wilma Bonvillian (Colin Heaton's aunt, who worked with me in New Orleans) can attest, just doing things every day was a struggle. Admittedly, I had mixed emotions about the success of this operation. I think we had some success, but not near the success I wanted, because we did not get the political support we were looking for from former Mayor Marc Morial and the leadership of New Orleans. I found that corruption ran deep, and the people I knew I could trust were just outnumbered by those I couldn't. Self-serving and mismanaged government was too deeply entrenched; long-serving personalities were difficult to work with and almost impossible to rely upon.

I also helped establish the University of New Orleans Technology Center, and I was instrumental in working with the late Dr. Stephen Ambrose on creating the National D-Day Museum, which has become the official national World War II museum. I am still a trustee for the museum. Ambrose had asked me to help him with the museum, and although I certainly procrastinated on that for a while, I finally agreed to help. We were able to successfully raise money, buy the initial facility that the museum is currently headquartered in, and get it underway.

I spent a couple of years as chairman of the museum board, but the heavy lifting was done by Col. Howard Lovinggood, USMC, a man I dearly love and who got it all together. He had worked for me as the G-3 of the 4th Marine Division, and I activated him to help. He was one of the principle developers of the Infantry Officers Course up at Quantico, with John Kelly and some other folks. Howard was sort of my guy Friday, helping me obtain all of the necessary start-up requirements. He and I left about the same time. Then we had Nick Mueller, who later took over the museum and is still doing a great job today. I stayed on the board, remaining engaged in the activities. Today it is the official United States National World War II Museum, and the great leadership in place has allowed it to prosper.

My personal crusade against the inability of the Orleans Parish School Board to properly manage state and federal funding for the benefit of students did not endear me to those I perceived as weak and lacking moral courage. Something needs to be done about that board; four or five people should not be allowed to destroy the lives of so many New Orleaneans. That school system was the greatest failure I have ever seen. Only the parochial and private schools were educating anyone, as they were beyond the corruption and incompetent influence of the city and parish.

My additional services included membership in the Business Council of New Orleans, the New Orleans and River Region Chamber of Commerce, and the Metropolitan Crime Commission. I have also been active in commercial and financial real estate services in New Orleans, serving as executive vice president of Columbus Properties, LLC, and on several boards, including as vice chairman of First Bank and Trust, Peoples Bank of Amite, and Inovus Incorporated. I also sit on a number of voluntary boards, such as the Boy Scouts of America, the American Red Cross, and the Louisiana State University Medical Foundation.

While I remained active in many roles politically and in business, most of my efforts were geared towards assisting the military, especially veterans in the current war on terror. I have been a presidential appointee to the Committee to Review Veterans Benefits, and I was very active in attempting to have elements of the Department of Homeland Security based in New Orleans. I have my supporters, although I also have my detractors. So be it. I was also a very outspoken advocate of limiting, if not completely preventing, the many military base closures in the New Orleans region. I didn't speak out against the closures just because of the jobs that would be lost in these areas. These bases were critical to our national security, not to mention the overall national economy. I simply applied common sense to the situation.

Although I clearly saw the city as having massive problems politically, socially, and financially, I also saw the city as having great potential. Cutting across racial and economic lines, I always strove to make integration and solvency a reality. Just as when I was a combat commander, I did not relent in my attacks against an enemy or what I perceived as injustice and incompetence from local, state, and federal politicians. If you want to hold those positions, you must be expected to accept accountability.

People came to know me as being someone who had certain expectations, and I was not going to bend on those expectations. I think New Orleans was much cleaner when I left than when I arrived. It was much more organized and much more focused. I was not going to put up with any horseshit. We had our fights, I put my stakes in the ground, and people knew where those stakes were. I may bend a little on small things, but on the major expectations, I was totally unyielding. I always have been. However, despite that, New Orleans was a town that I grew to dearly love, for all its warts, and I enjoyed my time there despite the difficulties. Finally, Sara and I sold out and decided to move to Mount Pleasant, South Carolina, where we live today.

In my retirement. I have worked with the Marine Corps Scholarship Foundation, which is a 501(c)(3) nonprofit organization helping the children of Marines and navy corpsmen receive college educations. These scholarships are made possible through the charitable donations of good Americans, who see the need, if not the privilege, to assist these young men and women. These funds are awarded to deserving sons and daughters of Marines, former Marines, and those naval personnel who served with them. Particular attention and consideration are given to those children whose parent was killed or wounded in action. This great endeavor is possible only when the American people recognize the service and sacrifice of the men and women who wear the uniform of United States Marines.

I firmly believe that Americans are the most generous, caring, and conscientious people in the world. That is not polemic, as our annual overseas contributions to developing nations and our own domestic charities clearly demonstrate these qualities. I am proud to be involved with such a wonderful organization as the Marine Corps Scholarship Foundation, and I can think of few others that are so worthy. I just wish that we spent more of our charitable dollars on our veterans and other deserving Americans, as opposed to throwing away good money into third-world black holes. No other nation on the planet would assist us financially or with charitable money, even if they could afford to.

I have also been involved somewhat with the Wounded Warriors Project and groups that assist that very fine organization. Men and women who serve in uniform do so with the knowledge that they may be placed in harm's way. Our nation was originally founded upon the concept of citizen service, and that sense of duty continues this day. Our nation, indeed the entire world, has prospered due to the willingness of young Americans to provide the manpower, materiel, and dedication necessary to maintain our freedom and to establish freedom for millions around the world.

By definition, our volunteer military has proven, by the service of our brave men and women, that our national identity, freedoms, and security will be forever maintained. Our veterans and active duty service members have been the template for all free nations to emulate. They are the guardians of our nation and its people. Their actions throughout our history, as well as their service today in the war on terrorism, have instilled confidence among our current and potential allies worldwide. Freedom-loving nations around the globe are keenly aware that when their freedom and security is threatened, whenever possible, Americans will assist their nations, support humanitarian relief missions; remove those threats, both internal and external; restore the sanctity, integrity, and hegemony of their societies; and set right that which threatens their security.

Many of these brave men and women, over 4,000 and counting, have been killed in our current war on terror. Many thousands more have been wounded, some grievously, while selflessly serving our nation. There is no greater honor than to serve one's nation, and there is no greater tribute to that service than assisting those who are in the most need—the fine people who have served so well and those who today assist our wounded veterans. These wounded warriors are truly the most deserving of our personal efforts and collective gratitude.

The veterans of the United States of America have been and continue to be the standard-bearers of our great nation. Our veterans have shouldered the greatest responsibilities of any nation in history. They have not only secured our own nation against foreign invasion, but they also have promoted free will around the world. Our military has liberated continents, given freedom to hundreds of millions of people, and educated and given hope to generations, and that legacy also continues today. Security through vigilance, freedom through service, success through sacrifice, and the belief that, if something is worth having, it is worth fighting and possibly dying for are concepts well known to Americans and second nature to Marines.

As an old wounded warrior, I can remember clearly the generosity of many people who I did not even know. These people did not know me, either. However, despite this fact, they were very friendly and compassionate and, to the best of their abilities, assisted us veterans returning. They saw in us those who had served and paid a heavy price, and I remember feeling humbled by their generosity and compassion. In most other nations in the world, wounded veterans are discarded. They are seen as a burden, to be placed out of sight and out of mind. The wounded are often viewed as reminders of military failure or, even if their military efforts were successful, of the horrors of conflict. These other nations do not share our value systems.

In the very near future, our nation will experience the highest number of veterans returning home from combat since Vietnam.

While politicians may debate and make promises to assist our veterans, the mantle of responsibility to help these wounded warriors has been taken up by others. If the people who read this book take away only one thing, I hope it is the belief that we, as a nation, owe a great debt and have a moral responsibility to assist those who need it due to their service protecting us. This is my personal plea. No one person will solve these veterans' problems. However, millions of us can make their lives better, and personally I feel they deserve it.

Obviously, I have my own perspective on many of the methodologies currently employed by the federal government, the military, and even the media, especially regarding the intense scrutiny of ongoing military actions and decisions in Iraq and Afghanistan. I understand from my time in Vietnam that no one is perfect, and we will all make mistakes, mostly associated with the emotions of the day.

For example, when I was in Vietnam, there was a battalion commander and a couple of other people relieved of their authority because of the decisions they made. Whether right or wrong, it is perception that mattered. In my mind, perception was simply second guessing. What I looked for was results. Did the action and its aftermath justify the effort and expense? Was there a positive lesson to be taken from the experience that would assist in future planning and war making? Did the leader actively operate in the field with his men, experiencing the same hardships and dangers, leading from the front, smelling the gun smoke, and not issuing orders from the rear?

Any commander who cannot answer yes to those questions should be relieved. The reality is this: a well-fed, comfortable leader sleeping in a warm bed out of harm's way cannot understand the actions and motivations, or even the thought processes, of a starving, sick, exhausted grunt sleeping on the frozen ground in a hostile environment. The leader must share the hardship and base his decisions upon first-hand experience, not theory or after-action reports alone. Save theory for the classroom. Practical application of real-world experience and logic are what make Marines different from most people. A man issuing orders from the comfort zone of a rear area, unless he has extensive field combat time, is nothing more than bureaucrat. That also makes him a dangerously misinformed person.

The great thing about the Marine Corps is that we tend to weed out these inadequate types during selection training, so only the best leaders and the most competent officers and NCOs end up leading our warriors. Mistakes are to be made in training, not in battle. Rapid assessment of a changing situation, working through the fog of war, and lucid contingency planning mean the difference between life and death. Cemeteries are filled with stupid people, as well as the unlucky. We eliminate the stupid factor from the equation starting the first day of boot camp. Being unlucky is up to God.

Some of the actions reported by the press in the current war remind me of what happened in Vietnam, where Marines and soldiers, on rare occasions, perhaps went over top in their activities against the enemy. Of course, there are limits; there are rules even in war, even in asymmetrical warfare against an illegal enemy, which is what we face today. But when you see kids next to you get killed, you build up some emotions inside of you that have to be released. Sometimes they are released properly, and in some cases, they are not. Some of those who are not a part of that process simply do not understand what it's like. Therefore, I do not care what a pundit's opinion is, and neither should the American public. I can assure you the grunt in the mud will not give a damn either.

There are many commanders today (and a lot of people in Washington, behind the scenes) making decisions who have never had a round shot at them. That is a bad recipe for long-range leadership. I completely understand the necessity of civilian leadership over the military. That is what prevents us become developing into a totalitarian dictatorship. Like Benito Mussolini said, "If I have a choice between 10,000 guns or 10,000 votes, I will take the guns. The votes will come later." Civilians must govern the military, but the military should be able to conduct its own operations, within political reason.

Unlike the fascist and communist states we have defeated, our nation is still and will always be a nation of law, respect, and opportunity, and we must maintain that image of integrity, hard work, and fairness that has defined us for over two hundred years. That is the reason why the global migrant community flocks to our shores. I do not seeing them beating down the doors of Chinese or North Korean embassies, wishing to emigrate to those countries.

However, the civilian leaders, once they have committed our forces into war, must allow the military commanders on the ground, not those behind a desk in the Pentagon, to conduct tactical operations unimpeded. Strategic military decisions can be made by the joint chiefs and the president, after evaluating the latest intelligence and focusing upon the long-range battlefield objectives. Military leaders should leave the long-range, post-conflict political strategy to the politicians and stay true to the tactical and strategic military objectives.

What we are again learning in this war in Iraq is that technology is not what wins the day; we have become more and more technologically sophisticated, and the threat we face is able to adapt and react to that. And how are they reacting to it? With human bombs. How do you stop a human bomb with technology? You cannot; you stop it with a bullet. Who is squeezing the trigger? The young infantryman. Therefore, the problems we have currently experienced are simple to correct: we went to Iraq to win this war with technology, and all we did was hit a beehive; we stirred it up, but we did not kill the queen.

The current military method employed is too soft. Some people think we need to go out and buy another airplane, but it's not about the hardware. I would say we are beginning to lose our mental toughness. I see people who are not physically and mentally in shape to handle the current crisis, and they do not appear to be ready to fight. They look for the soft way out, and you saw that happen in Iraq. The first thing you see is troops gravitating toward a McDonald's or Domino's Pizza and a soft bed and television and the recreation room. They want to maintain their constant familiarity with these creature comforts that are just like those back in the States. We are trying to overcome some of the objections to the war with our troops by giving them too damned much comfort. You need to totally deemphasize those kinds of things and emphasize the reason we are there. We need to learn to exist on the battlefield; that hardens you and makes you more combat ready. It sharpens your instincts, hones your skills. Warriors must integrate into the terrain, become a part of it, blend, and adapt. Our enemies live in it; therefore, we must also. You can bet the enemy is hardened by his field time and rarely finds himself sitting in a McDonald's. If I could do one thing, I would do away with the damned creature comforts. Go out, fight, and win. If it were up to me, the troops would be living off MREs and would be in the field until they won the war.

The surge of 2007 was long overdue, and it was the right call. General David H. Petraeus knew his craft, and I firmly believe that once we commit our troops to battle, we need to let the military commanders on the ground fight the war the way they know how. They have the experience, the training, and the understanding of the terrain, people, and events. Second-guessing politicians in Washington, who perhaps spend three days on the ground in country shaking hands, do not have that knowledge or experience.

One day I was on the treadmill, watching the battle going on in Afghanistan. What I saw of how the battle is being fought is not the way we can fight a war and win it. The journalistic pundits' combined military experience appears to have come out of watching an episode of *Combat!* with Vic Morrow. They divide the nation and distract the public from the objectives with their ridiculous rhetoric. I learned about these media tactics during my experiences in Vietnam and in subsequent postings around the world. Having press, like CNN or Fox News, with TV capability right there on the battlefield, watching the final protective fire being executed is absolutely ludicrous, because 99 percent of the people watching these clips do not understand what the hell is going on. The viewers look at the action almost as if it were a movie, and when they see a couple of guys get killed, they say, "My God, we've got more casualties." If the Battle of Dai Do had been jammed into people's faces through CNN, they would have probably said, "Let's get the hell out of there now."

All these people second guessing from behind the cameras is becoming more and more of a problem. They're out there with a microphone and a satellite TV uplink reporting in real time, and there is not enough time for analysis. If they report after the fact, they still do not always have all the facts. And wars are won as much by disinformation as they are by accurate, valid intelligence. In the first Gulf War in 1991, Saddam Hussein thought he was going to be invaded by Marines to the east in a massive amphibious and ground assault. This divided his forces, which allowed us to take his army apart in short order.

In World War II, General George S. Patton was used as a decoy in England and had a complete fictional army, including faked radio traffic and supply depots staged in England, to divert the enemy's attention and divide his resources. Had CNN been there in his headquarters or in Eisenhower's tent, broadcasting in real time, the Germans under Field Marshal Gerd von Rundstedt would not have been staged in the Pas-de-Calais, awaiting an invasion farther east that never came. They would have known our intentions and been sitting there on the five Normandy beaches on June 6, 1944. D-Day would have been the worst disaster in military history, and all of it would have been broadcast live for your viewing pleasure. The Germans would have loved it, the media would have justified it as free speech, and the military would have been blamed for the failure.

We cannot allow our operational capabilities and successes to be advertised through the media. By not exercising complete control over the dispensation of data, we are giving our enemies real-time intelligence on not only our capabilities and locations, but also any shortcomings we may have not yet addressed. Allowing embedded reporters unfettered access is fine, but there should be a time delay before information can be sent back to the world—five, six or seven days minimum, preferably at least a month, when it almost becomes meaningless from a graphic, visual standpoint. I believe that a free press, as guaranteed by the First Amendment to the U.S. Constitution, is critical in a truly free society. However, even constitutional rights have limits. If we ever want to win a war, we will have to place a leash on the media. Our enemies watch TV as well, and do not think that because they may not have running water that they are stupid.

CHAPTER 14

Personal Reflections

Always fight with your head, and not just the muscles.
—Lt. Gen. Dietrich Hrabak

THERE ARE MANY GREAT things related to military service. Certainly there are hardships. Separations from families, dangers inherent to the job, and low pay when compared to the private sector have always been obstacles to maintaining a voluntary career military force. Once service members complete their contracts and finish their college educations, most would move on to graduate school or better paying jobs. That is human nature, and if you have a family to feed, completely understandable.

However, what I have witnessed in the last few years is higher than normal reenlistments, albeit supported by the stop-loss program. These young men and women, 95 percent coming from the lower echelon of the working class, remained on active duty to serve their country even when they had the option to leave. Why would a young Marine making $23,000 a year remain in uniform, hoping to get a promotion and a slight pay increase, when he could carry that experience over into a civilian job making twice the income? The answer is patriotism, pure and simple. If our politicians, who make ten times that amount and do ten times less work, with zero risk and threat to their beings, cannot learn from our young warriors, then I believe we have greater problems than just a divided nation and terrorists knocking on the door.

These men of the Marine Corps, who are aggressive hunters and killers by nature, throw themselves at our enemies on battlefields all over the world, and we are good at it for a reason. The Marine Corps was a joint force before joint was sought after by everyone else, because we understand that although we have an infantry, it is a light infantry. In the early days, we did not have the artillery as we do now, and we did not have the heavy armor. Finally, by World War II, we adopted our own supporting arms and, accordingly, the doctrine that led to our success.

However, we have always understood that which gave us our unique capacity: the airplane and the helicopter. Helicopters gave us greatest mobility on the battlefield. Airplanes, along with naval gunfire, gave us depth, especially with regard to reconnaissance and the ability to reach out and touch someone where artillery could not reach. We always knew that we had to have a logistics mechanism in place to support both of these bodies. It must be understood that, given our unique capabilities, we were always organized as thirty-day warriors. This means that we go into a conflict to fight for thirty days, and we bring everything with us to fight for those thirty days. The army and air force would come behind us with a heavier force if the battle went on for any longer. Therefore, when we characterize ourselves as a first to fight, force in readiness, I think that sends a message; we come with all the capability to do those things, and that is what a Marine Air-Ground Task Force (MAGTF) is. It brings us the capability of maintaining the force in a short war, but not a long war.

I think the Marine Corps has to adapt to the new battlefield, and in my opinion, the Corps has done very well in doing just that. That is perhaps our greatest strength: the ability to adapt and be flexible, conforming to the scenario, overcoming adversity, shaping and framing the battle to achieve victory. When we need light infantry or heavy infantry, or whatever the situation requires, we must have these various capabilities at hand. And when we look at the battlefield and want to shape the battlefield, we shape it based upon the threat. The MAGTF gives us that capability.

That is the whole concept of the MAGTF, the ability to adapt. Saying we should be just light infantry is being too narrow; we need to look at what the battlefield threat consists of. How we shape and influence the battlefield is critical, and we must make sure we have the pieces on the battlefield to make up the MAGTF. If that means we need a hunk of the Marine Corps' infantry, a hunk of airplanes, a hunk of helicopters, or a hunk of this or a hunk of that, we say, "Commander, that's the threat over there; he has this certain kind of capability and these certain numbers. What do you need to shape the battlefield and win?" The answers should come immediately.

The moment you fail to control the battlefield, you have started down the path to defeat. Imagine driving a car to a destination, and you are in complete control over the machine. Now imagine you throw that steering wheel out the window and just go along for the ride. That is the difference of controlling a situation to direct an outcome, and being an observer just hoping for the best. We cannot be observers; we must be active direction controllers in every case. Never allow your enemy to control the direction of the fight, and that includes the enemy in the field and the enemy in Washington. Victory is earned, not given. In our current war, we cannot show mercy as in the past. Our enemies do not even know what that word means.

The sacrifices of over four thousand of our military brothers and sisters, who have given their lives to protect us at home and assist others abroad, maintain the momentum and strengthen our resolve to see through the completion of our mission statement. It is the U.S. Navy that still patrols hostile seas, protecting international shipping and thwarting terrorism and piracy at sea. It is the U.S. Army that maintains large occupation forces and logistical supply networks, supporting all the services as needed. It is the U.S. Air Force, with its great aerial strength, that secures the skies, protecting our warriors on the battlefield. And, last but not least, it is our Marines who are the first in, forging a path for others to follow, bearing the brunt of whatever our enemies have to offer. It is no doubt a daunting task, but one which they have accomplished before and shall successfully execute in the future. Marines know nothing else.

When it comes to training and preparing for war, I suppose I could be labeled a ruthless character. But I feel passionately that you cannot wait for war and then train for it. You must be at the ready, poised to launch and ready to fight once you hit the ground, wherever that may be. Warfare and the training associated with it are constantly evolving.

The battlefield of tomorrow will be always different than is the one of today or yesterday due to technology and the conflicting ideologies you face. Today we face an enemy that we have never dealt with before, an enemy that is not openly nation-state sponsored, an enemy that is not a true professional corps of soldiers. These are guerrillas and terrorists, and they do not adhere to the expected norms of warfare.

This is the problem of relying strictly upon old methods and tactics. We have to adapt to the current threat and then train and indoctrinate ourselves against any and all future threats. It does not take a genius to extrapolate the collective data on exactly who our future enemies may be. Likewise, we should not be comfortable and complacent with the friends we currently have, or those nations that may appear to be friendly towards us when the political and economic situation suits them.

If the Cold War and changing alliances following World War II are any kind of example, then the current war on terror, when completed, will only hit the pause button until the next war comes along. By creating a more flexible and cogent reactionary-force mentality, combined with better weapons and tactics, the Marines were forged into a twenty-first-century elite force, eclipsing the capabilities of their forbearers, yet still carrying on the tradition. We must be prepared, and I know the Marine Corps will be.

The eyes of the entire world are upon our nation and our military. The world also examines our politicians and our society, and these perceptions are greatly influenced by the media. The world takes a great interest in what occurs here because, whether they like to admit it or not, it is the United States that determines the fates of every nation in the world to some degree.

The French wrote us out of their history books regarding winning World War II in Europe. Likewise, the Russians do not even know that we and the British were involved, and the modern Japanese have never heard of the rape camps and massacres in China and Korea, or of the Bataan Death March. At least we tend to remain true to our history, which is something our politicians should remember. All they have to do is drive past Arlington National Cemetery and gaze upon those resting there. Remembering our history is their duty to the nation.

Evil has knocked upon the door of America, and it continues attempting to enter the perimeter. Our enemies underestimated our reaction, which was swift. They also underestimated our resolve, which was absolute under President George W. Bush. Time and our military actions have proven the judgment of our enemies to be flawed, and their causes to be illegitimate. This reality is also one reason why the world watched this most recent election (in 2008) and now watch our future actions with anticipation. They know us, although they tend to ignore us until they need our assistance. The entire world has had its hand out to us, requesting support. I say, place a shovel in those same hands and make them work for it.

In the words of Senator John McCain: "America is great not because of what she has done for herself but because of what she has done for others." No truer words were ever spoken. The same people who mock and hate us today would probably not even be alive had Americans not fought two world wars to give them the opportunity to have free nations. If they screwed it up, shame on them. We fought a revolution against an oppressive ruler. Perhaps they should do the same, instead of waiting for us.

The new generation of our military has lived up to Senator McCain's words. They have served long tours away from home and their families. Their service is perhaps the most difficult due to the unique nature of the profession and the divisiveness within the nation, which is a disservice to our service members. I believe that those in politics should at least be as capable and devoted to the nation as our military members are.

Many people wonder what it takes to become a Marine. Those who have not been Marines, but may have known Marines, probably have a basic understanding of the patriotism and discipline required. They probably also understand that stamina, attention to detail, cognitive thinking, and problem solving are part of the training regimen.

However, for those who have not been Marines, there is much more than simple military discipline and training. Unlike most other branches of the military, the Marine Corps does not make a man or woman. We recruit them and make them better men and women. The Marines do not simply create warriors. We screen, select, and choose those whom we wish to invite into our ranks. We finely tune the inherent nature of the American fighting spirit, add discipline, increase stamina, and build what we Marines call *esprit de corps*. As the commercial ad campaign states: "We don't accept applications. Only commitments." Marines do not search the want ads. They search their souls, and if deemed worthy and are accepted, they join a long, honored tradition of men and women who have made history and preserved our nation.

Also, a Marine is not just a warrior; he is an exceptional warrior. There are four primary factors that separate a Marine from all other human beings on the planet. *Discipline*, which is unyielding and second nature. *Duty to the Corps* and duty to our country, which simply put is duty above oneself, working for the collective good as a member of a team. *Honor*, which is such a simple word, but one that carries much meaning to a Marine. Honor is life, and without it, a Marine has no purpose and our nation has no future. When a Marine gives his word, he keeps it. When a Marine accepts an assignment, he completes it. Failure is never an option. Finally, *respect*. Marines are respectful, polite, and courteous, even when in the company of the enemy. We have a great record of being humane when the situation calls for it, despite our fighting reputation.

When a Marine fights for his nation and his friends, it is to the death of his enemy. Retreat and surrender are not parts of our operational paradigm. Marines are the best-known, most respected, and, likewise, the most feared group of American military fighting men in the world for a good reason. We love our country, God, and our fellow Marines with whom we serve. We do not leave our wounded or dead behind if we can avoid it. We do not hesitate to follow orders, and above all, we do not and will not hesitate to risk death or make that ultimate sacrifice to save our fellow Marines. Every Marine knows that no matter where he may be in the world, or how dark that situation may be, he is never alone and never will be alone.

Our Corps is a twenty-first-century fighting machine. We have the weapons, logistics, and technology to destroy our enemies anywhere on the globe, on short notice and in short order. Once unleashed, we will accomplish amazing things. However, once the fighting is over, Marines are also the most caring, supportive, and humanitarian people you will ever meet. Marines are respectful of life, polite to a fault, and firmly committed to doing good work on and off the battlefield.

However, all the technology in the world will not win a battle or bring victory in war, unless there is a man on the ground with a weapon, holding hard-won terrain, securing freedom of passage, and establishing human rights and providing freedom for those who ask for and deserve it. Wars are won by people, not by machines and computers. That is the truth, and winning those wars is the responsibility, or rather the privilege, of the United States Marine.

Our motto is "Semper Fidelis," which in Latin means "Always Faithful." This is more than a slogan; this is a way of life. Our emblem is the Eagle, Globe and Anchor. The eagle is the national symbol of our nation, and it is located above the globe and anchor, perched as a vigilant sentry guarding our nation. The globe denotes worldwide service. There is no single location, no environment, and no terrain that a Marine cannot operate in. The anchor displays our naval heritage, as infantrymen of the sea, linking us to the greatest navy in the history of mankind.

As our history has shown, from the deserts of North Africa and Iraq; to the jungles of the Caribbean, Central America, and Southeast Asia; to the subzero cold of Korea and the mountains of Afghanistan, the United States Marine will go where he is needed, accomplish any and all tasks he may be given, and do so comfortable in the knowledge that he is doing righteous work, preserving his nation, expanding freedom around the world, and carving another line into the wall of American history. Killing some terrorists is simply a bonus.

I think the nature of a theoretical democracy—and remember we live in a representative republic—is that we have to maintain the civilian control of the military. To do otherwise means that we may have certain people who could get out of line. That was the genius of the creation of the three branches of government: executive, legislative, and judicial. The system of checks and balances protects the rights of all Americans. However, I think that we have had the chance to witness the results of a lack of control, especially in Vietnam, somewhat during Korea, and a little bit in Iraq and Afghanistan. Now we are controlling the fight in Iraq and Afghanistan, not simply reacting to actions and perceived threats, and the policy and the surge are paying dividends.

I think that we Marines provide the civilian leadership with the assets, the guidance, and basic capabilities. But I also think that we should make sure that we constantly develop and maintain our officers, not only because of the loyalty we have to that process, but also because we must maintain the capability to influence the civilian leadership in a respectful fashion. The military knows how to win on the battlefield, earning the nation's respect, although with some of the activities going on now politically, and especially with the assistance of the liberal media, so critical of the military in general, I do not think that is the way to gain that respect.

I also think there is a prevailing attitude among some of our retired generals that is contrary to our long-term objectives, even though I agree with what some of them are saying. When we have Marines and soldiers on the battlefield, we need to be very cautious about how we comment and conscious of how our words can influence the stubbornness and attitude of the threat. I am very concerned about this. What we are doing is a little contrary to our democratic ideals.

The civilian leadership must respect the military and not be too damned stubborn to do so. I listen to their opinions. However, bear in mind that respect is a two-way street. Our military must also respect the elected officials, even if we disagree with them. In the military, we salute the rank, not the man, but we are obligated to respect the man, unless he has proven himself unworthy of that respect. Respecting elected officials is also good manners and illustrates true professionalism.

Authors Colin D. Heaton and Anne-Marie Lewis were our honored guests at the 2nd Battalion, 4th Marine Regiment, reunion in Charleston in 2007. We made them honorary "Magnificent Bastards" as they covered the event for *Reunions* magazine. As they made the contacts with many of the veterans who came, they began interviewing the men. Just as I have had my perspectives on the important persons with whom I have interacted, the people in my life also have their opinions of me. The comments interspersed within these pages are the opinions gathered from those interviews. I have had no input regarding their respective comments, but I feel that any book about a military leader would be incomplete without the comments of both his subordinates and his superiors. I decided that in order to have an honest and forthright book about my life, all opinions—whether good, bad, or indifferent—should be included. After two years of Colin twisting my arm to allow him to help me write my story, I thought that including others' opinions was the least I could do. I know that current, former, and future Marines will read this book, and I want them to have a very clear and unambiguous view of who I am and what I stand for. The same goes for the politicians who read this book.

The perspectives being given today are sometimes juxtaposed with opinions formed during Vietnam. Back then I did not become a Marine officer and combat leader to make friends and influence enemies. I became a Marine officer to serve my nation, to kill its enemies when necessary, and to convert those who may wish to become our enemy. Positive persuasion; focus; discipline; belief in yourself, your men, and your cause; and attention to the smallest possible detail often pay great dividends. My post-military career, as compared to the average retired Southern gentleman, may appear to be incongruous. But the person I was, the warrior many knew in the past, is still a big part of the businessman and advocate many know today,

Such is a human life. We do not live in a void. Good, bad, or indifferent, our actions become the catalysts for other events, and the ripple effect touches the lives of many more. This is why I think that we should choose our words carefully, think before we speak, and determine if we can handle the end result of our actions, analyzing both the potential positive and the negative outcomes. At the end of the day you have to be able to look at yourself in the mirror and say, "I like that guy," knowing that you have done what you believed was right at all time.

To this day, I still receive calls from Marines I commanded, and I receive such comments as, "You were a tough son of a bitch, but we are alive because you pushed us, and made us abide by a certain standard, physically and otherwise. And that's the reason we came home." Comments such as those make me feel that I did the job right, and I have no apologies if I ruffled a few feathers.

I know that in my career I kicked a lot of people in the ass. For that I have no regrets, as I always had a method for my perceived madness. Bringing Marines home alive and building stronger and more competent warriors was my job. If I hurt a few peoples' feelings along the way, so be it.

Echo Company Always Led
—1st Lt. Dave Jones

Jim Livingston has made it a point to attend almost all of our 2/4 reunions since 1988, even if only for a few hours. And it has been greatly appreciated. He understands that wearing the Medal of Honor includes an obligation to stay connected with the men who were there with him. He has told me many times that his MOH is a tribute to the troops he led. He would not have not have gotten the recognition he received if not for the efforts of his men.

I choose to believe that I was the perfect match for Jim Livingston. He was big on regulations, discipline, tradition, and all those other things that you think of when you think about Marines. On the other hand, I was not going to make the USMC a career. I joined because it was the branch of the service with the best reputation. I was teaching school and could have avoided the war [in Vietnam], but I wanted to be a part of it because I so respected combat veterans from previous wars. [I respected] the sacrifices they made, the fact that they felt an obligation to serve their county, and frankly, the "excitement" of going to war. I often wonder now what I was thinking when I thought war would be so exhilarating. Anyway, at the time, it was the only war around, and I didn't want to miss it. I felt my strength was in getting to know and work with the troops on a more personal level than Jim.

As Livingston's XO, I got around to all of the platoons regularly. I could help them understand what and why we were going to be doing certain things (even PT, which was not easy!). I think I was able to relieve some of the stress. Don't get me wrong.

I am certain that there is a lot more appreciation than consternation. I know for certain there are a lot of children and grandchildren who exist today because of the leadership we had at Dai Do, and other places. For those

Jim was excellent at his job, and we needed him as our leader, and we needed him to play the tough guy role. And I think the record speaks for itself. Echo Company in general, and Jim Livingston in particular, had an outstanding reputation during battles, and we were extremely proud of that and grateful to him for that status. Too much of him or too much of me might not have worked so well. I would like to think that we were a good balance.

The company's impression of Jim was varied. I saw him as being aggressive in order to have his men consistently prepared for any situation. His approach was that he had to be a hard ass. Naturally, some of the troops saw him as over aggressive and inclined to be too distant. For example, they thought that the idea of doing physical training in the field was crazy. But many of those same troops would also tell you that the idea of doing PT anywhere would not have been on their agenda. I believe he felt that being the "good guy" would get too many of his men killed or injured.

Jim Livingston was always aggressive, even before and during Dai Do. It seemed as though Echo Company always ended up as the lead company (did Jim always ask for that assignment?) and that whatever platoon I was leading ended up as the lead platoon. And because we had limited equipment (such as maps and compasses) I felt as though I had to be directly behind the point man during many of our operations. That probably isn't true, but it sure felt that way to me. Anyway, whenever Echo Company saw action, I was somehow in the middle of it. I don't know if that was because I was a good leader and Jim wanted me there, or because I was a bad leader and always ended up in the wrong place at the wrong time.[1]

factors, I think Bill Weise deserves a lot more credit than I or anyone else.

I have made it abundantly clear that I supported Senator John McCain during his run for the president of the United States. He was the only choice, given the necessities and experience required during the current international climate. John McCain is a good man, although sometimes indecisive; certainly he was not my first choice from the Republican Party, but there was nothing that I would feel would hold him back as president. He was clearly the better candidate, although the one thing that I have always been concerned about is his unpredictability. As a commander-in-chief, much like a general, you need to have an element of predictability. You have all these people trying to read and respond to you. If you are all over the damned map, then you are never going to get any focus. I think that was the good thing about President George W. Bush; he was consistent, he was predictable. You may or may not have liked him, but you could be pretty damned certain where he was going, what he was going to do, and who he was going to do it to.

Given the current political climate in our nation, I want to clearly state that I have always opposed the concept of economic socialism, and I see the redistribution of wealth as a failure on the part of individual Americans to take personal responsibility for their own lives. Pursuing an education and bettering themselves and their lives for the benefit of the nation and their children, not a government handout, should be everyone's paramount consideration. That socialist mindset destroyed New Orleans; it also proved to be the failure of Communism, and it creates a system of lazy people seeking handouts. There are people who legitimately deserve assistance, but this socialist mentality, created by Lyndon Johnson, has created a system of generational entitlements that is crippling this nation today.

Another thing that I want to make completely clear is this fact: President Barack Obama must not leave Iraq and Afghanistan unfinished. We must stay the course, as much for the military as for the larger political futures of both of those nations and their populations. We have been helping people achieve their freedom as long as we have been a nation. The world understands this. We must ensure that we leave those nations more stable, economically sound, and politically viable than they were before we became involved.

Eight years of Bill Clinton's timid and ineffectual actions against terrorists—even after the first World Trade Center bombing in 1993, the embassy bombings in 1998 in Tanzania and Kenya, the bombing of the USS *Cole* in 2000, and the multiple opportunities he had to get Osama Bin Laden in Sudan and Afghanistan prior to 9/11—speak volumes about political second guessing and a lack of resolve. It was his failure that Bush inherited and that is being dealt with today.

Liberal politicians who claim that we should be in Afghanistan and not Iraq all have blood on their hands. President Bush was relying on Clinton-era intelligence regarding the weapons of mass destruction (WMD). That was all we had, since the Clinton administration had effectively destroyed our foreign intelligence-gathering capabilities. I am talking about the human-intelligence sources, which are the most reliable. A dozen nations, including the British, Israelis, Swedes, Russians, French, and Germans, had all confirmed what Saddam Hussein had in his inventory—especially the French and Germans, since they were big chemical suppliers. The Russians supplied nuclear materiel.

Hans Blix and his U.N. inspectors counted, listed, and scheduled destruction of those biological and chemical weapons. Upon closing in on the mother lode, Saddam threw them out of the country. On top of that, President Clinton responded with little more than saber rattling while Saddam committed over a hundred violations of the 1991 cease-fire agreement. We had the moral and legal authority to lead another U.N. force into Iraq once he broke the first rule, but Clinton and the U.N. did nothing but make pronouncements and threats that weren't followed through on. Meanwhile, that maniac continued to kill his own people, ignore the 1991 cease-fire agreement, and posture and threaten his neighbors. Remember that this is the same U.N. that allowed the Rwandan genocide to erupt and did absolutely nothing.

President Bush did the right thing going into Iraq, even if he did not include the violations of the cease-fire as part of his plan. I do believe that not mentioning these violations, as well as the failure of the U.N. to even enforce its own agreement, were great strategic blunders. When the United States was attacked in 2001 and learned that the mission was planned and executed through Osama bin Laden in Afghanistan, and given the unpredictability of Saddam, as well as the unknown disposition of the WMD, securing the back door of

The Skipper Scared the Hell Out of You
—Lance Cpl. Steve Wilson

Over the course of seven months of a shortened tour, I had the honor of serving and listening to the Skipper on that cumbersome PRC-25 [radio]. Let there be no mistake, he scared the hell out of you. He looked, and his actions set, the precedent that was expected by the Marine Corps. There was never any doubt as to who was in charge. He was our leader, and it was by example; that was his mantra. The Skipper led Echo Company from [being] a VC-field-tested fighting unit in Quang Tri to [being] a "magnificent," tactically razor-sharpened, cohesive, trained Marine company. The company call sign was Dixie Diner Echo, and then there was the all-inclusive "This is Six" on the other end of the receiver when things were most critical and dicey. That pretty much cleared the net of any conversation. But let me be most pointed and state that there was never, never a time during the most critical event did the voice of the Skipper ever waiver. There were constant heated conversations over the

Iraq while crashing through the front door of Afghanistan in a double envelopment was the logical course of action. We could not take the risk of the WMD falling into Al Qaeda's hands. In addition, we could not allow Iran unfettered access to either country, given that it shares borders with them and has been a long-term sponsor of global terror.

However, I firmly believe that we should have gone into Iraq full force, just as we did in the first Gulf War, instead of sending in units piecemeal. Go in heavy and hard, like a sledgehammer, and then worry about the niceties when you set things right. This is what the last troop surge did. It put more boots on the ground, covered more critical terrain, and forced our enemies to retreat into smaller enclaves where they could be located and destroyed more easily.

net during the course of my time as radio operator by those of us with inexperience and then there was "This is Six!"

One thing that you are probably aware is that an RTO has a close, direct, yet unspoken relationship with his commander. Often when 3rd Platoon was in the lead, I was fortunate to sight the Skipper and Frank [Valdez] near the front, surrounded by antennae. Communication was always critical to the Skipper, and he communicated clearly what was expected. There were only two times he actually backed down from a fight. One was at Lam Xuan, when their artillery, 122s, had us boxed in, an enfilade of fire. He pulled us out because we were getting blasted. The other was May 1, as the left flank erupted in our plight to get to Dai Do. It was there that my antenna was shot off. Instead of taking on the enemy, we were instructed to break off and proceed. We only suppressed their green tracer rounds with red as we crossed the open rice paddy in our attempt to link up with the battalion, which we did. Again, Dave Jones and 3rd Platoon paved the way. The Skipper expected him to lead as he did. Dave Jones is a near carbon copy of the Skipper.[2]

The other reason the surge worked, and is still making things better, is that the average Iraqi sees more than simply a foreign occupation force directing traffic and hanging a dictator. We handed Saddam over to his own people and allowed their justice system to handle that issue, and we also allowed them to form and vote for their own government, which sends the public the message that we are there to help them.

The truth is, average Iraqis are in far more danger from their own radical countrymen and from the external Islamic radicals inside the country, than they ever were from an American or coalition soldier. We do not make and detonate car bombs in markets. We even have more respect for their places of worship than their own Muslim terrorists do, since the Shiites will bomb a Sunni mosque and vice versa, just to make a point.

Keep as Many Alive as Possible
—Brig. Gen. William Weise

[E]ven in combat, Jim Livingston was greatly concerned with his Marines and sailors. His main concern was to keep as many alive as possible. To do this, he held everyone to high standards and emphasized training. His highest standards were those he set for himself. He referred to his Marines as "my youngsters" when he talked to me. He had deep feelings for his men. He was a tough taskmaster and suffered no fools, because he loved his men and knew that was necessary for success in combat and to keep them alive. When you are eighteen years old, dead tired, hungry, wet, scared, and cold, you may not appreciate a leader like Jim who makes you keep your weapon clean and who pushes you to do what's necessary. But decades later, when you think about it, you realize that Jim Livingston is the reason you are alive today and able to play with your grandchildren.[3]

Understand that there is a simple fact regarding human nature: people tend to fear what they do not understand, and that goes for the vast majority of human beings. The small minority of people, the deep thinkers, examine rather than fear the unknown. We in the military look at the unknown from every angle and try to understand what makes up the components. We do not pass hasty judgment, but analyze the data and then plan a course of action that will be most beneficial to all. Most liberal minds cannot think that way. Liberals are not always realists, but are often idealists. There is nothing wrong with idealism; it is also a critical part of post-operational planning. Never destroy what you do not plan to rebuild, and never rebuild what you cannot protect.

Not long ago I spoke with a lieutenant colonel up at Carlisle Barracks, and I said that we have lost three years in this war by fighting it incorrectly. We went in and built these big enclaves, we wanted all

Mellower, but Still Determined
—1st Lt. Dave Jones

I think it needs to be said how much more mellow Jim is today. And that may be because he had to play a very different role under combat conditions. He is friendly, outgoing, and very sociable whenever he attends a 2/4 reunion. He makes a point of visiting with everyone there. And his recent experience with the VA [Veterans Administration] commission shows that he is very concerned about the health care that veterans receive, especially as it relates to PTSD [post-traumatic stress disorder], which manifests itself so often with Vietnam vets. (Other vets of other wars would probably argue that their peers suffer and suffered just as much, and they're probably right.) He seems very determined to see that VA services improve for all vets.[4]

these creature comforts, we wanted all this capability, and we wanted this base support set up before we went to war. That wasted time and energy. The longer we remain in a hostile environment without taking the operational initiative, the longer the threat has to analyze us, plan corrective actions, gather intelligence, and then strike the places we are weakest, which is, in fact, the stationary base camps. It is harder to hit a moving target than a stationary one.

This is what our enemies know, hence their highly mobile method and fluid nature. They have been fighting these hillbilly wars for centuries. They live, sleep, and fight hard. They know the cold, pain, and hunger of long-term commitment. These people may not be as technically proficient as we are, but they are definitely as, if not more, dedicated. They are willing to die for their cause, even if that means killing their own. When we keep on their backs, chasing them down hard and killing them in place, we can win by battlefield attrition. This is the only effective method: direct confrontation and elimination.

Our future leadership must understand the nature of this war. The next time, we have to understand that we do not need to worry about anything other than the mission, and we need to get out there to where the problem is. This has been the focus of the surge. This means that we cannot worry about getting back to sleep between sheets, using the Nautilus gyms, or getting on the computer or on the cell phone. A fighting man can never decouple mentally and disengage from the fight. That is what General Petraeus finally figured out. That is why, although we are three years behind where we should be at this point, things have been turned around. They should have read and executed the Marine Corps' small-wars manual when they first went in there.

There is no magic about what is going on in Iraq and Afghanistan now; the U.S. forces got out from behind these big enclaves, and there are no silver bullets. Petraeus is a smart guy, and he was the right guy at the right time; he was able to conceive a strategy, implement an operations order, and launch.

I believe that people who have not had their time in the barrel should not be second guessing the actions of those who have. And I am not too impressed with all these other guys who have not been in the barrel and are not aware of all the circumstances doing the talking now. I think the troop surge went fine. Before it, there was plenty of capability there; it was simply being misused. Getting outside the wire and becoming involved with the people was the only right way. The mistakes that were made were the same as those made in Vietnam, where we built up these base camps, and we spent a heck of a lot of capability defending all these damned logistics installations. I learned that by looking people in the eye, sharing the hardship, you earned their trust, and once you have that, you have their support.

I also think that the Iraqis taking on the Shiites in Basra and other places is one of the most positive steps, and the press is not picking that up. When they get this fat sheik who is, in fact, Iran's front man, out of power, that is going to isolate Iran more and more. We are seeing the results in Iran now; people want freedom, and they are willing to die for it. That same dedication is what made America great. That is what the future tyrants can expect, you can bank on it.

CHAPTER 15

Future Threats and Observations

The only thing stronger than military might is political will. Without the required political will, military might means nothing.

—Winston S. Churchill

M Y OUTLOOK ON GENERAL global political situations, especially those in the Middle East, is a bit grim. Syria had the Arab/Muslim conference, and the only country that showed up was Iran. Not even the Saudis showed up, thereby isolating Syria more. I do not think that having democratically elected governments in that region will have any effect upon the Jordanian or Saudi royal governments. Crowned heads tend to wish to remain that way.

The Jordanians have never had a very suppressive government, as they have a parliamentary monarchy. Jordan is a Hashemite kingdom like Morocco, and the people are free to move around. They do not have a Shari'a government, and as they do not have the oil wealth that the other nations do, the people are more dependent upon their government. The Saudis are gradually moving that way. The Iraqis and Iranians will move along much faster due to their oil wealth, which will allow them to join the global market on an even footing without needing world economic support—that is, if they can keep their own people from screwing things up. Once the next Iranian revolution takes place and the fanatics are driven out of power, I think the world will witness what could perhaps be the greatest economic miracle in modern history.

I have no hopes that the Israeli and Palestinian conflict will ever be resolved because first you must also solve the Iranian and Syrian issues. All Iran and Syria are doing (and will continue to do) is keeping Israel suppressed and engaged, because they are very concerned about what would happen if Israel was not tied down geographically and militarily with the Palestinians, Hamas, and Hezbollah. It is their way of trying to bleed Israel dry. The Arab and Muslim world does not give a damn about the Palestinians. If they did, they could have already resolved the problem. However, they do not mind spending their time and money spreading terror.

The only thing keeping the Islamic world from committing total fratricide is hatred of a common enemy. Without a collective hatred of Israel and the West, the Muslims in all camps would just continue killing each other out of radical and conflicting interpretations of their faith. What it really comes down to is resources, or the lack of them. If all Muslims had oil, money, water, and land, they would care less if a neighbor was a Sunni, Wahabi, Shiite, Christian, or Jew.

When you leave people with nothing much in life and nothing left to lose, you will get the results we are now experiencing. Look what happened in Germany after the Treaty of Versailles; the treaty's severe impositions led to unemployment, starvation, and economic collapse, which created the environment for Adolf Hitler to rise. A starving man will support anyone who feeds his family. Include a lot of religious ideology and zealotry and a promise of a better afterlife, and you have a recipe for a global catastrophe. I suppose history does indeed repeat itself.

I think our support of Israel was one of those things we had to do and should continue to do. Israel has the only true long-term democracy in the region, and it is the only real friend we have in the area. We have to make sure it survives.

With regard to Saudi Arabia, if not for oil, we would have no interest in that area at all. Oil is the reality of the reason we are there, and we have to be very clear about that. In the next five decades, when the oil runs out, or if we locate enough resources at home or move to alternative fuels, Saudi Arabia will rapidly become a distant memory.

It will also become a bankrupt third-world nation demanding foreign aid on the one hand, while trying to contain Islamic radicals with the other. The royal family is not the most respected collective within their own nation, hence their careful tightrope walking between the cash from the West and the zealots in their nation. These are tensions that have really yet to manifest themselves.

Russia, North Korea, and China want to be major players in the world, and they understand that the way to accomplish that is not only economically, but also through the perception of military capability.

Russia recently invaded Georgia because we're stretched out across Iraq and Afghanistan and Georgia is not a NATO member; thus, no united military action would be forthcoming by treaty. One thing is pretty certain: Georgia is a small nation, and if not for its oil and gas pipelines and the access it offers to the Caspian Sea oil rigs, Russia would have no interest in it. Also, if Georgia were as adequately equipped as Ukraine (which has over a third of all the old Soviet nuclear weapons following the dissolution of the Soviet Union), Vladmir Putin would have thought twice before invading.

Make no mistake, Dmitry Medvedev may be the president, but Putin—the former KGB colonel who ran the foreign desk—actually runs the country. Putin's successors will all be just figureheads. Putin will always be in control and will purge his opposition as well; that's just the nature of Russian society. You do not hear much about Russia from the American press because it does not know how to deal with Russian politics. We are so decoupled from that and recoupled with so many other things, if you look at it on the scale of our interests, Russia is not a very interesting press item. There can be only so many things that we have a political interest in.

Russia and China, just like America, Britain, France, Germany, and the rest of the major players in the world, understand that a nation cannot be a major military power without being an economic super-power. This has been true throughout history. If a nation has a strong economy, it can afford a strong military, but they seem to get it in reverse; they want to be a military power before they are an economic power. That is what hurt Russia before. There has to be a balance.

In China we created a hell of a market, but we have to be smart about how we play this thing. We must look at the millions of people there who work for western corporations, look at the things that they build for our markets. The thing keeping them off Taiwan is that they have too many internal problems right now. Look at Mongolia, where they have the Muslim problem cropping up, and the Tibet issue that is never going away. China's never going to give up Tibet. If they did, then the Chinese empire would start to become unglued. They will never show weakness. Taiwan is another situation; China and Taiwan both know that the focal point is economics. Besides, China would be foolish to upset the financial applecart. If they did make any aggressive moves, they risk losing the global economic machine that brought them out of an agrarian, second-world nation status.

The media and even certain members of our government are not taking enough of an interest in the future of Pakistan. This is especially true in the wake of the Benazir Bhutto assassination, the changing role of former president Pervez Musharraf, and that country's relations with the West. We made the mistake of placing too much faith in Pakistan. The Pakistanis are still not trying to deal effectively with the threats from Afghanistan, as those threats sort of got away from Musharraf. We should have been willing to step up to the plate more quickly and give him greater capability by training his forces.

However, we did not want to be seen as training his forces, which would have been contrary to some of the politics that were going on in this country, and I think we made some foolish mistakes by not engaging very quickly and providing Musharraf with the proper advisors. Doing so would have enabled him to get in there and take care of that sector in the northwest corner near Afghanistan, where all these threats are located. But Musharraf was appeasing the Pakistani public by keeping American forces out of their country. He was trying to keep a lid on a pressure cooker, and it would have boiled over if we had entered the equation in force. Then he would have had trouble keeping the fanatics in check, because our presence would have given them a jihadist platform. If you want to see just how modern minded the average Pakistani is, just look at the assassination of Bhutto, the government turning a blind eye to Al Qaeda and Taliban safe havens, and especially the policy of "honor killings" and the murder of women. That is our ally, and they have nuclear weapons.

The Guantanimo Bay detainment issue continues to be controversial, but look at the way the prisoners are being treated: we spend millions of dollars to take care of them. It is pure stupid politics. They are eating better food than most Americans; they have better health care than most, that is for sure. This is absolute foolishness. The tribunal method of adjudicating these cases is the way it should be. It is also justified by the laws of warfare.

These guys were caught on the battlefield, not wearing a recognized uniform, insignia, or any rank, and they have no national allegiance. Hence, they are either mercenaries or terrorists, neither of which have protection under the law, whether you use The Hague or Geneva Conventions. They are illegal combatants, not prisoners of war. They are criminals, as far as I am concerned, and are not expected to have the same rights as prisoners of war. They are not American citizens; they were fighting and killing Americans and their own people. Saddam Hussein was captured in his own country and dealt with by the very government that was being directly impacted by his actions for more than three decades and by the actions of the insurgents. We could have sent these captured criminals back to Saudi Arabia, Egypt, Jordan, or wherever they came from, to be dealt with. But the Saudis and others are not directly impacted by the actions of these criminals, so their attitude is quite different. Most of these nations just try to ignore the problem. In other cases, their people—truly victims within these nations—are not willing to take the necessary action that these criminals duly deserve because they fear of reprisals against them and their families.

Both The Hague and Geneva Conventions stipulate that, in wartime, any competent and legitimate military authority may hold its own investigative and judicial proceedings in the field. We could have just used the existing laws and held trials and firing squads in the field, away from the media, and it would have been completely legal. We did it in World War II, but we did not do that this time. We brought them into a detention facility, fed them the best food they have ever had, allowed them the opportunity to defend themselves, and interrogated them in a comfortable environment. And look where that has brought us.

Iran's Mahmoud Ahmedenijad has taken advantage of the current political situation. In any other circumstance, he would probably stop, but he's reacting to what is being said by the Democrats and Republicans, and he is manipulating the entire scenario. He knows that there is no global interest in invading his country. There is no serious European opposition to his wanting a nuclear capability, since most of our so-called allies have supplied him with the raw materials with which to create a nuclear program in the first place.

There is also a lot of tension in Iranian society; around 60 percent of the population is under the age of thirty, and the CIA ought to be pumping money into that society big time, creating more speculation and more tension. I think the youth have become very westernized and are very computer literate, and they don't like the crap that is going on. It is just another example of keeping the lid on the pressure cooker so that one of these days, it is going to blow. You are going to have a second Iranian Revolution, and I believe that day is not too far off. Just look at Iran's 2009 election.

Kim Jong Il's North Korea is another pressure cooker bound to explode, but he has that society so suppressed and isolated, there is no inflow of western information there like there is in Iran. I think at some point Kim is going to lose; he will pass on, just like Fidel Castro will, although he has named his younger son (who is another real genius) as his successor.

The South Koreans will end up in a position just like the one West Germany was in with East Germany, absorbing the latter's poverty and debt when the two countries were unified. The South Koreans will have to educate and feed the North Koreans, create jobs, and basically create a new marketplace. If that happens, Korea could surpass China as an economic power. The Koreans are certainly more reliable than China. I think the issue in North Korea is going to be a lot more subtle. They are sort of boxed in with China, and my sense is that things are going to become unglued in the next few years.

We seem to have lost focus on the Balkans. It was easy to do, and now we do not hear much about that region, which was held together by Josip Broz Tito for decades. Certainly, he had his issues in Yugoslavia with all the factions, religions, and ethnic groups. They have never been a cohesive entity on their own, and they never will be. They have this generational attitude about not getting along, and that attitude is embedded in that part of the world. That whole strip is a melting pot between East and West, ever since the fall of the Byzantine Empire and the loss of Constantinople to the Ottoman occupation in the fifteenth century. We have not heard the last from the former Yugoslavia.

Western Europe seems to be changing yet again. Nicholas Sarkozy of France is very pro-American, as is Angela Merkel in Germany, to a degree, and I hope they stay that way. I hope they change this notion that everyone in Europe hates Americans, which I find strange since European countries have American-style governments. They hate to be reminded that we had to bail their collective asses out of two world wars, and then we spent billions of American dollars to rebuild their shattered nations and economies. We have always had to pull the Europeans out of something. Gordon Brown in the U.K. and Kevin Rudd of Australia are interesting case studies, both being staunchly pro-American. All the stories in the press about negative attitudes toward the United States are exaggerated.

For all these reasons and many more, President Obama will have great responsibilities, and the U.S. Congress will have an equally critical burden. We have to make clear our mission goals and long-term plans, and if Obama is smart, he will stay the course. I naturally have my doubts. My fear is that Congressional leaders will continue the tradition of pork-barrel spending (as seen with recent the massive allotments of taxpayer funds) and back-slapping, good-old-boy politics, and they will forget that they are not only Americans, but also the very people responsible for passing laws and ensuring that we remain free through unity, not divisiveness. Perhaps there should be a boot camp for politicians, as in the Corps, where the individuality of a person is stripped away, and they are molded mentally into a team mentality, an *esprit de corps*, where there is a greater purpose than that of the individual. Politicians could learn a lot from Marines.

CHAPTER 16

The Future of Our Nation

You have to live and train like you will fight, otherwise you are not
prepared for the enemy who has trained to kill you. You will get all
the rest you need in the grave.
—Waffen SS Oberfuehrer Leon Degrelle

W E HAVE AN EPIDEMIC in this country of people coming
here not to be creative and go to work, but with expectations
of financial support. With regard to the McCain-Kennedy amnesty
plan, I think that the people who are here illegally should be leaving.
Those who are here legally, but who can't or won't find jobs, need to go
somewhere—and I don't mean Arizona and the other border states.

Look what happened to California. I would suggest Americans
examine that model closely, as it is just the start. If the immigrants
cannot get work, then we will not have to kick them out; instead, they
will kick themselves out. As far as the idea of sanctuary cities, that is
just immaturity and stupidity, spending taxpayer dollars to support
these people. It wouldn't be just the sanctuary cities' taxpayers, but all
taxpayers in the country that are paying the price, as these aliens are
able to tap into the great federal kitty—and they are doing that.

If we do not get the Mexican border under control, then we are also
setting ourselves up for a real issue with respect to future terrorism in
this country. The current drug wars and killings are simply the prelude
to the near future. The border issue is going to reach a head real soon,

and there is going to be a real backlash against the illegals that we have not yet felt. If the U.S. economy goes south a little bit more, then we are going to see them as part of the problem. There is an epidemic; just look at where the tax money is going, such as to medical care. The average American cannot afford health care, and if they do get service and cannot afford to pay, they risk having a lien placed on their property. Most bankruptcies in America are due to medical bills. Illegal aliens do not suffer from that problem.

With regard to immigrants serving in the U.S. military as a way to justify their being here, I would say no. Then what you are doing is allowing them, as their first act of citizenship, to break the law. Those who come here legally with the specific intent to serve in the U.S. military are fine; there is nothing wrong with that. If they serve their time and pay their dues, then they should become citizens. However, this is not to imply that we want a mercenary force.

As far as the Cuba foot-dry policy, I will always question whether we should have that, since we do not have that option for Haitians, Mexicans, or people from other Central American countries. That policy is based in large part to the great political power that the Cubans have in this country. The pre-Castro Cubans have always been very thrifty, generally very hard-working people, and they brought capabilities and their education to this country, where some of these other groups have not. When these others arrive, they are just an absolute burden, and many groups, such as the Jamaicans, Haitians, and others who brought drugs, have brought criminal elements and all this other crap here.

Regarding Cuba and the eventual demise of dictator Fidel Castro, I think it has already begun to happen. People there now have cell phones and computers (although these technological devices are strictly controlled); I think Castro's death will open a floodgate of opportunities. Fidel's going, Raul's going, and there's an entirely new generation that's tired of this stuff. The old guys are not going to be able to control it. The new Cuban generation is looking to have a better future, more opportunities, and to get out from under some of the holds that Castro's had on the population.

I don't think there will be a revolution in Cuba to the extent that there will be in Iran, because Iran is trying to keep a hold on the people through terror. Cuba's leaders are beginning to understand that they have to release this hold. You will see a relaxing on travel restrictions, and there will be more interaction. And then you have this huge enclave of Cubans right next door in Florida. There is no way Cuba's leaders can stop the revolution, due to geography and the power of the U.S. dollar.

Here in the United States, we need to become less reliant upon foreign oil, and opening up the reserves in the Arctic or expanding drilling operations in the Gulf of Mexico and off the coasts of California and Florida is an absolute necessity. The foolishness of not bringing those fields into play, to preclude us from being dependent upon all these other countries of the world and all their instabilities, is ridiculous. All these people in opposition to exploring and obtaining new oil resources are extremists. Other nations such as China are now securing drilling rights in our backyard. That is a violation of our national security and of economic and common sense.

We have already been successful in Alaska with the pipeline. Not being able to drill off Florida and California is crap, considering the distance out and the technology available, and considering what is already transpiring every day in the gulf without having any problems. We are not at the same stage that we were during the Jimmy Carter era, when people were lining up at the gas pumps, but people will tire of high prices and foreign dependence and say "find some." And this will be an issue that must be addressed rapidly.

We are also in trouble with regard to education. People say that our children are our future. This is very true and is completely logical. But look at the disastrous schools in the Washington, D.C., area. The politicians will tout their exceptional ideology on public education, and then they place their kids in private schools. This shows that not even they have faith in the public-education system; therefore, their diatribe is pure polemic. As far as I am concerned, we should put our education on a business model, just as has been done in some of the universities: eliminate the teachers' unions, stabilize the pay scale based upon merit, and hire and promote on merit.

The problem with public education is that it has been socialized. You have these big unions that dominate the public school systems, protecting those teachers who are unworthy, while stifling the exceptional. There was no real accountability until schools executed President Bush's No Child Left Behind Act. Before that act, there was no level of expectation or measure of success, and no one was to be held accountable. I think there should be a federal minimal expectation level on student scores, as Europe and Japan have, at every grade level, and that goes for the teachers as well. It would be good if the states could institute these levels, but they could never do it consistently, since local and state governments are at odds with each other. Once a minimum level was set by the federal government, the states could enhance it, and I would encourage them, over a period of time, to enhance that minimum level. Raising the standard benefits everyone. Then you could reward the states for enhancing it.

I also think we should use the school-uniform method, just as Great Britain does. It gives the appearance that everyone is the same, eliminates the fashion statement, and removes from the equation what a family's economic capability may be.

I think that the establishment of teachers' salaries is a local matter, as economics differ from location to location. But again, teachers' salaries should be based upon merit.

Never hesitating to make the hard calls, I have always had the ability to rapidly assess a situation, sum up the school solution, and take immediate action to resolve the issue as presented. That is not really saying anything special about me. I would say that this is a quality inherent to any good, well-trained, well-seasoned Marine combat officer. However, I have always tried to be a thinker, and as stated by Brig. Gen. William Weise, "Jim Livingston, like Jay Vargas and my other officers, was a thinking man, but it is also important to remember was that he was also a man of action. You always knew that if he was involved, the problem would be resolved satisfactorily. That gave me great comfort."[1]

I feel humbled to have such words written about me. I cannot state how much pride and caring I have for all the Marines I served with. Bill Weise holds a special place in my heart.

Epilogue

I am certain the killing will continue long after I am gone. I would like to think that perhaps we would have learned something from the entire process. It should be everyone's right to live in peace.
— Pieter Krueler (last living participant of the Second Boer War)

MY WIFE, SARA, AND I moved to Mount Pleasant, South Carolina, in our twilight years, and we have two daughters, Kimberly and Melissa.

Kimberly started her education when I was the commander of Marine Barracks in London, England, and handling security duties for the nuclear-weapons sites and navy headquarters. She completed Camp Lejeune High School and was selected for the United States Naval Academy at Annapolis, Maryland. Upon graduating in 1991, she attended the Medical University of South Carolina in Charleston, earning a medical degree and specializing in dermatology. She later served on active duty in the U.S. Navy as a flight surgeon. She also served at Bethesda Naval Hospital, where she was dermatologist to the president of the United States. I am very proud of her. At the time of this writing, Kim works at Balboa Naval Hospital in San Diego, and her husband is a former naval doctor currently practicing family and sports medicine.

My younger daughter, Melissa, graduated from Tulane University and lives in Chapel Hill, North Carolina, where she works for Blue Cross and Blue Shield. She has a daughter named Chloe and a son named Charlie, and her husband has his Ph.D. in economics.

I must say that I am very proud of my daughters. They were wonderful children, and they have become outstanding women and solid American citizens.

In what I would consider as the height of irony, but also a great honor, on November 19, 1993, the state of Georgia dedicated a historical marker in my honor at the intersection of U.S. Highway 341 and State Route 19 in Lumber City. I could not imagine why they would do that, but I was quite humbled by that great gesture, and my mother was very proud. She passed away in 2008, and as I write these thoughts, I remember her gentle ways—her wisdom and her smile—and reflect upon how proud she was of me, my brother, my children, and her family in general. I am the man she and my father made me.

If men's lives may be evaluated by the opinions of others, especially those with whom they have served, and that opinion is measured and evaluated by personal conduct and service, then our Marine Corps' legacy is secure. These attributes are deeply intertwined with the Marines, sailors, and soldiers mentioned in this book. Their dedication to duty and their love of America and freedom have continued to secure our nation. Their history and legacy is carried on today by Marines who continue to provide security and freedom in a very uncertain world. However, one thing is certain: wherever tyranny and terror raise their heads, either at home or abroad, U.S. Marines will be vigilant and prepared to address those threats. Count on it.

The men of 2nd Battalion, 4th Marines, in particular, and of the United States Marine Corps as a whole, have always made history. Even more important, we have made a difference. Our nation and the world at large are better places for our service. All people who enjoy or desire freedom should always remember that our service, focus, and loyalty often come at great personal expense. They should also understand that this service has provided the liberty that we all enjoy, and they should be thankful that we have such Americans who will willingly sacrifice, without question, to provide that freedom.

I am thankful to God just to have been a Marine.

Personal Awards and Decorations

Medals

Medal of Honor

Navy Distinguished Service Cross

Silver Star

Superior Service Medal

Bronze Star with Combat V

Purple Heart (three awards)

Defense Meritorious Service Medal

Meritorious Service Medal (two awards)

Navy Commendation Medal with
Combat V

Marine Corps Expeditionary Medal

Armed Forces Expeditionary Medal

Humanitarian Service Medal

Vietnam Service Medal

National Defense Medal

Awards and Ribbons

Combat Action Ribbon (two awards)

Navy Unit Commendation

Navy Unit Citation

Joint Meritorious Unit Award

Sea Service Deployment Ribbon

Overseas Service Ribbon

Basic Parachutist Insignia

Navy-Marine Parachutist Insignia

Foreign Awards

Vietnamese Cross of Gallantry
with Palm

MEDAL OF HONOR CITATION

For conspicuous gallantry and intrepidity at the risk of his life above and beyond the call of duty while serving as Commanding Officer, Company E, in action against enemy forces. Company E launched a determined assault on the heavily fortified village of Dai Do, which had been seized by the enemy on the preceding evening isolating a marine company from the remainder of the battalion. Skillfully employing screening agents, Capt. Livingston maneuvered his men to assault positions across 500 meters of dangerous open rice paddy while under intense enemy fire. Ignoring hostile rounds impacting near him, he fearlessly led his men in a savage assault against enemy emplacements within the village. While adjusting supporting arms fire, Capt. Livingston moved to the points of heaviest resistance, shouting words of encouragement to his marines, directing their fire, and spurring the dwindling momentum of the attack on repeated occasions. Although twice painfully wounded by grenade fragments, he refused medical treatment and courageously led his men in the destruction of over 100 mutually supporting bunkers, driving the remaining enemy from their positions, and relieving the pressure on the stranded marine company. As the 2 companies consolidated positions and evacuated casualties, a third company passed through the friendly lines launching an assault on the adjacent village of Dinh To, only to be halted by a furious counterattack of an enemy battalion. Swiftly assessing the situation and disregarding the heavy volume of enemy fire, Capt. Livingston boldly maneuvered the remaining effective men of his company forward, joined forces with the heavily engaged marines, and halted the enemy's counterattack. Wounded a third time and unable to walk, he steadfastly remained in the dangerously exposed area, deploying his men to more tenable positions and supervising the evacuation of casualties. Only when assured of the safety of his men did he allow himself to be evacuated. Capt. Livingston's gallant actions uphold the highest traditions of the Marine Corps and the U.S. Naval Service.

Selected Biographical Sketches

Col. Jay R.Vargas, USMC (Ret.)

Jay Vargas was born in Winslow, Arizona, the son of immigrants—an Italian mother and Hispanic father—who came to the United States in 1917. His family taught him that the price of success is hard work and the cost of freedom is personal sacrifice. Each of the four sons wore the uniform of their country in time of war; brothers Angelo and Frank served at Iwo Jima and Okinawa during World War II, brother Joseph served in Korea, and Jay served in Vietnam.

Before joining the Marines, Vargas attended Northern Arizona University and graduated with a bachelor of science in education. He completed a master of arts in education with honors at United States International University, and received a doctorate from Northern Arizona University.

While in the Marines, he commanded and led at every level, from a rifle platoon to an infantry regiment. Of his many accomplishments as a Marine officer, the most widely publicized was achieved in combat. In the spring of 1968, while serving in the Republic of Vietnam, Vargas's unit engaged in fierce combat with the enemy at the village of Dai Do. During the battle, he was able to free one of his platoons, which was pinned down by heavy fire, by personally destroying three enemy machine-gun positions. His actions left fifteen of the enemy dead, while he was wounded three times. For his actions at Dai Do, Vargas was presented with the Medal of Honor by President Richard M. Nixon in a May 1970 ceremony at the White House. His Medal of Honor citation states:

> For conspicuous gallantry and intrepidity at the risk of his life above and beyond the call of duty while serving as commanding officer, Company G, in action against enemy forces from 30 April to 2 May 1968. On 1 May 1968, though suffering from wounds he had incurred while relocating his unit under heavy enemy fire the preceding day, Maj. Vargas combined Company G with two other companies and led his men in an attack on the fortified village of Dai Do. Exercising expert leadership, he maneuvered his Marines across 700 meters of open rice paddy while under intense enemy mortar, rocket and artillery fire and obtained a foothold in 2 hedgerows on the enemy perimeter, only to have elements of his company become pinned down by the intense enemy fire. Leading his reserve platoon to the aid of his beleaguered men, Maj. Vargas inspired his men to renew their relentless advance, while destroying a number of enemy bunkers. Again wounded by grenade fragments, he refused aid as he moved about the hazardous area reorganizing his unit into a strong defense perimeter at the edge of the village. Shortly after the objective was secured the enemy commenced a series of counterattacks and probes, which lasted throughout the night but were unsuccessful as the gallant defenders of Company G stood firm in their hard-won enclave. Reinforced the following morning, the marines launched a renewed assault through Dai Do on the village of Dinh To, to which

the enemy retaliated with a massive counterattack resulting in hand-to-hand combat. Maj. Vargas remained in the open, encouraging and rendering assistance to his marines when he was hit for the third time in the 3-day battle. Observing his battalion commander sustain a serious wound, he disregarded his excruciating pain, crossed the fire-swept area and carried his commander to a covered position, then resumed supervising and encouraging his men while simultaneously assisting in organizing the battalion's perimeter defense. His gallant actions uphold the highest traditions of the Marine Corps and the U.S. Naval Service.

In addition to the Medal of Honor, Vargas's personal decorations include the Silver Star, the Purple Heart with four Gold Stars, the Combat Action Ribbon, the Meritorious Service Medal, and the Vietnamese Gallantry Cross with Silver Star and Palm.

His final tour of duty as a Marine was on the staff of the Commander, U.S. Naval Forces, Pacific, where he served as Force Marine. He retired from the Marine Corps with the rank of colonel in 1992. He served as secretary of the California Department of Veterans Affairs from 1993 to 1998.

Vargas was appointed veterans liaison for the United States Department of Veterans Affairs (USDVA) by the secretary of Veterans Affairs on July 9, 2001. He is responsible for maintaining contact with federal and state elected officials, state directors of veteran affairs, USDVA network directors, directors of V.A. medical centers, regional offices, national cemeteries, and veterans and community organizations involved in the exchange of information on issues affecting veterans. He is based at the USDVA regional office in San Diego, California. His region includes nineteen western states, Guam, and the Philippines.

For his dedicated service in caring for veterans, Vargas has received a Veteran of the Year Award from the Veterans of Foreign Wars (VFW), a Civil Servant of the Year Award from the American Veterans (AMVETS), and a Citizen of the Year Award from the Jewish War Veterans of the Unites States of America.

Brig. Gen. William Weise, USMC (Ret.)

William Weise, a native of Philadelphia, entered boot camp as a private at Parris Island, South Carolina, in 1951, during the height of the Korean War. He retired from active duty at Parris Island as a brigadier general in 1982. During his thirty-one-year career, he had combat tours in Korea and Vietnam. In Korea he served as a 60mm mortar section leader, a rifle-platoon commander, and rifle-company executive officer with George Company, 3d Battalion, 5th Marines, 1st Marine Division.

In Vietnam he commanded the Magnificent Bastards of the 2nd Battalion, 4th Marines, during some of the heaviest fighting of that conflict, in 1967 to 1968. His personal decorations include the Navy Cross, the Silver Star, two Legions of Merit (one with Combat V), three Purple Hearts, and the Vietnamese Cross of Gallantry with Gold Palm. In addition, his Battalion Landing Team 2/4 was awarded the Navy Unit Citation "for outstanding heroism in action against insurgent communist forces in the northern I Corps Area, Republic of Vietnam, from 5 March to 31 May 1968."

His peacetime assignments have included rifle-company commander for Foxtrot Company, 2nd Battalion, 1st Marines, from 1959 to 1960; Force Reconnaissance Company platoon commander, operations officer, officer, and inspector-instructor for the 1st and 3rd Force Reconnaissance Companies from 1960 to 1965; and infantry-regiment commander for the 9th Marines from 1975 to 1976.

He also held various staff positions and taught at the Naval War College, Army Command and General Staff College, and the Marine Corps Officers Basic School. He graduated with highest distinction from the Naval War College. He has a bachelor of science from Temple

University and a masters in business administration from Arizona State University. Other schools attended include Army Ranger School, Army Airborne School, Special Warfare Officers School, Navy SCUBA Divers School, Army Command and General Staff College, Marine Corps Basic School, Supply Officers Course, and Marine Corps Boot Camp.

General Weise participates in a number of veteran and community activities. He co-chaired the Marine Corps Heritage Center Committee for five years and led the small group that furnished the vision for the National Museum of the Marine Corps. He spoke at many reunions and small groups to generate interest in the museum and get the project started. He helped found the 2nd Battalion, 4th Marines Association and chaired the committee that raised the money and built the "Two Four" Monument in Semper Fidelis Memorial Park, next the National Museum of the Marine Corps. Weise has been an active church member for many years, serving as lay reader, Sunday School teacher, and vestry member.

He was married for forty-three years to the former Ethel Jaeschke, who died in 1997. He has three children, nine grandchildren, and three great-grandchildren.

Col. James Laney Williams, USMC (Ret.)

Born in Winona, Minnesota, in 1938, Jim Williams served the Marine Corps for twenty-nine years in a wide variety of command and staff assignments, including commanding officer of Marine Barracks, Newport, Rhode Island; assistant naval attache, Rome, Italy; and program coordinator for the U.S. Navy's Hovercraft Program at the Pentagon.

Williams served as the company commander of Hotel Company, 2nd Battalion, 4th Marine Regiment, during the Cua Viet River battles in Quang Tri Province, Republic of Vietnam, in the spring of 1968. For service during that time, he was awarded two Silver Stars and a Purple Heart.

Over the years, Camp Pendleton has been his home port. Command assignments there included CO of 1st Reconnaissance Battalion; CO of 3rd Battalion, 5th Marine Regiment; and CO of the School of Infantry. Staff assignments included operations officer for 3rd Force Reconnaissance Company; executive officer for 5th Marine Regiment; and assistant chief of staff, Operations and Training, Marine Corps Base.

Colonel Williams is a graduate of both the Naval War College and the Army War College and holds a master of science from George Washington University's Elliot School of International Affairs. He has been a frequent contributor to various military professional journals in the United States and abroad.

Since retiring from the Marine Corps in 1989, Colonel Williams has been employed as the executive director of a Boys and Girls Club and in several community-relations posts. He and his wife, Cynthia, have four grown children and reside in Oceanside, California.

Lt. Col. George Frederick "Fritz" Warren, USMC (Ret.)

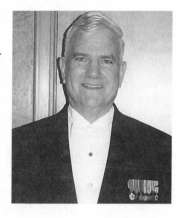

On June 28, 1950, at the age of seventeen and not yet a graduate from St. Paul's High School in Jacksonville, Florida, Warren joined the Marine Corps to fight against the North Korean forces that had invaded South Korea and were threatening to push the American forces into the sea at the southeastern Port of Pusan. Warren never arrived in Korea. After boot camp at Parris Island, South Carolina, he became a Marine bugler and was ordered to the famous battleship USS *Missouri* (BB-63), where he served for eighteen months. A young ensign, William "Billy" Earl, taught Warren enough geometry, at night in his personal stateroom, to pass the exam for entry into the U.S. Naval Academy prep school.

During his four years at the United States Naval Academy, Warren played varsity football and lacrosse. He was elected president of the class of 1957 and would remain in that office for some thirty-three years. He served as both a member and the chairman of the Brigade Honor Committee. Upon graduation from the U.S. Naval Academy, Fritz was commissioned a second lieutenant of Marines. One week later, on June 15, 1957, he married Barbara June Minga; Fritz and Barbara Warren have three living children and have been married for almost fifty-three years.

In July 1957, Warren was ordered to Okinawa and sent directly to join the staff of Special Landing Force Alpha, operating in U.S. Navy ships off the coast of Vietnam. As the assistant operations officer, he helped plan and execute six successful amphibious-combat operations into the Northern I Corps Tactical Area of Operations. He served in a number of assignments that are typical for young Marine officers, including some fifteen months as the executive officer to Capt. William "Bill" Weise, who was his company commander on Okinawa. In 1962, Captain Warren was selected to attend the United States Naval Postgraduate School, where he earned his second bachelor's degree, this time in communications and electronics engineering.

In February 1968, he rejoined Bill Weise (then a lieutenant colonel) who was the commander of BLT 2/4 (the Magnificent Bastards), the ground element of Special Landing Force Alpha. Major Warren was assigned as the BLT 2/4 operations officer and remained in that position until he left Vietnam in mid-July. During his time in country, BLT 2/4 was engaged in heavy combat across the Northern I Corps tactical front stretching from the mountains on the Laotian border in the west to the South China Sea in the east. While all of the combat during this period was heavy and significant, it was the Battle of Dai Do (sometimes referred to as the Battle for Dong Ha) that severely tested the mettle of the officers and men of the Magnificent Bastards over a the three days of April 29 to May 1, 1968.

Upon Major Warren's return home, he was an honor graduate at the Marine Corps Command and Staff College at Quantico, Virginia. He was selected to attend Georgia Tech University, in Atlanta, Georgia, where he earned a master of science in information and computer science.

Lieutenant Colonel Warren's final Marine Corps assignment was as the plans and programs officer for the Military Technical Assistance Group, which was attached to the U.S. embassy in Jakarta, Indonesia. His personal decorations include a Legion of Merit and two Bronze Stars (all with the combat V device authorized), as well as several awards from the South Vietnamese government and the Marine Corps Good Conduct Medal.

After retiring from the Corps in August 1975, Warren worked in Indonesia for eight years in a number of capacities for Arthur Young and Company (accountants and auditors) and for an oil company while supervising the construction and installation of oil production platforms in the Java Sea.

Returning to the United States, Warren earned his second masters degree—this time a master of business administration—and an advanced professional degree in business administration from Chaminade University of Honolulu in Hawaii. He became a certified public accountant and took a position as the business manager of Chaminade University for two years.

Warren worked as the chief financial officer for three organizations (an upscale printing company for five years, a Catholic charitable organization for two years, and the Navy-Marine Corps Relief Society for eleven years). He has recently agreed to serve as the chief financial officer for the American Heroes First Foundation, a charitable organization whose intent is to solicit funds from the general public and pass those funds to approved charitable organizations who are efficiently serving military personnel and their families.

Bibliography

3rd Battalion, 21st Infantry Regiment, 196th Infantry Division, Combat
After Action Report for April 30–May 16, 1968. Date of AAR: June 5, 1968.
Courtesy of Wally Nunn.

Battalion Landing Team, 2nd Battalion, 4th Marines, Combat After Action
Report for April 29–May 3, 1968.

Butler, David. *The Fall of Saigon: Scenes from the Sudden End of a Long War*. New
York: Dell, 1985.

Cerasini, Marc. *Heroes: U.S. Marine Corps Medal of Honor Winners*. New York:
Berkeley Books, 2002.

Dunham, Maj. George R., USMC, and Colonel David A. Quinlan, USMC.
U.S. Marines in Vietnam: The Bitter End, 1973–1975. Washington, D.C.:
History and Museums Divisions, Headquarters, U.S. Marine Corps, 1990.

Dyhouse, Tim. " 'Magnificent Bastards': Battle at Dai Do," *Veterans of Foreign
Wars*, Vol. 94, No. 7 (March 2007), 40–43.

Engelmann, Larry. *Tears Before the Rain: An Oral History of the Fall of South
Vietnam*. New York: Da Capo Press, 1997.

Hammond, William M. *Reporting Vietnam: Media and Military at War*.
Lawrence: University Press of Kansas, 1998.

Jordan, Kenneth N., Sr. *Men of Honor: Thirty-eight Highly Decorated Marines of
World War II, Korea and Vietnam*. Atglen, PA: Schiffer Publishing, Ltd, 1997.

Nolan, Keith William. *The Magnificent Bastards: The Joint Army-Marine Defense of Dong Ha, 1968*. Novato, CA: Presidio Press, 1994.

Shulimson, Jack; Lt. Col. Leonard A. Blasiol, USMC; Charles R. Smith; and Capt. David A. Dawson, USMC. *U.S. Marines in Vietnam: The Defining Year 1968*. Washington, D.C.: History and Museums, Headquarters, United States Marine Corps, 1997.

Steinman, Ron. *The Soldiers' Story: Vietnam in Their Own Words*. New York: TV Books, 1999, 2000.

Taylor, Lt. Col. Vic, "Hotel Company: Day Three," *Marine Corps Gazette*, April 2004, 71–72.

Weise, Brig. Gen. William, "The Battle of Dai Do," *Marine Corps Gazette*, September 1987, 16–34, 70–73.

Notes

Preface

1. Wally Nunn in email to Colin D. Heaton.

Prologue

1. Telephone interview with Ruth Livingston by Anne-Marie Lewis in March 2007.
2. Ibid.

Chapter 1

1. Email from Dave Jones to Colin D. Heaton, November 12, 2007.
2. Keith William Nolan, *The Magnificent Bastards: The Joint Army-Marine Defense of Dong Ha, 1968* (Novato, CA: Presidio Press, 1994), 127.
3. Corrections courtesy of George "Fritz" Warren.
4. Nolan, 30.
5. Brig. Gen. William Weise, "The Battle of Dai Do," *Marine Corps Gazette,* September 1987, 18–19.
6. Nolan, 30; see also Weise, 18.
7. Email from Jones to Heaton, November 12, 2007.
8. Nolan, 27.
9. Ibid., 28.
10. Email from William Weise to Colin D. Heaton.
11. Nolan, 31.
12. Ibid., 34.
13. Ibid., 47.
14. Ibid., 127.
15. Weise edit to in-progress manuscript.

Chapter 2

1. The A Shau Valley actions included the famous Hamburger Hill episode with the 101st Airborne Division, among other critical battles. See also Jack Shulimson; Lt. Col. Leonard A. Blasiol, USMC; Charles R. Smith; and Capt. David A. Dawson, USMC, *U.S. Marines in Vietnam: The Defining Year, 1968* (Washington, D.C.: History and Museums Division, Headquarters U.S. Marine Corps, Marine Corps Historical Center, 1997), 312–327.

2. Ibid., 291.

3. Ibid., 291.

4. Interviews with Gen. William Westmoreland by Colin D. Heaton in January–March 1994.

5. Nolan, 35.

6. Ibid., 35.

7. Weise, 18.

8. Tim Dyhouse, "'Magnificent Bastards': Battle at Dai Do," *Veterans of Foreign Wars*, Vol. 94, No. 7 (March 2007), 42.

9. Weise, 18.

10. Weise edit to in-progress manuscript.

11. Ibid.

12. Ibid.

13. Ibid.

14. Weise, 21.

15. Ibid., 19–20.

16. Weise edit to in-progress manuscript.

17. Ibid.

18. Ibid.

19. Ibid.

20. Ibid.

21. Westmoreland interviews.

Chapter 3

1. Nolan, 32.

2. Weise edit to in-progress manuscript.

3. Weise comments made by telephone to Colin D. Heaton.

4. Weise edit to in-progress manuscript.

5. Ibid.

6. Ibid.

7. BLT 2/4 Combat After Action Report (AAR), 31.

8. See Shulimson, et al, 291–292.

9. Weise edit to in-progress manuscript.

10. Nolan, 13.

11. Ibid.

12. Ibid.

13. Ibid.

14. Weise edit to in-progress manuscript.

15. Nolan, 6.

16. Shulimson, et al, 298.

17. Nolan, 7.

18. Weise, 19.

19. BLT 2/4 AAR 31.

20. Ibid., 32.

21. Ibid., 14.

22. Weise edit to in-progress manuscript.

23. BLT 2/4 AAR, 16.

24. Weise edit to in-progress manuscript.

Chapter 4

1. BLT 2/4 AAR, 18.

2. Nolan, 19.

3. Tim Dyhouse, 40. Fritz Warren clarified this data.

4. Ibid., 42.

5. Information courtesy of Fritz Warren.

6. The U.S. response to this NVA incursion became the Battle of Dai Do, as it was officially known by the Marines. The U.S. Army's "American" Division classified the action as a continuation of Operation Napoleon.

7. Weise, supplemental timeline data sent to Heaton.

8. See Shulimson, et al, 292.

9. Weise edit to in-progress manuscript.

10. BLT 2/4 AAR, 32.

11. Ibid. See also Shulimson, et al, 292.

12. BLT 2/4 AAR, 32.

13. See Shulimson, et al, 293.

14. Ibid., 294.

15. Ibid.

16. Nolan, 22. This information has been corroborated by all the officers concerned, and was critical on the spot intelligence.

17. Shulimson, et al, 294.

18. Ibid., 295.

19. Dong Huan, as noted in the after-action reports and Nolan's book, is actually Dai Do 1, or the first numbered hamlet in the collective area. The village called "Dai Do" in the text is Dai Do 2. This information also came from former Viet Cong guerrilla chief Dung Tu Ahn, via Weise, in the latter's email dated May 12, 2008. The names of the villages noted in Nolan and the other sources have been maintained and endnotes have been added for clarification.

20. Dyhouse, 42–43. BLT 2/4 AAR, 32.

21. Nolan, 39–40.

22. Shulimson, et al, 296.

23. Nolan, 41. See also Weise, 21.

24. Shulimson, et al, 296.

25. Ibid.

26. Courtesy of Warren. See also BLT 2/4 AAR, 32.

27. Shulimson, et al, 294.

28. Ibid., 297.

29. 174th Assault Helicopter Company website at www.174ahc.org/daido.htm, courtesy of Wally Nunn.

30. Nolan, 46.

31. Weise, 23.

32. Ibid., 22.

33. Nolan, 48.

34. Ibid., 49.

35. Telephone interview with Jim Williams by Colin D. Heaton.

36. Ibid., 55. See also Dyhouse, 41.

37. Weise, 23.

38. BLT 2/4 AAR, 32.

39. Weise, 26.

40. Fritz Warren email comments to Colin D. Heaton.

41. Ibid.

42. Ibid.

43. Weise, 20.

44. Shulimson, et al, 294.

45. Weise, 26.

46. Ibid., 23. Weise, following his visit to Vietnam with Livingston, noted that the actual Vietnamese name for An Lac is *Xoi* (pronounced "Soy"). From this point forward, the names of all the villages will be presented as they appeared in Keith Nolan's book and in other records. These names were clarified by former Viet Cong guerrilla chief Dung Tu Ahn during the tour of the battlefield in May 2008. Email from Weise to Heaton, May 12, 2008.

47. Telephone conversation with Weise by Heaton, October 4, 2007.

48. Dyhouse, 41.

49. Weise, 24.

50. Ibid., 22.

51. Nolan, 82–83.

52. Jordan, Kenneth N., Sr., *Men of Honor: Thirty-eight Highly Decorated Marines of World War II, Korea and Vietnam.* (Atglen, PA: Schiffer Publishing, Ltd, 1997), 276–278.

53. Weise, 24.

54. Shulimson, et al, 298.

55. Weise, 25.

56. Ibid.

57. Dyhouse, 43.

58. Ibid., 41.

59. Nolan, 94–95.

60. Dyhouse, 41.

61. Shulimson, et al, 299.

62. BLT 3/21 Combat After Action Report (RCS AVDF-GC), 14. Courtesy of Nunn.

63. BLT 2/4 AAR.

64. Shulimson, et al, 299.

65. Ibid.

Chapter 5

1. Email from Jones to Heaton, November 12, 2007.

2. Weise, 27.

3. Ibid.

4. Ibid.

5. Weise, 25.

6. Dyhouse, 43; Jordan, 266–268.

7. BLT 2/4 AAR.

8. Ibid.

9. Nolan, 103. See also BLT 2/4 AAR.

10. Weise, 25.

11. Ibid., 20.

12. Ibid.

13. Nolan, 105.

14. Letter from Steve Wilson to Colin D. Heaton, October 17, 2008.

15. Nunn telephone interview, October 3, 2007.

16. Nolan, 105.

17. Weise, 27.

18. Courtesy of Warren.

19. Ibid. See also Shulimson, et al, 301.

20. Nolan, 119.

21. Dyhouse, 41.

22. Weise, 27.

23. Email from Weise to Heaton.

24. Nolan, 122.

25. Line of departure.

26. BLT 3/21 AAR, 15.

27. Ibid. See also Dyhouse, 42.

28. Nolan, 125.

29. BLT 3/21 AAR.

30. Weise, 28.

31. Email from Jesse Brooks via Rod Forman, November 14, 2007.

32. Vic Taylor, "Hotel Company-Day Three," *Marine Corps Gazette* (April 2004), 71.

33. Ibid., 128.

34. Weise, 28.

Chapter 6

1. Weise.
2. Nolan, 130.
3. See Weise, 20.
4. Taylor, 71–72.
5. Nolan, 138–139.
6. Email from Frank Valdez to Colin D. Heaton via Dave Jones.
7. Nolan, 140–141.
8. Ibid., 141.
9. Ibid., 142.
10. BLT 2/4 AAR. See also Shulimson, et al, 301–303.
11. Ibid.
12. Ibid., 28.
13. Nolan, 154.
14. Ibid., 152.
15. Letter from Weise to the authors. He also supplied the copy of Taylor's article, "Hotel Company: Day Three," written for *Marine Corps Gazette*, in April 2004.
16. Nolan, 147.
17. Ibid., 154.
18. Taylor, 71.
19. Nunn.
20. 174th Assault Helicopter Company website at www.174ahc.org/daido.htm, courtesy of Wally Nunn.
21. Weise, 33.
22. Letter from Wilson to Heaton, October 17, 2008.

Chapter 7

1. BLT 2/4 AAR.
2. Dyhouse, 43.
3. BLT 2/4 AAR.
4. Weise, 27.
5. Nolan, 154.
6. Weise, 31.

7. Nolan, 156.
8. Ibid., 158.
9. BLT 2/4 AAR.
10. BLT 3/21 AAR, 14–15.
11. BLT 3/21 AAR, 15.
12. BLT 2/4 AAR.
13. Ibid.
14. These were comments expressed by Livingston and Weise during their discussions with Colin D. Heaton.
15. BLT 2/4 AAR.
16. Ibid.
17. Shulimson, et al, 303.
18. Ibid.
19. Courtesy of Wally Nunn. See his unit's website at www.174ahc.org/daido.htm.
20. Ibid.
21. Dyhouse, 42–43.
22. Nunn. See also BLT 3/21 AAR, 16.
23. Nolan, 162.
24. Ibid., 166.
25. Nolan, 286.
26. Jones mail, November 12, 2007.
27. Nolan, 162.
28. Ibid., 167.
29. Warren email to Colin D. Heaton.
30. Ibid.
31. Weise, 27.
32. Ibid., 32.
33. Ibid., 34.
34. Ibid., 70.
35. BLT 2/4 AAR.
36. Email from Weise.
37. Weise, 70.
38. Email from Weise.
39. Warren comments. See also BLT 2/4 AAR. Warren assumed temporary command at approximately 6 p.m.

40. Shulimson, et al, 303.

41. Ibid.

42. Ibid., 303–304.

43. Weise, 70.

44. Nolan, 349.

45. Ibid., 113.

46. Shulimson, et al, 304.

47. Weise edit to in-progress manuscript. See also the DVD *Memories of Dai Do*, specifically account of 1st Lt. Judd Hilton.

Chapter 8

1. Weise, 34.

2. Ibid., 70.

3. Email from Jones, November 12, 2007.

4. Email from Weise to Heaton, October 22, 2008.

5. Weise, 72.

6. Ibid.

7. Email from Jones to Heaton, November 12, 2007.

8. Email from Warren to Heaton.

9. Email from Weise to Heaton.

10. Email from Warren, August 6, 2009.

11. Weise, 26.

12. Ibid., 72.

Chapter 9

1. Email from Frank Valdez to Colin D. Heaton, October 22, 2008.

2. Weise, 17.

3. Camp's letter courtesy of Weise.

4. Ibid.

5. Nolan, 112.

6. William M. Hammond, *Reporting Vietnam: Media and Military at War* (Lawrence: University of Kansas Press, 1998), 1.

Chapter 10

1. David Butler, *The Fall of Saigon: Scenes from the Sudden End of a Long War* (New York: Dell, 1985), 50–53, 231, 256. Larry Engelmann, T*ears Before the Rain: An Oral History of the Fall of South Vietnam* (New York: Da Capo Press, 1997), 29.

2. Butler, 89–90, 243.

3. Ibid., 16, 21, 22, 98, 244–245, 248, 340. See also Engelmann, 84–86, 122, 137, 260.

4. Ron Steinman, *The Soldiers' Story: Vietnam in Their Own Words* (New York: TV Books, 1999, 2000), 334.

5. Engelmann, 69, 134, 159, 161, 267, 286–287, 292, 300, 308–309.

6. Maj. George R. Dunham and Col. David A. Quinlan, USMC, *U.S. Marines in Vietnam: The Bitter End, 1973–1975* (Washington, DC: History and Museums Division, Headquarters, U.S. Marine Corps, 1990), 168. See also Engelmann, 43, 72.

7. Engelmann, viii, 43, 72, 140. Steinman, 293

8. Butler, 95.

9. Dunham and Quinlan, 299.

10. Ibid., 160.

11. Butler, 155, 293, 296–297, 334–336, 360–361, 367–368.

12. Ibid., 292–295.

13. Engelmann, 125–127.

14. Dunham and Quinlan, 174.

15. Ibid. See also Butler, 292–294, 405–407, and Steinman, 302–303.

16. Aarib Bank interview with Colin D. Heaton, 1986.

17. Steinman, p 319, 336-42.

18. Butler, 419. Engelmann, 56, 57, 101, 105, 120-41. See also Steinman, 333-36.

19. Dunham and Quinlan, 174. Engelmann, 127.

19. Jordan, 239.

21. Email from Ken Crouse to Colin D. Heaton, February 6, 2007.

22. Steinman, 293.

23. Butler, 6–7, 16, 18, 21–22, 25, 236, 290–291, 299, 385, 489–490, 503. See also Dunham and Quinlan, 169; Englemann, 42; and Steinman, 318.

24. Dunham and Quinlan, 174.

25. Ibid., 174. See also Butler, 65, and Steinman, 301–307.

26. Butler, 415–416. Engelmann, 71–73.

27. Engelmann, 60.

28. Dunham and Quinlan, 174.

29. Ibid.

30. Ibid. 174. Butler, 426.

31. Butler, 87, 276.

32. Engelmann, 44, 75–92, 98.

33. Dunham and Quinlan, 171. Engelmann, 166–167, 196, 205–206.

34. Dunham and Quinlan, 172.

35. Butler, 251.

36. Engelmann, 98, 125, 141.

37. Dunham and Quinlan, 171.

38. Ibid., 178.

39. Butler, 231; Engelmann, viii.

40. Dunham and Quinlan, 178. See also Butler, 94, 279, 395, 399, 402, and Steinman, 293, 296–301.

41. Dunham and Quinlan, 178.

42. Ibid., 182.

43. Steinman, 295.

44. Dunham and Quinlan, 178.

45. Steinman, 293–296.

46. Engelmann, 98, 101, 104, 124, 130, 165-68, 171, 195, 204.

47. Dunham and Quinlan, 172.

48. Butler, 279, 281.

49. Dunham and Quinlan, 181.

Chapter 11

1. Dunham and Quinlan, 183.

2. Butler, 452. See also Steinman, 287.

3. Dunham and Quinlan, 184.

4. Steinman, 307.

5. Dunham and Quinlan, 184. See also Engelmann, 103.

6. Dunham and Quinlan, 184.

7. Ibid., 185. Butler, 446.

8. Dunham and Quinlan, 183.

9. Ibid., 184.

10. Steinman, 299.

11. Ibid., 299, 317.

12. Dunham and Quinlan, 191.

13. Ibid., 295–296.

14. Ibid., 332–333.

15. Dunham and Quinlan, 192. Engelmann, 89, 104.

16. Dunham and Quinlan, 193.

17. Steinman, 337.

18. Ibid., 195–196. See also Butler, 442.

19. Ibid., 326.

20. Steinman, 337.

21. Dunham and Quinlan, 197.

22. Steinman, 309.

23. Dunham and Quinlan, 197.

24. Ibid., 198.

25. Ibid. See also Butler, 462.

26. Steinman, 337.

27. Dunham and Quinlan, 199.

28. Steinman, 336.

29. Dunham and Quinlan, 199.

30. Butler, 467.

31. Butler, 464. Steinman, 39.

32. Butler, 390–391.

33. Steinman, 341.

34. Ibid., 334.

35. Ibid., 297–298, 301, on Hasty's involvement.

36. Dunham and Quinlan, 199. Engelmann, 189.

37. Dunham and Quinlan, 201.

38. Ibid., 202. See also Steinman, 310–314.

39. Steinman, 309–314, 321.

40. Dunham and Quinlan, 201.

41. Ibid., 204.

42. Email from John Valdez to Colin D. Heaton, February 5, 2007.

Chapter 12

1. Michael Bedford, "Mangyans Forced to Evacuate Homeland in Philippines," *Cultural Survival Quarterly*, Fall 1988.

2. James Neilson, "Nick Rowe: U.S. Intelligence Knew Independently of Threat to his Life." *U.S. Veteran News and Report.* http://www.pownetwork.org/bios/r/r077.htm

3. *Far Eastern Economic Review*, June 1989.

Chapter 14

1. Email from Jones to Heaton, November 12, 2007.

2. Letter from Wilson to Heaton, October 17, 2008.

3. Email from Weise to Heaton, December 31, 2007.

4. Email from Jones to Heaton, December 31, 2008.

Chapter 16

1. Email from Weise to Heaton, November 12, 2007.

ABOUT THE AUTHORS

Major General James E. Livingston retired from the U.S. Marine Corps following more than thirty years of service. He was one of two Medal of Honor recipients for actions on May 1–3, 1968, in the Dai Do region of Quang Tri Province, Republic of Vietnam. He and his wife, Sara, live in Mount Pleasant, South Carolina.

Professor Colin D. Heaton served in the U.S. Army and later the U.S. Marines under Livingston's command as a Scout Sniper. He was a guest historian on the "Secret Weapons" episode of the History Channel series *Dogfights* and has authored several books on military history, including *German Anti-Partisan Warfare in Europe: 1939–1945*; *Occupation and Insurgency: A Selective Examination of The Hague and Geneva Conventions on the Eastern Front, 1939–1945*; and *Night Fighters: The Luftwaffe and RAF Air Combat over Europe, 1939–1945*. He taught history and military history at American Military University from 2002 to 2009 and is currently working on a series of military history books based on first-person interviews.

Anne-Marie Lewis received both her BA with honors and her Masters in International Relations from American Military University and is a professional photographer and researcher. She co-authored *Night Fighters: The Luftwaffe and RAF Air Combat over Europe, 1939–1945* with Professor Heaton.